THAT'S GOLF

THAT'S GOLF

THE BEST OF AL BARKOW

AL BARKOW

BURFORD BOOKS

Library of Congress Cataloging-in-Publication Data
Barkow, Al.
     That's golf : the best of Al Barkow / Al Barkow.
          p.   cm.
     ISBN 1-58080-096-3
     1. Golf—Anecdotes.   2. Golfers—Anecdotes.   I. Title.
GV967.B315   2001
796.352—dc21   2001043222

CONTENTS

FOREWORD

BY JACK NICKLAUS

Throughout my 40 years on Tour, I have established what I consider a special relationship with several writers in the golf media. Al Barkow has been one of those special guys. Whether it's been in the interview room at a major championship, or a locker room at a Tour stop, or under the oak tree at Augusta National, it seems as if I have had as many memorable exchanges with golf writers as I have had memorable matches on a golf course. Throughout my career, these writers have become trusted friends, confidants, and familiar faces I enjoy seeing each time I step into a press room. We've shared some good stories, lots of laughs, and a few good-spirited needles. Most of all, we've always shared a mutual respect and love for golf – the greatest game of all. I believe this respect has been at the foundation of my relationship with the golf media.

As a child in Columbus, Ohio, I grew up loving all sports, not just golf. Yet it was golf that appealed to me and challenged me in many ways. I've always embraced a challenge, and with golf, you compete more with yourself and the golf course than you do with an opponent. More intriguing is the fact that golf is a never-ending pursuit. No matter how good you are or think you are, golf challenges you to be even better. Just when you think you've got the game solved, it provides another mystery to puzzle you. Combine all these pieces, and golf is a sport for a lifetime. The same sport that intrigued and challenged me 50 years ago does the same for me today.

This, it seems to me, is what makes golf writing so diverse and interesting. It is also what to keep in mind as you read this collection of Al Barkow's work. In his long career covering golf, Al has reached out to touch the complete range of elements the game presents, and perhaps also added a few. Al's gone as far as to write about the dreams of golfers, including the late Ben Hogan, who once told Al that he dreamt of playing a round of golf in 18 shots – all aces. When Hogan lipped out on the last hole for a 19, he was very angry. That kind of story-telling enriches the "literature" of golf, and adds fresh insight for fans of the game.

Al's unique and comprehensive perspective on the game likely stems in part from Al's background as a competitive golfer. He has played in numerous prestigious amateur events, including a U.S. Amateur, and, as he has reminded me more than once, we competed against each other in a college quadrangular match. So often, if you have lived the subject, you are better at writing about that subject. If you have competed in the sport, there is usually an added credibility to your perspective on that sport. Al fits both of these categories.

Al Barkow and I are products of the same golf generation, which is why I feel comfortable introducing this collection of his fine work from the past 35 and more years.

Read and enjoy!

—Jack Nicklaus

INTRODUCTION

For the first ten years or so of my life in golf I didn't want to do anything but play the game. I had little to no interest in its history. Knowing the Scots were the perpetrators was enough for me. I did not have the deep sense of awe others display for the legendary sites of the game—St. Andrews, Carnoustie, Augusta National. I just wanted to play, and get good enough to make it to the pro tour.

I played some decent amateur golf around Chicago, was on a small-college (NAIA) national championship golf team while at Western Illinois University, qualified for a U.S. Amateur championship one time. If I had stuck with it I probably would have been a middle- to lower-middle-range grinder as a pro, picking up the occasional small check. I didn't wait to find out.

One of the best, or in another sense discouraging, things about golf is that success or failure is measured very simply, concisely, unequivocally. There is the score, which is a clear-cut, undeniable, not to say unavoidable truth. I didn't shoot often enough in the 60s to think I had a chance as a pro. Therefore, I took up my other main interest, writing. Actually, that came first. As a seventh grader, and before I got into golf, I had completed a writing assignment for my English teacher that was a journalistic account of a baseball game. If I didn't exactly copy it right out of the *Chicago Tribune,* I did one hell of a job of paraphrasing, a term and technique I had no clue to at the time. Anyway, after getting a top grade for the piece, plus some live classroom commendations, I said to myself that I wanted to be a sportswriter. So it came to be.

It could be said I am a classic case of the old adage, reworked a little, that says those who can do, those who can't write. Maybe there was a bit of that in the beginning of my career as a writer, but that wasn't my intention. I was interested in producing the Great American Novel, or at least some good short stories. But before I could get to those achievements, I needed to earn my living. So I began to write about golf. After all, as the writing teachers tell you, write about what you know. So I did.

After a couple of years learning the magazine editorial trade working for trade magazines dealing with road construction, I moved to New York City and, by chance, got a job as golf writer with the original *Shell's Wonderful World of Golf* television series. After six years of that, I hired on as an associate editor at *Golf* magazine, and a year or so later became the editor in chief. I was off and running as a golf journalist, and perhaps in part out of necessity found myself getting more and more intrigued by the game's history, the complications of playing technique and the intense mental energy it takes, the interesting and occasionally even fascinating personalities the game engages, and how the social structure of the game intertwines with the society at large. I began to think a lot more about how the game came to be and how and why it grew, and who did the seeding, the personality of golfers in general and individually; what motivates people to devote their lives to this very hard game?

I had been hooked on golf as a player (still am), and now was hooked on it as a writer. I found so much to contemplate, examine, research, divine. We who are deep into golf like to say the game is an extension of life. Those not involved say that is silly, that it is only a game. Well, it isn't only a game. Golf is yet another venue by which to express your personality, life-view, attitudes toward all things encountered in your passage through time and place. In my experience, for example, those who kept the black African-American out of mainstream American golf also supported keeping those people in the back of the bus and eating and drinking out of their own restaurants and fountains. On the other hand, many golfers who extol the fact that their game is essentially self-governing, each player responsible to uphold the rules of play, and themselves play with such devotion to the rules, cheat in business and on their wives. Then again, I caddied as a youth for Chicago mobsters who made their living by murder and mayhem, but adhered carefully, thoughtfully to the Rules of Golf. Point being, golf and those who play it can be and are as contradictory, mercurial, inconsistent as the game itself. Which is what has made my career in golf so absorbing, the hook on which I've hung my work.

Not for me the mere reporting of scores, and the play-by-play. My interest has always been in the interior dimensions of the game and those who play it, administer it, write about and broadcast it, and just watch it from the periphery. The serious guys, the funny guys, the serious things and not-so-serious things, and everything in between the cracks.

—A. B.

HERE'S TO THE PEOPLE WHO GOLF

LEE—THE PEOPLE'S PRO

(Golf Magazine—1971)

In the middle of the 14th fairway during the fourth round of the '71 U.S. Open, at Merion, Lee Trevino is tied for the lead. But he doesn't know what club to use for his second shot. You know this because he's saying so . . . out loud, in that medium-high voice and mixture of Texas and Chicano accent. He finally pulls a five-iron from his bag.

"This isn't the right club," he says, "but I'm going to hit it anyway."

He hits is perfectly, 10 feet from the cup.

If he holes the 10-footer he takes the lead for the first time in the tournament. A good time to do it, with only four more to play. It's funereal around that deep, swaley green. Trevino comes out of his crouch from behind the ball and as he moves up to position says,

"Man, how I'd love to make this little dude."

Everyone in the gallery breaks up. It's what they themselves say at the Burnt Fairways muni when they need a putt to win a two-bit, bingo-bango-bongo.

The laughter subsides, but now everyone is easy, relaxed. Including Trevino, who holes the putt and becomes the leader on the golf course.

He walks off the green gabbing away, only the gab is just a touch faster than usual and is broken up by hard, dry, hacking coughs that bring up little white pellets, which he hawks to the beautifully manicured lawn of mainline Merion. He'd been nervous all day, tugging at the back of his shirt and freeing it from his thick round shoulders. But the vise has just been turned that extra little bit, and don't let anyone tell you that just because a man has already won the Big One and has a bank full of money, the winning of another U.S. Open is "just another tournament."

Four holes later, on the 18th tee at Merion, Lee needs a par-four to win. That's not a dead cert, but it seems likely. Jack is struggling just behind him. Lee has eased in a great saving putt for a par on 17. There is a slight pause on the tee to clear some people from the overgrown quarry and the fairway ahead. It's a small, narrow tee. Very intimate. Lee is pacing—anxious to go. The marshals give him the high-ball. Trevino puts his ball on a peg, gets upright, slaps his hands together loudly. He goes for his driver. It should be right there. It isn't. Inexplicably, his caddie has dropped back a few feet into the close-hugging crowd. Trevino's club is not at hand. His rhythm is broken. He looks for an instant like someone who has just been struck behind the ear by an invisible fist.

"Where's my club?" he whines.

The caddie appears. Lee says to the boy, "What's the matter, you choking already?"

Again, everyone breaks up.

"I'm doing all the playing and my caddie is choking."

More laughs. The audience has been tight with the pressure of the moment, and Lee takes everyone off the hook. Now it's fun to watch him work the ball. What he says, very often, is not very funny in and of itself. It's the circumstances in which he says things. His timing is pluperfect.

Lee Buck Trevino has made a shambles of the Hoganistic school of golf course concentration, that severely tight-lipped and expressionless manner that turned almost all of an entire generation of golf players into walking mummies. Sure, there was your Jimmy Demaret, and there is your Doug Sanders and Chi-Chi, with their snappy clothes and little jigs. But they didn't, and haven't won like Hogan. Which proves the point, right? The only way to play the game well is to close out the world . . . completely. And give no outward hint of inner trepidation. Crank out one perfect shot after another like a soft-drink machine. With each coin dropped in the slot above, a soda bottle comes into the chute below. Every time. Perfectly, and with the same icy, impersonal bang.

Wrong! Because with Lee Trevino, who won three national championships in the space of four weeks, the only man to ever turn such a trick, you have a champion who from start to finish, before, during, and after every shot he plays, is nattering like a Wednesday matinee audience of little ladies from Long Island. Make no mistake, Trevino's constant stream of verbiage does not mean he's always loose; that his attitude is don't-give-a-damn. Lee Trevino's mouth is his relief valve—the escape hatch from which all his fear, doubt, downright anxiety, and his confidence and sheer love of what he's doing, gushes forth. He wears his emotions on his sleeve. If he didn't talk all the time he'd explode like a steam engine with its exhaust pipe stuffed with steel.

Will Trevino institute a new era, a new generation of professional golf players who will resemble real live human beings instead of Tussaud wax figures? Maybe. And why not? After all, it *is* only a game.

Last November this writer went to El Paso to do a column and get some instruction articles from Lee, who is a member of *Golf*'s instruction panel. In the column he predicted Nicklaus to win the PGA, Yancey to win the Masters, Jack to win the U.S. Open ("I don't know that Merion course, but they say you have to move the ball around a lot—play a lot of shots. I might have a chance.") and himself to win the British Open ("I love that Royal Birkdale course"). The work done, we drove to the nearby New Mexico University golf course, in Las Cruces, where Lee was playing in a small pro-am. It was a favor he was doing for some of his old buddies—helping them make a few bucks. It's the kind of thing he does often, everywhere. Last year he heard of a pro whose shop burned to the ground and was out of business. Lee had never met the fellow, still hasn't, but he played an exhibition and turned his fee over to the pro to reestablish himself.

Anyway, Lee put me in with him in the New Mexico pro-am and we were last off, starting at about one. A couple of hundred people materialized out of the sage and dry brown earth on this Monday afternoon to watch—and listen—to Trevino play golf. He was in good form. He hit shots off the hardpan no higher than a snake and stiff to the pin. And at a par-three I decided to use a four-wood.

"That's too much, if you hit it," Lee said.

"Well," I said. "I'll just feather it in there."

So I hit my patented little snaphook, and Lee came out fast with, "If that's feathering the ball I'd hate for you to pluck my chickens."

I sneaked back into the crowd, laughing with everyone else.

"I don't know where I get lines like that," Lee said a few moments later. "They just come out."

The play was slow. It had been chilly and windy the whole day, and now that the sun was just about gone it was getting desert cold, which is . . . cold. But the crowd of 200 never diminished. It seemed, in fact, to be bigger than at the start. They stayed with Lee right to the dark and bitter cold end.

Next to Arnold Palmer, there is only one man on the tour whose announced presence at a tourney will bring people through the gate who might not have come otherwise. That man is Lee Trevino. In a *New York Daily News* headline for the British Open, it said: LEE TIES FOR OPEN. That's all it took to identify Trevino—just Lee, and that puts him up there with Arnie and Jack and Gary. The people know him on a first-name basis. It figures.

Even Arnie, who, more than any pro before him, with his flailing follow-through and animated grins and grimaces, captured the empathy of the masses, is not as truly identifiable with the average man as is Lee Trevino. Arnie, for all his special appeal, is sleek and powerfully built, obviously stronger and better than Joe Golfer. He's the ideal.

But if you like your folk heroes bigger than life don't look to Lee Trevino. Right down from his foreign name to his oversized cap to the sometimes raunchy joke lines to his wide-open stance and awkward-looking swing that is straight out of the public golf course, Lee Trevino is the stuff of the American proletariat. Lee Trevino is the people's pro—pure.

MY ROUND
WITH JOE

(Golf Journal—1993)

I recall that no one was impressed, not even surprised, when I told them. The reaction was kind of "Uh yeah, sure, uh huh." Understandable. I was just a skinny neighborhood kid who wore glasses. But I wasn't making it up. I had, in fact, played seven holes of golf with Joe Louis, the Brown Bomber himself, heavyweight champion of the world. We played for the price of my putter, when it was new: 13 bucks. I won. I probably should have given him the putter after collecting my loot, as a nice gesture to a great man. But I didn't understand that sort of thing at the time; it didn't fit my stolid, practical working-class background. Hey, if I give Louis the putter, I have to buy another one. So what's the point of winning the bet? Besides, I liked that putter. It was a Golfcraft Lloyd Mangrum Model with a gray soft metal half-moon mallet head, goosenecked. Gooseneck is what is now called offset.

I played the seven holes with Louis at the old Bunker Hill Golf Course, about two blocks into the town of Niles from the north end of Chicago's Milwaukee Avenue streetcar line. Bunker Hill has been a housing development for years now, but it was a public course back then that let blacks play. Not all courses did in 1950. I was enjoying a round there by myself after caddying at nearby Tam O'Shanter Country Club to earn money to pay my green fee. I knew the group ahead was Louis and his retinue. He had three or four people who were just hanging around, or on, and a personal pro who was playing with Louis. Sometimes the pro was Ted Rhodes, but not this time. Too bad. Rhodes was the best black golfer before Charlie Sifford and Lee Elder, and maybe ever—he had a wonderfully smooth swing and classic moves.

I caught up with the Louis group on the second green, when I was waved through. Louis was sitting on his bag at the side of the green watching me putt out. There was nothing at all pretentious or self-important about him. There seemed to be a certain passivity, even, but that couldn't have been, because you don't become the world's heavyweight champion by being passive. Anyway, he said he liked my putter. I said I did, too. He asked me how much it cost, I told him, and he said he'd play me for it. So our game was on.

He was by all means a big man, and it wasn't just presence. He was probably bigger than in his pre–World War II prime, because he had been retired from the ring for a couple of years and had bulked up. Still, he made a pretty good pass at the ball—good form, fluid. After all, he was a superb athlete. But he wasn't especially long off the tee. I was in my teenage grip-and-rip days and actually hit it a little past him. Naturally this got Louis's attention. "How do you hit it so far?" he said, with a light tone of incredulity.

I remember only three shots from the affair. First there was a drive hooked into some trees that was longer than his in the fairway that prompted his incredulous question. Then there was the iron out of those trees that reached the green. Louis just looked over at me after that one. I can't interpret that look. The third shot was at the ninth, a long par-three. I was one up on the tee, and I hit the green. So did Louis. He was away, on a line close to mine. I had marked my ball, but he nicked my coin with his putt, which just missed going in. I got a little anxious about that, a pang that the heavyweight champion of the world would get angry at a little squirt in blue jeans. But of course he didn't. He made a soft remark with a small smile about my coin costing him the putt. Then he paid me the 13 bucks, and we shook hands. Mine was swallowed up, let me tell you. Then I went my way, he his.

The next time I saw Louis was on television. He was in the ring with Rocky Marciano. The thing that I remember, as does everyone who saw the fight on the tube, was Louis going down with his back on the ropes and the bald spot on the top of his head a sad symbol of his fate at the hands of the powerful, young Marciano.

I'm afraid I have to recall the old gentle giant cliché. For a man of such controlled violence by profession, in my experience Joe Louis was very good-natured, a soft touch. And that was his reputation, that he always had a few bucks for a down-and-out fighter or a hustler with a good story. And he was definitely an easy mark on the golf course. The 13 bucks I got off him, as I later discovered, was a mere pittance compared to what the tour pros made playing Louis. There were many stories of how tour pros when they visited Detroit, where Louis lived, played the champ for very big money, and made enough to pay their expenses on the road for a good while.

I was reminded of this last year when Michael Jordan made news losing big bucks to a couple of golf hustlers—another superstar from one sport thinking he could, or should, be able to carry over his talent to golf and discovering that the old Scots game just doesn't work that way. I also saw for myself how Louis got nicked by the pros. When the big tournaments were played at Tam O'Shanter—the All-American and "World" Opens—I caddied in them. The sponsor of the events and owner of the course, George S. May, let Louis play in the amateur division of his tournaments. When people remarked that Louis wasn't good enough and should have been made to qualify, May simply said, "Joe Louis qualifies as the heavyweight champion of the world." That was that. May was a master promoter, and Joe Louis drew crowds just as celebrities do playing in the tour's pro-ams.

The pros didn't complain about Louis being at Tam. They lined up for practice rounds with him—they might well have had a lottery—even those who were either outspoken against or made no effort to let blacks like Teddy Rhodes and Bill Spiller play on their tour. The PGA of America was running the tour in those days, and still had the "Caucasians only" membership clause in its constitution. That's the main means by which they kept the blacks out. May was one of the very few tour sponsors (the Los Angeles Open was another) who let Rhodes, Howard Wheeler, Bill Spiller, and other good black golfers play. He got away with it because his purse money was a bonanza—$25,000, and eventually $50,000 (not counting a $50,000 exhibition deal) to the winner alone in a day when the *total purse* elsewhere on the tour averaged maybe $15,000. To mollify the protesting white pros, May paired the blacks together. He was a gradualist in regard to the race problem, but at least he was that.

Louis did a good bit to help black golfers play the game. For a number of years there was the Joe Louis Open, played in Detroit for black players—although whites were allowed to enter and did, taking a week off from the PGA Tour and sometimes winning it. Out of pocket, Louis saw to it that black pros had some money to play on the black tour. As Walter ("Chink") Stewart, a black who for many years was head pro at Carroll Park Golf Course, a Baltimore municipal course, recalled, "Only once I went up to Detroit, and I remember the lady in the registration booth saying my entry fee had already been paid. Well, *I* hadn't paid it, so I talked to Clyde Martin, who was Joe Louis's golf teacher, and he told me Joe paid my entry fee. He paid for all the black pros. He was that type of man. And after the tournament was over, he chartered a plane and flew a lot of the black pros up to Canada for a tournament up there."

On balance, Louis was by his own nature and background—born very poor in the Deep South, with little formal education—from the "go slow" school of integration. But he was capable of taking direct action. He did in 1953, and thereby played a significant role in changing the way things were.

THE CASE
OF
E. HARVIE WARD

(Golf World—1997)

In 1957, Harvie Ward was the best amateur golfer since Bobby Jones. He might well have become even better. Ward was odds-on favorite to win an unprecedented third straight U.S. Amateur title, and had made very strong showings in recent U.S. Open and Masters tournaments. He might also have become golf's Arnold Palmer, instead of Palmer himself. He had many of the same charismatic properties that made Palmer so welcome a change from the tight-lipped, laconic Ben Hogan–dominated era of professional tournament golf. Ward was a good-looking, good-natured, easygoing, unpretentious young man. And with a rhythmic and uncomplicated golf swing, he was a winner.

But at the very moment when Ward had reached the highest point yet in his burgeoning golf career, he got caught up in the illusory doctrine of amateur status. As a result, a lustrous present was deglazed, and an almost certain radiant future ended up in a murky wasteland. Ward is perhaps the most tragic mightabeen or, better to say, almostwas in golf history.

Born in Danville, Virginia, and raised in Tarboro, North Carolina, Ward made his first mark in golf in 1940 as the 15-year-old winner of the

Carolinas Junior championship. He successfully defended the title. The onset of World War II slowed his progress in golf, as it did the game itself. Ward served in the U.S. Army from 1944 through 1946, and was discharged with an inner-ear problem that affected his balance but not his golf. Returning to Tarboro, Ward put in the extended, concentrated hard work at the game that sets up the rise to its ultimate height.

"From June through September of 1947," Ward recalled, "I hit balls every day from 9 to 12, and played every afternoon." He got some professional advice, but by all accounts didn't need much instruction. Bill Campbell, the one-time U.S. Amateur champion, described Ward's game this way: "He had outstanding instincts for golf. A simple swing with no mechanical problems. He was a very straight hitter, with adequate length, and could read greens wonderfully."

In 1948, Ward's exceptional facility for golf bore its first national-level fruit. He won the prestigious North & South Amateur championship. The field included such future stars as Julius Boros, Doug Ford, Dick Mayer, and 19-year-old Arnold Palmer, who Ward defeated 5 & 4 in an early round. In the final, Ward beat Frank Stranahan, the best amateur in golf at the time. Ward was now counted a definite comer, a position reinforced when he won the 1949 NCAA individual championship representing the University of North Carolina. Not long afterward, Ward became "establishment."

It took Ward a little longer than expected to win the U.S. Amateur, which Arnold Palmer once said was the hardest of all to win, but he had good showings while working up to it—he twice went to the fifth round, twice to the sixth round. In the meantime, Ward won the 1951 British Amateur, defeating Stranahan once again in a final, 7 & 5. He also won his singles and doubles matches while playing for the 1953 U.S. Walker Cup team. And in 1954 Ward won the Canadian Amateur.

In 1955, Ward won his first U.S. Amateur, crushing Bill Hyndman, Jr., in the final by 9 & 8. That same year Ward again was a strong member of the victorious U.S. Walker Cup team. And in the '55 U.S. Open, he was tied with Tommy Bolt for the lead after 36 holes and eventually finished seventh. He retained his U.S. Amateur title the next year, and then, in the 1957 Masters, his sixth appearance at Augusta National, Ward, along with Palmer and Stan Leonard, was a shot off the lead with one round to play. He concluded with a 73, to finish fourth. (Palmer had 76, Leonard 78; Doug Ford won.) Ward at this point in time was widely considered one of the ten best golfers, professional or amateur, in the world. Which is precisely when he was cut down.

The ax fell the day he arrived home in San Francisco, following his fine '57 Masters performance. Upon stepping from the plane he saw a crowd of reporters on the ramp. Ward recalled the moment: "I wondered who the celebrity was they were looking for. Bobby Brown, the president of the National League and a friend of mine, met me at the plane and showed me the the headline on the front page of the *San Francisco News*— HARVIE WARD'S AMATEUR STATUS QUESTIONED! That was the first time I heard about it."

What happened? In early May 1957, Ward was cited by the USGA as having accepted expense money over the past five years to compete in golf tournaments. The man who gave him the money was Eddie Lowery, a San Francisco automobile dealer for whom Ward worked as a salesman. Lowery had a claim to golf fame from the game's periphery. He was the 10-year-old caddie for Francis Ouimet when Ouimet, an unheralded amateur, won the 1913 U.S. Open in a historically poignant playoff against the British professionals, Harry Vardon and Ted Ray. Lowery stayed involved in golf, and from 1953 through 1956 was a member of the USGA's executive committee, a critical factor in the Ward affair.

Ward did not have a shadow job with Lowery. He sold cars out on the lot, and earned commissions for his sales. Certainly, Lowery also wanted to help further Ward's golf career and he made it possible for him to play during normal working hours. "I usually played twice during the week," said Ward. "Friday for sure there was always a big game." But Lowery also knew Ward would attract customers by the very fact of his golfing reputation. Ward himself could count on that.

Herein lies the germ of an intrinsically fallible, basically unenforceable section of the Amateur Code, and the one that effectively, if not precisely, brought Ward to grief. In Rule 1, Paragraph 6 of the code as it read in 1957: [You are in violation of the code for] *receiving or contracting to receive compensation or personal benefit, directly or indirectly, for allowing one's name or likeness as a golfer to be used in any way for the advertisement or sale of anything, whether or not used in or appertaining to golf.*

Eddie Lowery didn't put up a sign on his showroom window saying U.S. and British Amateur champion Harvie Ward sold cars there, which would have been a blatant violation of the code. But people knew by word of mouth, including Lowery's and Ward's. The question, then, is whether word of mouth is a form of advertising? The answer is yes, of course it is.

Such a business practice did not originate with Lowery and Ward. Not by a long shot. It has always been the case, and remains so to this day, that amateur golfers who gain some prominence at the game as winners of anything, from a club to a city to a national championship, use their reputation to help further business careers, which are almost invariably in sales. It is generally a subtle, but not always unspoken strategy. Dale Morey once told me that after trying the pro tour as a young man and deciding he couldn't make it, he resolved to get into selling something at which "I could use my golf." He went into furniture, and did very nicely while also finding time to play Walker Cup golf and win many significant amateur titles. No less an icon of amateurism than Bobby Jones advised Jack Nicklaus, when he was contemplating his future, to remain an amateur. Said Jones: "The right amateur in the right boardroom could make tons more [money] than any tour pros, and still bring a pure glory to golf." *Pure* glory!

The Dale Moreys of amateur golf, strictly speaking, violate the Amateur Code. They trade on their reputations as excellent golfers. But are they really any less amateur golfers because of it? The best answer lies not in the definition of an amateur, but of a professional: that is, someone who plays or teaches golf as his or her *primary* or *only source of income*. If this simple and legitimate distinction between an amateur and pro was the case, Harvie Ward's life in golf would have been much longer and happier. Even today, any faintly felt or subconscious sense of guilt experienced by an insurance man, say, who uses a reputation gained through success in amateur golf competition, would be dispelled. (Insurance men seem especially prevalent in the category—Jay Sigel, before he turned pro, comes to mind; Jack Nicklaus, by the way, sold insurance while a university student.)

Ward was undeniably in violation of Rule 2, Paragraph 1 (now Rule 1, Paragraph 10) of the Amateur Code, titled Expenses. The discovery, however, was accidental. Only because Lowery had been brought up on federal tax evasion charges and his financial files were made public did it come out that he had paid Ward's expenses to play in tournaments. At that, as those dismayed at the Ward ruling pointed out at the time (and still do), Lowery only had to increase Ward's salary or commission rate to cover the expenses and it wouldn't have appeared in his books as it did. Which is to say, this portion of the code can also be sluffed or easily circumvented.

Ordinarily, the suspension for Ward's infraction is two years. But it was reduced to one year because of a "mitigating circumstance," which Joseph Dey, Jr., the USGA executive secretary at the time, explained as being the fact that Lowery was a former USGA executive committee member who assured Ward that the expenses were permissible. Ward immediately applied for reinstatement as an amateur, and was allowed to compete in the '57 U.S. Open as "an applicant for amateur reinstatement." (He tied for 26th.) Furthermore, although he didn't compete in amateur golf for the next year, Ward was selected to the 1959 U.S. Walker Cup team.

On the other hand, during the suspension period Ward was invited to play in every prestigious non-USGA amateur tournament in the country—the Western, Trans-Miss, and Southern Amateurs, among others—but the USGA warned that if Ward played the amateur status of all the other players in these events would be jeopardized. Thus, Ward did not play. "I guess they thought I would contaminate everyone," he said.

So Ward's punishment was a confused, and confusing mixed bag. It was as if the USGA wanted to appear strong, virtuous, strict, and at the same time merciful, lenient, understanding. It was a fence straddling that may well have contributed to Ward's eventual response to the entire episode. Ward did get back into amateur action after his suspension, but with little enthusiasm, as his record would indicate. He got to the fourth round in the 1959 and 1960 U.S. Amateurs, to the third and fourth rounds in 1961 and 1962 respectively. Compared to his presuspension play, this was mediocre stuff. After 1962, he quit altogether.

Why didn't Ward turn pro? "There wasn't enough money in it then," he says. "I couldn't foresee the money that was coming in tour golf any more than anyone else. It started in 1960, with Arnie, but even then not right away. I could make more working for Lowery."

Ironically, Ward went back to work for Lowery, who had started an auto leasing business. "Lowery made me a partner, gave me shares in the company, did a lot of things to sort of make up for what happened," said Ward. "But eventually we got into a dispute, and we each went our separate ways."

Then why didn't he take the reduced suspension, and come roaring back as an amateur? Says Ward, some 40 years later: "Basically, I said to hell with it. No one in California [where he continued to live] pushed me to get back into the game, because they knew I wasn't interested. I sort of said I'd show those guys by not playing anymore. Kind of silly, I guess. I took up tennis, played some social golf, went about making a living."

Ward's decision to quit cold seems odd. Anyone who reaches such a high level at golf and is willing to test his talent in the biggest arenas must have a powerful urge to be on top. By the same token, it would take something just as strong as that desire to turn a head the way the suspension did Ward's. Four decades later he talked in general of the affair with what seems a life-goes-on, water-over-the-dam shrug—with an easy smile, a gentle twinkle in his eyes. But when Ward gets down to the nitty-gritty of this singular life-changing incident, the smile and the twinkle have a less benign register.

"It would have gone right by the boards," says Ward. "Nobody would have cared and nothing would have been done if I hadn't been the Amateur champion at the time. And Lowery being in tax trouble and getting the notoriety, the USGA had to do something. I don't know it for a fact, but Lowery told me that a number of people on the USGA board at the time resigned after it all happened. So there must have been a lot of dissension or disagreement in that group. An attorney friend of mine called me right after it happened and asked if I wanted a lawyer. He said I had them dead to rights, a sure win, they couldn't lay a glove on me. I said no, because it would look bad.

"Kenny Venturi took it differently. [Venturi was a contemporary of Ward, a friend and fierce golf rival, and also a Lowery car salesman.] I don't know whether Lowery told him it was coming or not, but he turned pro right about that time. [Venturi's name never came up in the aftermath of the Lowery tax disclosures.] I was very hurt, and bitter. Not about Kenny, about the suspension. The assumption was that I wasn't earning the money by work. But we were promoting cars."

Ward may not have made long, involved personal business calls when he traveled to play tournaments, but he did make the calls. So did Frank Stranahan, who justified the expense money he used for his extensive amateur golf schedule (which also included playing in pro tour events) that came out of the public relations budget of the Champion Company (spark plugs) his father owned. Stranahan's amateur status was never questioned.

Promoting cars! That remark skips back past the more enforceable expenses section of the Amateur Code by which Ward was in fact taken down, and to the extremely vulnerable advertising section. Ward felt he was doing what so many other salesmen who played good golf did. To give Lowery his due, being he was cast as the villain in the affair, he was probably also going by that unwritten "gentleman's agreement." Ward, then, was trapped by the USGA's desire or need to enforce where it could—expenses received—and avoid having to confront a portion of its amateur status code that was indefensible; to wit, cashing in on a golf reputation. As Bill Campbell, a one-time president of the USGA, said in reference to the Ward incident: "Much of the rule about taking expenses was honored in the breach."

If that be the case, then perhaps we have a clue to Ward's decision to drop out. Could it have stemmed from a profound disillusion that was not uncommon among young men of his generation following World War II? Consider this scenario, admittedly broad-brushed but I think valid. Harvie Ward grew up in a small town in the Midsouth at a time when, for example, Mickey Rooney's Andy Hardy gee-whiz movies were very popular. In small-town Andy Hardy Land father knows best, the Judge is firm but fair and consistent, and folks are good, helpful, honest. Life is simple, if not simple-minded.

Then, at 19, Ward is witness to and takes part in the meanest, most vicious war of all time. When it's over, Andy Hardy's innocence is hokey, jokey, passé. The world is not nearly as safe as it seemed to have been, people not as honorable and sincere. It's pretty clear that the naive are not about to inherit the earth. In the postwar world, morality has a different face. One must do a little *dealing* to make out in a harder-nosed materialistic society. Well, all right. One gets worldwise and learns to adapt to the new ways. But vestiges of those halcyon first-impression teenage days remain, and are searched out for their comfort in a world not as ordered as it was. Amateur golf is under the aegis of upright old-school gentlemen professing "traditional" values. Staying an amateur is for Ward a throwback to those lovely Andy Hardy days.

But wait a minute. Even in golf things turn out to be not as pure as one thought. Amateurs, according to the code, are supposed to pay the going market price for their golf equipment. But Ward knew very well that was not the case in real life. He also remembered that when he tied for 24th in his second Masters, in 1952, he was approached by John Danforth, a USGA bigwig out of Boston, a member of Augusta National Golf Club, and a friend of Lowery's, who told Ward that there was a spot open for the British Amateur that year and asked if he would be interested in playing. A spot open? "It meant my expenses would be paid," Ward explained. "It happened a lot. You didn't know who paid them. An airplane ticket just came in the mail, and the hotel bill was picked up."

Returning to our Andy Hardy metaphor, Ward is told by Eddie Lowery that he is not breaking the rules by taking expense money. Lowery is a Father Who Knows Best, and Ward believes him. But it turns out Lowery does not know best. What's more, the USGA, the Judge, says out of one side of its mouth that Ward did wrong and must be disciplined, and out of the other side that he wasn't all that wrong so we'll sort of go easy on you.

"If I was guilty, then give me the whole penalty or give me none at all," Ward mused many years later. "You can't be a little pregnant. Why not go the whole hog or just forget about it?"

Ward, said Campbell, "was a pure amateur. He didn't have a professional bone in his body." Totally disenchanted, Ward tells everyone to go to hell and walks out of golf. It wasn't all that serene. Ward had always been a partying type. Some say, and Ward agreed, that he might not have had the discipline needed to succeed on the pro tour. But when he quit golf he began drinking more heavily. His first marriage, the one that friends say gave him the stability that made him a star golfer, ended. He would marry four more times. Eventually, Ward did turn pro. In the early 1970s he tried an Arizona mini-tour, but it was too late. "I couldn't beat those kids," he said. He became a club pro, first in North Carolina, then Florida. Finally, with his fifth wife, he moved to Pinehurst, North Carolina, where he has settled in for the duration. He gives the occasional lesson, plays casual golf, and generally lives the life of a country gentleman. (His wife brought considerable wealth to the marriage; she even gave Harvie a Rolls-Royce for one of his birthdays.)

Harvie Ward was always a charming gentleman with a warm smile, and he was one hell of a golfer. When asked if he would have done well as a tour pro, he nodded, chuckled, and said, "Oh, I think I'd have done pretty well." All those who knew Ward in his prime said he would have done *very well*. "But we'll never know, will we?" Ward concluded.

American golf lost a player of outstanding talent to the hazy and inherently hypocritical doctrine concerning amateur status, which in the real world should read very simply: Any person who makes his living playing and teaching golf is a professional. Everyone else is an amateur. Period.

THE IMPOSSIBLE DREAM OF MARTY FLECKMAN

(Golf Magazine—1971)

If you were a 23-year-old golfer who had just led the U.S. Open through three rounds of play, as an amateur, and a few months later turned pro and won the very first tournament you played for money, what would you do? You'd work that hot streak as long and hard as you could, right? Wear the same socks every day until a law said you had to change them, take only cold showers, and never, *never* alter a blessed thing in that blessed golf swing you're using. It works. Let it be. Don't tamper with the gods, man. Not Marty Fleckman. Marty actually managed the heroics mentioned above. In the 1967 Open at Baltusrol he sent thrills of delight up the spine of Mr. Simon Pure before folding to a final-round 80, and at the end of the same year he won the Cajun Classic, then the last stop on the regular PGA tournament circuit. Yet when he was at, or at least quite close to, the pinnacle of the golf pile, that's when Marty Fleckman decided to take his golf swing apart. He hasn't put it back together yet. He may never, and time could be running out on him.

The fellow was mad, you say. Perhaps. Marty is afflicted with something of a disease. He wants to be perfect. In his search for infallibility

Marty did not try a do-it-yourself kit. He took lessons, the first formal ones to which he had ever subjected himself. And he did not go to the corner filling station garage with what everyone else assumed was his beautifully working machine. He went to a Cadillac dealer in golf mechanics, Byron Nelson. It could be that a local grease monkey would have done him better. Since his involvement with Nelson, Fleckman has been careening on the outside rail of the golf track. He shot 78–79 in the 1968 U.S. Open, quite a contrast with his performance in that event the previous year, and in defense of his Cajun title he finished out of the money. He won some $27,000 that year, partly on the strength of a tie for fourth in the PGA championship and a high finish in the San Diego Open, but the following year near-total disaster set in. He won less than $5,000, had no finishes in the top ten, had a stroke average of 74-plus, and missed the cut in 75 percent of the events he entered. He entered a lot of them, too, because playing tournament golf is all Marty wants to do. He also lost his automatic exemption and so became another one of the mass gangsome struggling on dewy Monday mornings to qualify for the tournament proper. In the brief span of two years he had gone from glittering luminosity to dismal ignominy, which is where he resides most of the time these days.

If Marty Fleckman had not shown such real talent at the highest levels of the game (he was also an NCAA champion) his would be the case of just another hot-rod who finally opened his eyes. But he did, and so we have not a case, but a "story"; one that in the end transcends this individual and pings a universal string that runs through all of us, no matter how good or bad we play golf. Fleckman's quest for the ideal, an errorless golf swing, touches everyone who has ever hoisted a length of tooled pipe called a golf club and sought to put it properly to a small ball.

Some people in golf feel that the teacher, Byron Nelson, has messed up the pupil, Marty Fleckman—given him the wrong advice, or too much advice. Marty is aware of this sentiment, but he's not buying it. He absolutely idolizes Nelson, and believes in him as in the Lord, if you'll excuse a play on Byron's old nickname. Marty told me he would rather spend a week with Byron at Nelson's Roanoke, Texas, ranch working on the practice tee, than playing in a $100,000 tournament. When I called Byron "down home" to chat about Marty, guess who was out behind the barn slugging six-irons while the rest of the pros were in Los Angeles teeing it up in the 1971 tour opener?

It's probably unfair, and incorrect, to blame Byron Nelson for Fleckman's descent from golfing grace. Anyone who had as much success as Marty but still felt he had to make important changes in his swing, must have been carrying seeds of self-doubt within himself. Marty would not call it self-doubt, only a problem of mechanics, but we are not always our own best analyst. Fleckman's father, who runs a lumber business in the family hometown, Port Arthur, Texas, tells of a time when Marty shot 60–62, that's 60–62, in a small local tournament. Now how much more perfect can you get at the bloody game? Everyone thought a dinner for the phenom was in order. Everyone showed up, too, except the honoree. Was Marty off on his own celebrative toot? Not at all. He was out practicing, for God's sake, trying, one presumes, to fine down the three-wood shot so the ball went *in*. With this in mind I asked Marty, "Why don't you forget all the mechanics and just go out and play a game of golf? Tee it up, hit it, then go hit it again." A distant look came into his brown eyes, he smiled somewhat ironically and said with a negative shrug that he's just not capable of playing golf that way. He believes you must consciously swing the club into the proper position. He wants to be a swinger in the Hogan, Nelson tradition, and know exactly what he's doing every time he goes at a ball. To Fleckman, men like Hagen, Palmer, or Trevino play instinctively. When they lose it, whatever it may be, it takes longer to get back. If Marty hits one bad shot he wants to know why immediately so the next one will not suffer similarly. A debilitating business, as this writer sees it, and as Marty's last couple of years would seem to indicate. A human being is swinging a golf club, and given all the variables of day-to-day metabolism (we just don't feel the same all the time) it's just not likely that we can ever really develop the kind of precision Marty is after. Then again, Hogan and Nelson became great following this pattern, and that's who and what Marty Fleckman sees as right for him.

Fleckman is total commitment personified. He has one hobby, gardening, which he got from Nelson, but his affair with rosebuds is not too heated. It's that dimpled white ball he's after, and just about every thought and action is related to it. He eats brewer's yeast in the morning, along with a high-protein breakfast, which he says calms the nervous system. He abjures what he calls "waist" foods, i.e. potatoes, bread, etc., takes vitamin supplements, and with his perfectly proportioned, well-muscled, smooth-skinned, flat-stomached body he is a walking advertisement for calorie counting. Fact is, Fleckman is a health nut. If he wasn't such an easygoing, self-effacing fellow he might come off like Gen. Jack D. Ripper, in the film *Dr. Strangelove,* who lectured maniacally about our "vital juices."

When on the road Marty takes in an occasional movie, reads not very much, will have a glass of beer from time to time, attends a synagogue, although usually only for high Jewish holidays, and normally beds down early. He and his wife Sandy have no children, and in fact, no home of their own. When off the tour they stay at Sandy's folks' home, in Port Arthur. At "home" Marty practices six and seven hours a day. It all sounds a little boring, and to some of Marty's compatriots on the tour it most certainly is. Ascetic golf à la Ben Hogan has just about gone out. Marty Fleckman is holding the line. I asked Marty if he might consider knocking off for a few weeks, or months. Stack the bats in a corner and forget the game completely, then come back to it fresh. Again the gentle smile. (For a man searching so hard for lost valuables, Marty is one of the most untense persons I've ever seen . . . on the surface, anyway. Maybe the brewer's yeast works.) No, he replies, he wouldn't dream of doing such a thing. The only way he's going to find his way back from the boondocks is by playing and practicing, and that's about all he does. It's a single-mindedness that could be his downfall. Even Pablo Picasso, the most prolific artist of our time, takes time out for a glass of wine and a song now and then.

Marty is financially independent, at least for now, which helps his situation. He borrowed some money from a bank when he first went on tour, but paid that back quickly and has traveled on his own hook ever since. His money winnings have obviously not been enough to pay all expenses, but his manager, Eddie Elias, is still able to get his man about $25,000 in off-course endorsement money, and that's what makes the difference. Elias, an Arab, and Fleckman comprise perhaps the only Arab-Jewish relationship currently working in the world. One happy note. However, Elias feels, and Nelson and Marty's father feel the same, that the first six months of this year is the make-or-break point for Marty. Such a long period of frustration, as they see it, must finally affect Marty's attitude. Seeking perfection, as he has, could become an obsession that gets in the way of its own goal.

As Marty Fleckman sees it, there are three kinds of pros on the tournament circuit: the ones who are just after scraping the ball around well enough to make a few bucks; those who would like to win a tournament or two, but have no illusions of, or desire for, greatness; and finally, those who want to be big champions, all-time winners, the stuff of which record books are made. Modestly, but firmly, Marty says that the third category is his target.

Golf is not Marty Fleckman's business, it's his life. There are great risks involved in such aspirations. If he doesn't make it, and most who try don't, he can be a most unhappy fellow for the rest of his life. I'm not sure anyone would like to see Marty fail, not because he's such an agreeable man, but because Marty Fleckman is shooting for the moon. We like to identify with those who take such a chance. It may be a barren, lifeless dustbowl up there, but as the man has always said, it's there. It's there.

THE MAN FOR
ALL SEASONS

(Golf World—1994)

Timing is not quite everything. There is also context. When Arnold Palmer threw his visor twirling into the air with joy after completing his great rush to victory in the 1960 U.S. Open, he broke the ice of near-solemn propriety that had always frozen the on-field demeanor of professional athletes. It was a rare moment when DiMaggio would so much as lightly tip his cap to a crowd roaring its approval of a superb catch or a clutch hit. After Unitas engineered one of his miraculous last-minute touchdown drives to victory, he trotted industriously off the field with his head bowed, and the receiver of the pass that took the trick merely handed the ball to the referee. It was a point of their professionalism to not act out their feelings, especially after a winning play.

Golfers, their game deeply rooted in a 19th-century gentleman's code of conduct, were perhaps even more inclined toward nontheatrical behavior. The ultimate example was Ben Hogan, the icon of the generation of pro golfers Palmer succeeded in 1960. Asked once if, when he was playing tournament golf, he ever thought of himself as an entertainer, Hogan responded quickly and unequivocally: "No." Even Hogan's good friend, Jimmy Demaret, for all his flashy clothes, wonderful smile, and gift of gab, played in competition with a serious mien. Grandstanding was simply not done.

And yet, when Palmer reacted with animated physical and facial emotion to his own play and to the shouts of the gallery and went so far as to actually chat up the rope-huggers during a round, it was readily accepted. More than that, it was refreshing. Palmer reflected a new mood germinating in the national psyche. Enough with the morbid tension of the Depression 1930s, the numbing fear of World War II, the cautious skepticism of the 1950s Silent Generation. Let's let it all hang out for a change. Palmer helped usher in the celebrated '60s decade of open rebellion by the youth of the nation against established authority, mores, politics. It was pretty much accidental, for Palmer was already 30 years old and had an ingrained conservative mind-set shaped in a semi-rural working-class hometown, and by a stern disciplinarian of a father. But symbolism is not necessarily pegged to personal details.

Actually, the upbringing that molded Palmer's essential character enabled his popularity to cross the entire spectrum of popular culture. Had he worn his hair long and sported a beard, worn raggedy jeans, mouthed off, he would have been an idiosyncrasy. His unabashed enthusiasm was attractive to youth, countercultural and otherwise. His trim, muscular physique, battering-ram golf technique, and willingness to make conversation with one and all appealed to the man in the street (and, about as importantly, to a media worn out from, or bored by, trying to make lively copy out of the grim Hogan). Noncommittal in his world views, his speech pattern uncomplicated, his clothes neat and conventional, and his manners appropriate, he did not threaten the corporate world. Indeed, this son of a die-hard FDR Democrat would become the darling of the GOP, Andy Hardy in white buck shoes.

Context, and timing. Palmer bolted onto the scene when television was still a mesmerizing miracle and just beginning to expand its enormous reach into golf. And an exceptionally popular President Eisenhower was smitten by the old Scotsgame, and Palmer ("They were in truth kindred spirits," says Palmer's wife, Winnie). An exquisite synergy. It made Arnold Palmer not only an athletic idol whose celebrity would persist far longer than his golf exploits would warrant, but a larger-than-life folk hero who would finally transcend the narrow bounds of his game.

In this day of camera-conscious, ball-spiking hotdoggers, to whom Palmer opened the floodgates and which it could be said is his one negative contribution to sport, it is tempting to speculate that Palmer's engaging histrionics—the pants hitching, for example—was contrived, an attention-getting gimmick. In 1971, a news item noted that during one round of golf, Palmer hitched his pants 345 times. But the habit was rooted in his childhood.

"You know, when I was a little kid," Palmer recalled, "my shirttail was always coming out. The reason was my build, big shoulders and no hips. My mother was always saying, 'Arnie, tuck your shirt in.' I became very conscious of it. Also, back then I sometimes didn't have pants that fit me right, so they'd slide off my hips and I tugged them up. It was a way of life, a natural thing. It wasn't meant for show, it was meant to hold my pants up. Then people got onto it and thought it was funny."

He didn't have *any* "actor" in him? "Not when he was growing up," says his sister, Lois Jean Tilley. "He didn't have the self-confidence then. He developed the ability to joke with people and grin and so on when he became more sure of himself. But he was always that way around the house. He couldn't contain himself when he was really happy about something. When he won the Open, when he met Winnie and said he was going to marry her, everything. He was always an emotional guy. We all are. We got that from our mother, who has never gotten enough credit for Arnie's career. You know, she drove him to every tournament he played all over western Pennsylvania until he was out of high school. And waited for him. He never spent a night away from home."

The stuff of Palmer's charisma was genuine, which is another reason it worked, but it would have been merely a diversionary sidebar if he hadn't been a big winner at the same time. I remember when he first came out on the pro tour, in the mid-'50s. Some friends and I, who fashioned ourselves golf purists, sidled over to watch this guy Palmer everyone was talking about hit some balls. We saw, and heard, a slugger with a bunched-up, quick-swing action. The ground shook at impact, which sounded like a rifle shot, and his finish was gyroscopic. Naaah, we nayed, he hits everything hard. Can't last. We went back to admire the smooth, classic moves of another new guy on the block, Gene Littler.

It's interesting to realize that Palmer won 17 pro tournaments prior to his 1960 U.S. Open "breakthrough." Among them was the 1958 Masters, his first major, also seen on television. But that victory didn't lend itself to any Palmerian dramaturgy, the come-from-behind flourish he exhibited in Denver two years later. It was that flourish—bold, chance-taking golf featuring last-minute heroics brought off with a workmanlike swing and a fine smile—that gave the golf world *Arnie, the King, Arnie's Army.* Again, had he played with the coldly calculated, prudent precision of Ben Hogan, not to say Hogan's complex swing, Palmer would have only been appreciated, not loved. The amiable ball-beater was an Everyman.

From 1955 through 1964, Palmer won a total of 35 events, including two British Opens and four Masters. The '64 Masters would be his last major title. But Palmer's prime was the period from 1960 to 1962, or more specifically, June of '62 and the playoff for the U.S. Open at Oakmont. That was when Jack Nicklaus began to spoil the fun.

The most vivid memory of that Palmer-Nicklaus playoff was a sense of astonishment that Palmer was being routinely outhit off the tee by 10, 15, even 20 yards. Much of Palmer's mystique came from his power off the tee, especially after he drove the first green at Cherry Hills in 1960, the drive heard 'round the world that set him off on his final-round charge. Palmer was long, no doubt, but at Oakmont the realization began to come home that the vigor of Palmer's swing, the crash of impact, the seemingly supersonic speed of a low trajectory were worth an imaginary 20 extra yards. The incredible height of Nicklaus's shots somehow masked the greater power—until everyone got used to seeing it. (Palmer understood, and could be protective of his power image. In a match he played in the mid-'60s against Julius Boros for the original *Shell's Wonderful World of Golf* television series, on the island of Eleuthera, the players could use either the American or the then-smaller British ball. Boros opted for the latter and was outhitting Palmer. Midway through the round, Palmer suggested to commentators Gene Sarazen and George Rogers that mention should be made of the ball Boros was playing.)

Anyway, as the playoff round at Oakmont progressed, it became increasingly clear that Nicklaus was not only longer off the tee, he was just a better player. He controlled his ball well and was surely a better putter. What's more, he was not in awe of Arnie or his Army of loyal and loud fans. Clearly, Nicklaus beating Palmer, 71 to 74, was not a fluke.

Such was the strength of Palmer's popularity by 1962 that Nicklaus was cast in the role of a regicide for what he did to Arnie at Oakmont, and was abused accordingly. Nonetheless, while Palmer had 12 more victories afterward, including another British Open and Masters, the King was—though he would never say so publicly—stung. It was not only his athletic pride. Nicklaus had grown up a member of a country club and had the bearing of privilege that reminded Palmer (and the blue-collar segment of his following) of his having grown up the son of a club pro/greenkeeper who had impressed on him his lower place on that particular social ladder. Palmer's self-esteem was surely wounded, too, when in 1963, after Nicklaus won his first Masters, the much-revered Bobby Jones expressed doubt that Palmer would ever beat Nicklaus consistently. Four years earlier, Jones had said Nicklaus had the game to become one of golf's all-time greats, and in '63 he said, "I haven't changed my opinion. Nicklaus must be rated an even bet to win every time he plays." Then came the faint praise that kills. Jones added that he "felt certain Palmer will snap out of his slump and have his victories."

Was it only Jack Nicklaus that sent Palmer on his gradually descending spiral? Of course not. For one thing, Palmer was 11 years older than Nicklaus and by 1962 had been grinding on the tournament circuit for seven years in the days when the travel was more arduous than now—at one time he and Winnie pulled a house trailer. Mainly, though, it was self-inflicted pain, if *pain* is the right word, because Palmer was playing out a classic scenario arising from his social/economic birthright and a stormy relationship with his father Milfred, known as Deacon or Deke.

Arnold Palmer was born about two weeks before the infamous 1929 Wall Street Crash, from which the world sank into the Great Depression. Palmers, of German descent ("We think it was Balmer way back," said Jerry Palmer, Arnie's younger brother), have been living in the Latrobe area for the last 150 years. A great-grandfather Palmer had been a landowner, but by Deacon's time the family fortunes had diminished significantly. Deacon worked on the Latrobe CC course as a young man, and took some classes in agronomy at Penn State University that led to him becoming the club's greenkeeper. Despite a withered right leg left over from polio he contracted as a boy, he also had a talent for playing golf. When the Depression hit and the club could not afford both a pro and a greenkeeper, Deacon was given both jobs. The pay wasn't much, but it was pay and he meant to keep it coming. As Lois Jean Tilley, Arnold's younger sister, recalls, the members of the club probably wouldn't have minded if she and her brothers used the swimming pool and golf course freely, but Deacon, by force of nature, would not allow it. He imposed the restrictions on his children. "Daddy knew his place," Lois Jean remembers. "He'd never go in the clubhouse or dining room. He took all his meals in the kitchen. But he was also worried he might lose his job. He didn't want to take a chance that the members would complain." The upshot was, "we were made to believe we were just a little bit second class."

When success on the tour came, Arnold Palmer was strongly inclined to take every financial advantage possible. Money was both security and status. Mark McCormack, who founded what has become a giant, octopal athletic management firm (International Management Group) on the strong back of his first client, Arnold Palmer, was very energetic and resourceful in making Palmer's pull on the public pay off. Palmer's income in 1961 from outside sources—endorsements, exhibitions, and so forth— was quoted as $200,000, a lot of money in 1964. A company was formed to sell Arnold Palmer sportswear, Palmer's name was put on a chain of laundries, dry-cleaning establishments, and a maid service. Palmer bought a string of quarter horses and opened an inn near Latrobe. He also began buying up a lot of property around his hometown, and in 1971 purchased Latrobe CC. He was flying some 10,000 miles a year to service all his off-course business accounts, such as attending the opening of a bank in Wichita Falls, Texas, and signing autographs and hitting shots in a chill rain. Little wonder that doctors were advising him in the early '60s to get more rest, and would reiterate the warning regularly. Little wonder that Palmer came out in favor of cutting the entire tour down to 30 tournaments "to do justice to pros and sponsors." And little wonder that the quality of his golf began to diminish.

A regular refrain rent the golfing air beginning in 1962. Arnie wasn't playing as well as he used to because he was devoting too much time to his outside business interests. And his voracious manager was ruining him by sending him all over the world grubbing for dough, of which the manager was taking a nice piece of the action. Demaret had a player's take on the matter, remarking once that Palmer was discovering he couldn't keep holing 40-foot putts all his life. In any case, in 1986, Palmer recalled: "There were a couple of things I wanted to do. One was, if I had to go back to being a club pro, which was always a possibility when I was younger, I wanted to have some control over it. I wanted more than just going back and having to take a job for a living. I had set a standard and knew that by getting myself into business I could reach it, or maintain it. I wanted to own my own club if I had to be a pro there. That was important to me, to establish myself solidly. So I had reasons for getting involved in business while I was still competing a lot on the tour, and I can tell you without a flicker of doubt in my mind if I had it to do over again I would do it the same way."

He wasn't thinking in a vacuum, either, as Winnie Palmer, who came from a family of businesspeople, made clear recently. "Oh yes, Arnie wanted to make money because he grew up without much," she said. "And if IMG had left him alone he would have won more, although at the time he could shut it out pretty well when he wanted to. But he wanted to do the business, and I wanted him to also, because I wanted him to be more than a pro golfer. I have always been proud that Arnie became a successful businessman, as well as a golfer. He's done some good things, and has had a much more well-rounded life than many athletes from his decade have had."

But Palmer was still torn, because in the end he was (and still is) first, and foremost, an athlete. There was the Nicklaus factor, as well, but more compelling was Palmer's need to keep proving to his father that he had the goods. Deke and Arnie had a helluva relationship. "My goodness, they fought like cats and dogs," Winnie recalled. "About anything, putting stances, breaking your wrists, but not only golf stuff. Anything would do, and especially when they had a couple of drinks under their tummy. Arnie would sometimes say, after a fight with Deke, 'Come on, babe, pack your bags, we're getting out of here. We're moving.' The next day, they were walking down the fairway with their arms around each other, and Arnie's mother and I would watch them and shake our heads because we thought they would never speak to each other again. Deke just wanted Arnie to be perfect, and Arnie wanted his father to think he was wonderful and Deke would never give in and tell him that."

Deke was also Arnie's only golf teacher. Arnie did not open up to the advice of others, and by all accounts Deke Palmer was not much into swing theories, fancy or otherwise. Bruce Rearick, the current head pro at Latrobe C C and a young man who likes to delve in the maze of golf technique and equipment technology, says, "Sometimes we'll get to talking about hitting the ball a certain way, and Mister Palmer just says, 'Well, let me hit a few and see how to do it.' He doesn't even want to know how much loft is on a club, he'll just hit it and if it gets the trajectory he wants, that's it. Mister Palmer plays by feel." Deke Palmer insisted strongly on a good grip, and Arnie has always had an envious one. Other than that, Deke simply told Arnie to take it back slow then give it everything he had. In the mid- 1960's when Palmer thought about trying to hit the ball a little higher and perhaps add a soft shot with a bit of cut to his repertoire, Deke told him to just hit it hard at the target. And Arnie obeyed. And all that hard ball-beating inevitably started catching up with him. In 1966 he developed a problem with his right hip that was at first diagnosed as bursitis. In 1969, a doctor discovered he had a lumosacral strain; the right hip was not in the proper position. A chiropractor designed a heel wedge for his right shoe. The cosmic irony is unmissable. As a result of Deke Palmer's polio, for the rest of his life he needed a big buildup in his right shoe.

Palmer's last victory on the PGA Tour came in 1973, the Bob Hope Desert Classic. It was nice to see him win again, but no one thought it meant anything in the way of a comeback. He was wearing glasses, and a hearing aid was in the works. His vanity was ruffled, but he had no choice on the glasses. When he began using a hearing aid, he did so only in private conversations. Although he has always stayed trim at the waist, he was bulking up through the chest and shoulders and his swing was getting tighter than ever. Jack Grout, Nicklaus' mentor, of all people, was quoted as saying Palmer's body turn had diminished terribly in the last four or five years. His putting was often pathetic. In one tournament, he three-putted from two feet.

None of this made a difference in his popularity rating. A clerk helping him fill out an entry blank for a tournament wrote in the space for hometown, "Heaven." He won a Washington, D.C., poll to determine the favorite sports idol of the day. In 1970, Palmer was considered one of the most wanted personalities for product endorsements. He had sold his business conglomerate, Arnold Palmer Enterprises, to NBC for $15 million, and a few years later bought it back. Pennsylvania Republicans asked him to consider running for governor. (Winnie didn't have too much trouble talking him out of it: "He would have been miserable. He didn't want to take the time, wasn't qualified, and is too sensitive to criticism. Arnie wants everybody to like him.") His commercial saleability was (and is), presumably, no longer dependent on his being an active, or even a contending competitor. In the same way that Joe DiMaggio, some 35 years after playing his last ballgame, was representing banks and coffeemakers and being cheered by people who weren't even born when he was in Yankee pinstripes, Palmer could have quit the competitive stage and still done fine financially and otherwise.

But Palmer kept banging away on the regular tour, increasingly to little or no avail. In 1979 he won but $9,276. Thank goodness for the Senior PGA Tour. Arnie had a place to play where he had a chance to win. And win he did, 10 times between 1980 and 1988, with total earnings to date of more than $ 3 million. The senior tour can also thank goodness for Arnold Palmer. Once, while at the far end of the course playing a late afternoon round prior to the 1986 Legends tournament in Texas, spectators began heading toward the clubhouse as if laser-beamed from outer space. What had happened? Arnie had just arrived to play a practice round, that's what.

Even at 64, he still has the magic, but its high gloss has been muted to a matte finish. Have all the hero's off-course troubles in the past few years fouled the image? Palmer was involved in a new-car dealership that went sour—multi-million-dollar losses. A golf course/real estate project in Orlando, Isleworth, in which Palmer had a notable interest, went into receivership. Ignominiously, law officers came one day to take possession of golf carts, pro shop goods, and other tangible assets. Palmer tried to sell his Bay Hill GC to a Japanese group, which did not make his members happy (the deal never went through), and he didn't please them either when he moved into a new house at Isleworth. Celebrity residence enhances property values. People began to listen more closely to anecdotes about Palmer's contribution to the golf courses designed under his name, and how he sometimes shows up for the opening of a new one and has to ask the whereabouts of the first tee. Still, the "street talk" seems to absolve him of any fault in these affairs—another example of the Teflon shield that protects many athletic and folk heros. What the hell, it's probably that bunch of sharks who manage his business who are to blame.

But the quality of his golf is no longer a ballast that keeps his people afloat. It's hard on everyone to watch him duck-hook a 2-iron from the fairway. The flight of his shots is lower than ever. Too low. At this year's Masters in the first round, his drive didn't quite reach the top of the hill on the first hole, and someone in the gallery remarked, "I guess ol' Arn can't get it up there anymore." The cheers for a good shot, or a run of two or three good holes, by a gallery now almost exclusively from his own graying and leathery generation, is sympathetic rather than anticipatory of more to come. Palmer's own body language says it won't last. In his prime, Arnie, like all athlete-heroes, was the power and strength and verve of those who came up a little short in those departments. He filled in that gap in their lives. Now those people see him play as he does and are reminded of their mortality. Whether that is Palmer's responsibility is a question with no final answer.

Palmer says his appearance in this year's U.S. Open and the PGA Championship (both by special exemption) will be his last in those events. He had already given up the British Open. But there is a feeling of dread that he is going to look really bad, especially at Oakmont. It was here where the decline began. Will it also be where he falls? No one expects him to make the cut. The worry is he'll shoot in the 80s.

"Arnie has intuitive good sense," says Winnie Palmer, "and has his own program for winding down without making a big hurrah about it. I think this is the dignified way to do it. Getting all the awards and exemptions he's been getting will help him make the decision."

In the meantime, from mid-April through mid-May of this year, Palmer played all five tournaments on the senior circuit. And when he gets home, he practices. "I asked him the other day," says Winnie, "after he'd just come home from a trip, 'Why is it so important that you go out and practice and play? You have all these business things to take care of. Surely you can miss a day.' He gave me that look that says, 'How can you ask such a question after all these years?' He can hardly stand not being on the golf course all the time."

Never much of a reader, only an occasional moviegoer ("He goes when he can pick the movie," says Winnie), an old-fashioned steak-and-potato man at the table, reticent about spending much time with his grandson ("I don't think he knows how to be comfortable with children," Winnie says), Palmer seems able to define himself only when at golf. Promoters of the game like to tout it as the game of a lifetime. Yes, but that can be a curse for those who have reached such heights as Arnold Palmer and need to stay on or within the vicinity of its competitive front line. Does it feed needs he may not even dare to articulate? Ghosts? His once mighty youth? Surely. That damn Nicklaus? Maybe. The gallery, even if its roar has become a murmur? Depends on who's listening. A father he could never satisfy? Hmmm. The damnable game? You bet.

Quitting is never easy, especially for those who have *been there*. For some, it is harder yet.

HOGAN: CONSTANT FOCUS ON PERFECTION

(New York Times—1996)

The brusque side of Ben Hogan's personality is the stuff of legend. A struggling tour pro once asked him for help with his swing and was told, "Dig it out of the dirt, the way I did."

When Nick Faldo, only a couple of years ago, asked Hogan how one wins the United States Open—Hogan won four; Faldo had won none and was getting anxious—Hogan replied, "Shoot the lowest score."

Faldo thought the great man was having a bit of fun. He asked again, got the same reply and was told in so many words to change the subject. Faldo did. Hogan did not suffer fools at all.

Hogan, who died Friday at the age of 84, was without question one of the greatest golfers ever. And like all those who reach such a level of excellence, his style was out of the ordinary. The sound of a Hogan golf shot with an iron—metal against balata and turf—was somehow different from everyone else's.

No word, onomatopoeic or otherwise, can describe it. The flight of Hogan's shots was also uncommon. The casual observer would call him a low-ball hitter; it certainly wasn't high, but it wasn't that low. Hogan carved out his own exclusive channel in the sky. It sounds ridiculous, but the effect he had on everyone who watched him play was mesmerizing. Those who missed it live will never get the real sensation. Film doesn't capture the Hogan aura.

The way he hit the ball was fascinating, but there was more than that. There was the unbending intensity and the total absorption in his work. Byron Nelson remembered rooming with Hogan one week when they were both young tour players and waking up in the middle of the night to a forbidding grinding noise. Rats? He woke Hogan, who told him it was just him grinding his teeth.

Nowadays, a tour pro has in his retinue, on the payroll, a caddie, a swing coach, a physical therapist, and a sports psychologist. Hogan in himself was all of the above. His caddie was but a bag toter; Hogan knew the distances, not by yards but by sight, and made his own decisions on club selection. His knowledge of his swing was beyond the mere proprietary.

When he revealed his "secret" in 1953, *Life* magazine paid him a then-phenomenal $25,000 for it. Few understood it, and those who did couldn't do it.

Nearly crushed to death in a collision between his car and a bus in 1946, Hogan played and lived the rest of his days in pain. He once hinted that after the accident he played with little to no sight in one of his eyes. His badly damaged legs deteriorated gradually, and before every round of golf he soaked them in a solution and wrapped them just so with special bandaging.

Focus has become a big buzzword in sports psychology. Ben Hogan practically invented it 40 years ago. In the second round of the 1948 United States Open, George Fazio, paired with Hogan, holed out a four-iron second shot on a par-four hole. There was a huge gallery, and it responded with a roar. But Hogan apparently missed the moment.

At the end of the round, Fazio's eagle was not recorded on his card, which Hogan was keeping. Hogan would not put down the two. He said he didn't see it. Obviously, he didn't hear it, either. It took an hour to persuade Hogan to sign off on the score, else his friend Fazio would be disqualified.

I asked Hogan once if as a tournament golfer he ever considered himself an entertainer. His response was immediate, unequivocal, and, of course, terse: "No."

Indeed. His life was defined by the game. It was his decision not to have children, because, he said, it would be unfair to them. He could not give them enough of his time. He had to practice, you see.

Why so hard a guy? Was he shielding himself from hurt? He grew up in grinding poverty, and when Hogan was a boy, his father committed suicide.

Hogan was not a natural at golf, and until he was in his late 20s it looked as if he would fail miserably at what he knew could make him special.

And yet, there were the occasional hints of a more human being beneath the hard, secretive exterior. I asked Hogan once if he had ever had golf dreams. He said yes, one, that he was going to make 18 holes in one, a perfect round of golf.

And? He made the first 17, but on the 18th his drive lipped out. He made a two. How did he feel about that? Angry. Angry? At shooting 19? Sure, he had planned on 18.

There was a trace of a smile on his face when he said he was angry about the end of the dream. It was a smile I read to say that he did, after all, have some perspective. Nothing, nobody was perfect.

He came pretty close, though.

FILLING DADDY'S SHOES: ON SONS OF CHAMPIONS

(Golf Magazine—1980)

Allll of you who wish your father was Gary Player, Johnny Miller, or Jack Nicklaus, raise your hands!

The guess here is that the sky has just been filled with a forest of hands. Think of the lessons you would get, the opportunities to meet famous persons, the thrill of your parent's celebrity, some of which would rub off on you.

The children of famous golfers in real life will tell you, however, that it is not necessarily a piece of cake. As Bruce Devlin's wife, Gloria, says, "We've seen sons of famous people who have had very sad experiences. It can be a tough thing."

Walter Hagen, Jr., the son of one of golf's all-time greats, has looked objectively at both sides and claims there are more pros than cons attached to being the son of athletic royalty.

"On the plus side," says Hagen, "my name alone allowed me to meet the British royal family, play in a lot of celebrity golf events, things like that. I know I got my first job after college, with a radio station in Chicago, because of my name. Sure, I studied radio journalism at Notre

Dame, but so had a lot of other guys. It may not be fair, but that's the way life is."

On the other hand, Hagen, now in his 60s, recalls with regret that as a youngster in military school he wanted very much to play baseball but was sidetracked because of his name. "I was a pretty good catcher, had some heft, and was a pull hitter. But they made me captain of the golf team, because of the publicity it would bring the school. I never did get to play baseball."

Eventually, Hagen, Jr., became a better-than-average golfer, competing in two U.S. Amateur championships, and shooting a 68 in a Canadian Open. "I learned to play pretty much out of self-defense," Hagen says. "I felt a responsibility to my name—and to Dad. The trouble with being the son of a famous golfer, though, is that you don't get any credit. When you make the shots, it's expected. But when you miss, you're a bum."

Which is to say, sons of champions are not entirely masters of their destiny. There is a lot of pressure on them to follow in their fathers' footsteps during their formative years, when they are young and unprepared to handle it. Some of this pressure is self-imposed, since it is in the nature of the relationship that a son wants to emulate his father. In sports, that means being as good a player, or even better. This natural inclination can be particularly frustrating in golf, because great players generally continue to compete at a high level into their 50s, by which time a son has matured and feels he can—or should—knock off the "old man."

At that point some unique elements come into play. One, the younger man must be an exceptionally good player to beat someone who, after all, is or has recently been one of the world's best. For another, the "old man" may want his boy to be an outstanding player, but not at his expense. The intense competitiveness that helped make Dad a champion is to some extent going to override his paternal feelings. Thus, Julius Boros says that for any of his three oldest sons to beat him on a golf course—the youngest is 19, and all have tried or are preparing to try for the tour—that son must play his best and Julius must play poorly. Julius, Sr., doesn't say this in the way of an of an overbearing father who must retain his supremacy in the family, but as a man who does not like lose to anyone. Awed by their father's competitive record, the Boros boys need all the self-confidence they can muster.

At the same time, a champion father can demand of his children his own high standard of performance and be less than patient when it is not reached. A close friend of Jack Nicklaus recalled a round Jack was playing with his firstborn son, Jack, Jr. The latter sprayed a long iron well wide of a green, and Jack, Sr., expressed his dismay for all to hear. "How are you going to play this game with a swing like that?" asked the master.

"Jack probably should have taken the kid off to the side and spoken quietly to him," says the friend. "Lately, he's been getting better about that; he's becoming less demanding."

Indeed. We now have Guy Boros and Dave Stockton, Jr., who, based on their play on the 1994 PGA Tour, indicate they may one day equal if not surpass the achievements of their celebrated fathers. There may be more to come from sons of Johnny Miller, Raymond Floyd, another Stockton boy, and Gary Nicklaus.

There are two interesting aspects suggested in this development. For one, by the time the youngest Boros and the Stockton boys, et al., decided to make a serious try at their father's game, their fathers had become seniors. And seniors not merely as defined by the 50-years-old requirement to play the Senior PGA Tour. For another thing, the boys themselves brought to the situation something of a New Age attitude.

Gary Nicklaus, who is eight years younger than his brother Jack, Jr., is the first Nicklaus son to win a professional tournament. It was only a Florida mini-tour event, but it was highlighted by a closing-round 63 on a very good Tom Fazio–designed course. It could be that Gary is the beneficiary of having come along at a time when his father had gained a certain wisdom from the experience with his oldest son, and from his own maturation.

Let's set up some watershed-year markers. They are somewhat arbitrary, but not unreasonable. Fathers tend to reach a new, or at least different level of maturity starting at age 35. On the actuarial table, they are close to midway through their lives and are getting their first sobering inklings of their mortality. What's more, they have had 10 or so years of the trials and tribulations of making a marriage work, raising children, etc. Professionally, they have become masters at their craft and have had gratifying results. They can now be somewhat less detached from that aspect of their lives.

As for the sons, at age 13, at least biblically, young boys become men. Also, they begin to focus more on what they might want to be when they grow up. Let's say that it is to be in their father's game. Okay. When Guy Boros was 13, his father was 57 and essentially retired from competitive golf. When Dave Stockton, Jr., hit prime time, his father was 40 and had won two PGA championships and a number of other regular tour events. When Johnny Miller, Jr., was 13, his 36-year-old father had won a U.S. and British Open, and was on his way to retiring. Jack Nicklaus was 42 when his son Gary came of age (Dad was 34 when Jack, Jr., did) and of course had won everything.

How are the kids doing? Dave Stockton, Jr., tied for first in the 1993 Q-School, to earn his tour card the first time he tried. That same year he earned over $64,000 on the Nike Tour, and won twice. In his first year on the PGA Tour (1994), he won over $182,000, which earned him a full exemption in '95.

Guy Boros also earned his card in his first try at the Q-School, in 1993, and won over $75,000 on the Nike Tour. In 1994, Boros won just over $240,000 on the PGA Tour. Johnny Miller, Jr., is struggling, so far. However, his brother, Scott, 18, is on a golf scholarship at Brigham Young University, and in 1994 won a 72-hole junior tournament with an eight-under-par total. Raymond Floyd, Jr., and his younger brother, Robert, are on golf scholarships at two college golf powerhouses, Wake Forest and the University of Florida, respectively. Gary Nicklaus won the prestigious Porter Cup amateur event.

What has been done right that these sons of top pros are breaking through, where the sons of Gary Player, Billy Casper, Bruce Devlin, and others before them did not?

"When my brothers were coming up," says Guy Boros, "it was easi-er for me, in part because Dad was a little older and wasn't playing much in competition anymore. Also, by that time he may have gotten it straight-ened out a little bit and had become a little more mellow."

"I purposely didn't give David my whole name," says Dave Stockton. "I gave him a different middle name, Bradley. For about two weeks when he was eight he went by Bradley. He didn't want to be called Dave. But then he went back to Dave, and when he went on tour he started calling himself David, Jr., even if he's not really a junior. So obviously, having the same name as me hasn't bothered him.

"From the start David really wanted to play. It's all he wanted to do, so I tried to keep him from doing it because I didn't want him to get burned out. My father did the same with me. He wouldn't let me play summers. I worked construction, and never played or even hit balls. I just played during the school year. It didn't seem to hurt me. I think that was the best thing my dad ever did. I've seen too many parents who push their kids too hard."

As with Dave Stockton, Johnny Miller was deeply influenced by an indulgent father who conscientiously trained his son for golf. Miller brought tenets of that grounding to his sons, with important modifications. "My dad was a good player and an amazing motivator," Miller recalled. "The only trouble was, while he gave a lot of praise he also stretched you. He had patience, but was so desirous of excellence and the sacrifice involved that most kids would probably not choose his regimen. There were never enough shots to hit for my dad. He would always say, let's hit one more. He was smart enough to say just one more, not let's hit another bucket. Of course, there might be 200 of those one-mores in a session, but by saying let's get another bucket he knew I was liable to say I was tired and didn't want to hit anymore.

"I haven't done that with my kids. I'm sort of a stop-frame teacher. I watch the boys hit shots one week, then not again for a week. That way, the next time around I can see what changes they've made. If you see them every day you can get lost in the thing. Also, I believe there are times when you have to be a little critical. My father took the road of eliminating the negative and accentuating the positive. He'd never say stuff like, 'Gee, what the heck is wrong with you being so quick at the top.' He'd just say, 'Try this, because that shot is gone so forget about it.' I'll say to my boys, 'See those hooks you just hit? Here's what's causing them.'

"The one negative and positive I have passed on to my kids," Miller continues, "is with their name being Miller, if they can play a good game of golf and have a knack for teaching it, they will always be able to make a good living teaching golf. The negative is, trying to become a champion can beat you up a little. If you don't make it, it can leave a little scar tissue and some self-doubt about your ability in everything else."

It's interesting to consider that when Dave Stockton, Ray Floyd, Johnny Miller, and Jack Nicklaus became fathers, it was during a memorably evocative period in American social history, the '60s, which actually spilled over into the 1970s. There is no evidence, and it is unlikely any will turn up, that these men were actively involved in the bearded and sandaled counterculture of that time. But it is not unreasonable to assume that they were touched to some extent by at least one component of that turbulent period.

Beneath the brash defiance of received customs and politics, there was in the "hippie" movement a kind of empathy for people and the realities and trails of ordinary life that had been missing in the culture. "Have a nice day," that code-phrase of the flower-child '60s, became a terribly trite phrase, but its real sentiment may well have resonated into the fabric of day-to-day life, even unto that of the conservative, status-quo world of golf. Thus, these golf champion fathers may well have opened up in more effective ways than they might otherwise have to the problems of being a kid, and especially a kid with a celebrated, accomplished father.

Surely their kids were or have been products of that '60s generation mind-set. The young Stocktons and Boroses and Floyds and Millers were and are proud of their fathers, and impressed by their accomplishments and renown. But they have also brought to the party a degree of sophistication to this aspect of the relationship that may best be illustrated by a remark 19-year-old Robert Floyd made: "I like being the son of a famous father, because then he doesn't have to live his life through me."

The other source of pressure on champions' children comes from strangers, and it is no less daunting. Of course, a kid doesn't have to feel the responsibility Walter Hagen, Jr., speaks of, but how does he ignore a gallery of a thousand who have come to watch him play when he knows he doesn't have the record to earn such notice? That it is simply because he has a famous father? And, perhaps, because his famous father is also part of his gallery? That happened to Jack Nicklaus, Jr., while trying to qualify for the U.S. Amateur championship recently.

USGA president "Sandy" Tatum remembers that many in the crowd were "just gawking" at the Golden Bear. His son must surely have realized this. And his father certainly recognized the impact of his presence. But if he had stayed away, he would have been depriving himself of his rights as an involved parent. Sons of champs have it tough, but sometimes so do the champs.

Walter Hagen, Jr., recalls the time in the 1940s when he tried out for the Notre Dame golf team. "A hundred guys came out to see me tee off on the first hole. I cold-topped my drive, and they all scattered. Left to myself, I ended up captain of the team, and one year won the Indiana Intercollegiate."

In the end, each child of a champion must make his own peace with his advent into unsought prominence and expectations. Tommy Armour's son took the genetic gift of his father's famous golf hands and became a fine surgeon. Joe Kirkwood, Jr., son of the famed trick-shot artist, "hated" the role he was expected to play in golf and operates a bowling alley in Los Angeles. Jay Boros, Julius Boros's eldest son, is satisfied he gave the tour his best shot, and is now happy running his father's pro shop at a club in Florida. Gene Littler's son decided he had traveled enough on the tour as a child, "was not tempted by it," and has gotten into tennis and medical school.

But whether they make it or not as golfers, the ultimate conclusion champions' children must come to is probably best expressed by Walter Hagen, Jr. "When I was older and people told me that I was a nice golfer but couldn't play as well as my dad, I answered, 'Who in hell could?'"

BEN HOGAN'S DAY IN COURT

(Golf Magazine—1971)

In 1921 Honus Wagner, one of the greatest shortstops in baseball history, sued a company for manufacturing and selling baseball bats with his name on them, without his consent or recompense to him. The case went to the U.S. Supreme Court, and Wagner lost. Some 20 years later Davey O'Brien, a brilliant football quarterback, brought suit against a beer company for putting his name and picture on a widely distributed calendar. O'Brien received no money, but even more disturbing to him was that, as a crusading teetotaler, he was associated, however indirectly, with beer drinking. O'Brien also lost his case. The decisions against Wagner and O'Brien were based essentially on the legal ground that they were public figures; thus their name and/or picture could be used for commercial purposes without their being consulted or paid.

But laws only represent social attitudes, and at the core of those decisions, which seem so incredible today, was a notion of an athlete's place in society. It seemed to say in effect that when a man exhibits himself on a playing field he lowers himself in the eyes of his fellow men, becomes something of a clown, a second-class citizen who merely entertains and thus can be taken advantage of freely. In 1955 that concept was put to the test by Ben Hogan, and the story is yet another example of this rather unique man's strength of character, and will.

At the 1954 U.S. Open at Baltusrol, pictures of Hogan were taken as he was putting on the practice green. He did not give his permission and had no knowledge of what they would be used for. About a month later Hogan received a letter from a sportswriter named Dave Camerer telling Hogan that the pictures would appear in a book Camerer was writing on the various golfing styles of some of the top pros of the time, including Hogan. Camerer asked Ben to sign a release waiving all literary rights, and for the right to use Hogan's name and pictures in the book. He offered as payment two copies of the book, and a $100 "honorarium." Hogan's response had the directness and pungency of a six-iron he might hit to win a Masters. General McAuliffe at the Battle of the Bulge beat Ben by only two words in the terse comment department. Ben replied, "Are you kidding?"

Just as the Nazis did not know the full measure of the man from whom they heard "nuts," neither did Camerer and his publisher know Hogan. The book, entitled *Golf with the Masters,* was brought out with Hogan's portion included. On the day Ben was to tee it up against Jack Fleck in a playoff for the '55 Open, he was handed a copy, and was asked to autograph it no less. Along Seventh Avenue that is known as super *chutzpah.* Few people can say "no" with the finality of Ben Hogan, and one can imagine with a shudder the glacial glare that accompanied his refusal. Ben now knew that against his express wishes his name and picture were being used for the commercial benefit of someone else. The "someone else" was the A.S. Barnes Co., publisher of Ben's own book of instruction, *Power Golf.* This meant, of course, that the company and Ben were good friends, or at least had been. But this could not deter Hogan from doing what he had to do. There was a matter of principle involved, and when it comes to matters of principle Ben Hogan is what might be called, in currently popular language, a strict constructionist. He began proceedings against A.S. Barnes.

Just as Hogan can know the best part of a fairway to be 6½ yards in from the right-hand rough, which is where he will hit the ball, he knows how to select legal talent. His man was Francis W. Sullivan, a Philadelphia lawyer. The term *Philadelphia lawyer* has a special connotation deriving from the time when the U.S. Supreme Court was at home in the City of

Brotherly Love. That circumstance brought many fine attorneys to the city, and there evolved a tradition of high professionalism and integrity that exists to this day. Francis Sullivan is very much a part of that tradition. From the time he obtained his law degree at Temple University, all he's ever wanted to do was practice his profession . . . and play golf when he finds time. In his late 60s, Sullivan scores in the early 80s most of the time, but was a near-scratch player in his younger days. A member of Merion and Pine Valley, he has consorted on golf courses with some rather good players. Hogan and Tommy Armour are but two. Armour was an old friend, and as Sullivan puts it, he never took an actual lesson from the "Silver Scot"; simply playing with him was lesson enough. No doubt. But it is the law that is his main calling. Sullivan may be the only man in the world to turn down an invitation from Ben Hogan to spend a week play-ing with Ben and hearing out his theory of the swing. In anyone's jargon that is plain madness. But Sullivan has turned down other enticing offers. He has been proposed for commissionerships of professional football, and golf, and was tendered two federal judgeships. All, including Hogan's offer, were refused, because the one thing that comes first with him is the practice of law. In an unassuming, minimally staffed downtown Phila-delphia office, that is exactly what he does. And as further evidence of the individualistic strain in his character, he is one of a vanishing breed, a general practitioner.

There are other traits of personality that make the Hogan-Sullivan relationship more than a legal business one. They are both smallish, slen-der men with a no-nonsense facial expression not easily broken through. Both take a serious approach to life, particularly the professional end of it. Sullivan, like Hogan, is careful and methodical, as are all good lawyers . . . and golfers. Both came from similar economic conditions. Sullivan took his bar exam with the last five dollars he owned. Hogan scraped for enough money to hire shag boys and enter tournaments. Both became successful and relatively wealthy by dint of their single-minded sense of purpose and perseverance. They are quietly proud of their achievements and have the same perception of a man's rights. Hogan's are wholly instinctive, Sullivan's articulated through his knowledge of, and skill at, the law. These two bantam Irishmen made a formidable team in that Phila-delphia courtroom.

The trial had some ironies of passing interest. The defendant, Barnes, carried the same name as a great player in past golf history. Hogan was already a legendary figure, and a judge named Hagan presided. Witnesses included Leo Fraser, president of the PGA; George Fazio, who along with Lloyd Mangrum lost a playoff for the '50 U.S. Open to Ben; and Charlie Price, one of the country's premier golf writers and the first editor of *Golf* magazine.

Hogan on the stand was little different from Hogan on a golf course. Only the spiked shoes and white cap were missing. There was the same intense concentration on each question put to him, and, following Sullivan's instructions to the letter, he answered only when he fully understood what he was being asked. If he had to ask Sullivan what "club" to use, once on the "tee" Hogan knew precisely how to use it. When asked to produce evidence of his earnings as a professional golfer, Hogan surprised even his lawyer, producing a folder with neatly typed pages filled with an accounting of every cent he ever made, including $16.16 for something called the Coral Ridge. The meticulousness of the man was absolute. Judge Hagan remarked after the trial that Hogan was perhaps the finest witness he had ever had before him. And 15 years later the judge recalls that Hogan was clearly a man who knew where he was going, how to get there, and what he would do when he arrived. Indeed.

Sullivan built his argument on five counts: invasion of Hogan's right of privacy; unfair business competition damaging to Hogan's rights as an author of existing and future literary property; an unauthorized and uncompensated appropriation for commercial purposes of Hogan's right of publicity; libel, since the book in part was believed to disparage Hogan's ability and standing in his profession; and a breach of fidelity, good faith, and fair dealing required of Barnes by a written contract between them and Hogan. You don't always expect to win every round in such a fight, but Sullivan provided for all possibilities. In fact, Judge Hagan denied the claims of invasion of privacy and libel. He did, however, uphold that Barnes had committed an act of unfair competition, a misappropriation of Hogan's right of publicity, and a breach of fidelity and good faith. The three counts were actually interrelated, as the judge determined in his brief, and rather than go into all the legal reasoning here, let it suffice to say that Hogan was awarded damages of $5,000. Hogan had won, and a new law was made.

The $5,000 was not a great sum, but that wasn't Hogan's main aim. He was out to prove a point. He dispelled the concept of the athlete as it had been directed toward Honus Wagner and Davey O'Brien. He showed that he was not to be taken for a Roman gladiator, performing for his masters solely on their terms and grateful for the few shekels thrown to him.

Such an idea is repugnant to the man. He demands the respect he has earned by virtue of his own hard work, and insists on controlling his destiny as far as that is possible. His approach to golf has always been that of a professional in the highest sense of that word. What may be only a game to others, a fine way to avoid work, is to Hogan a life's labor. All the endless hours of practice and play are to him equivalent to the scientist poring over test tubes and equations. That Hogan made so capricious an endeavor as the golf swing into something many feel is the ultimate of perfection attests to the seriousness of his purpose. Francis Sullivan remarks that given his remarkable powers of concentration and clear thought Hogan would have been a success in anything he may have tried. Those who appreciate golf at its finest are pleased it was the Royal and Ancient game he opted for.

Man makes laws to order society and to protect what he deems are his rights. Those laws are not static, but to change them is never an easy matter, for men's minds have to be turned to a new light. Those who do alter established concepts are usually of a rather special nature. Ben Hogan is one of them.

DUSTBOWL DANDY

(Golf Magazine—1980)

 One day back in the 1930s Ben Hogan was having a nap in the rear seat of a car driven by Ky Laffoon. The two were on their way to the next stop on the pro tour. When Hogan awoke from his kip he was startled. The car was moving at highway speed but he saw no one at the wheel. What's more, sparks and smoke were rising up just outside his window. Ben thought the car was on fire and about to go out of control any second. What was going on?!

It was this. Laffoon was bent low and, while holding the bottom of the steering wheel with one hand, with the other hand was holding his wedge out the slightly open door of the auto. Ky wanted to grind down the flange of the clubhead and was running it along the pavement as the car sped along. Route 66 was not only "America's Main Street," it was Ky Laffoon's workbench–grinding stone.

That is a Ky Laffoon anecdote, one of many, for Ky Laffoon was an "original," a character from an era we will never see again. Had Ky won but one major title such stories would be better known and Laffoon would probably be more than the footnote he is in golf history. But footnotes are sometimes more interesting and evocative than the main text, which tends to focus only on *big* winning and *big* losing. To know Ky Laffoon is to know something more elemental about American golf.

That's *American* golf. To be sure, the gentlemen on the East Coast who imported the game to this country and first organized it were Americans. Yet in manners, in social cast of mind they were more in the way of Old World genteel. Some of that still exists—USGA officials at the Open wearing coats and ties in Oklahoma's summer heat, the ambience of the Masters tournament, where mention of prize money is as crude as a tailor dunning his liege lord. A touch of such is not so awful, and far be it from me to say it is un-American. But the game in this country might ever have been a sedate lawn party if not for the likes of a Ky Laffoon, who gave it a more homey texture, a New World coloration marked by yeasty language, a flair for innovation, individual enterprise, and an urge for movement that defines the popular conception of our American "character."

A fair share of the above was kept well moist by tobacco juice. Ky Laffoon chewed (still does), and those who chew spit. For good luck he often immersed the head of his driver with chew goo before firing away, and after a particularly bad hole was apt to drench the bottom of the cup with it—*after* removing his ball.

"Lighthorse" Harry Cooper remembers that in his playoff with Laffoon for the 1934 Western Open his all-white outfit was freckled brown at the end of the day. "Anyone who played with Ky got it," says Harry.

Laffoon recalls a yellow Cadillac he drove that was flecked like a bird's egg with the residue of his plug. He was once stopped for speeding along Chicago's Outer Drive by a cop who did not write a ticket after recognizing the famous golfer, but who did ask Ky to refrain from spitting out the window of his moving vehicle. Another motorcycle cop on the chase ran off the road when a flying gob caught him in the eye. Admittedly, that is all a trifle gamey, but that's how golf was "Americanized" in the first half of this century.

In 1915, at age seven, Ky Laffoon moved with his family from a failed farm in Zinc, Arkansas, to Miami, Oklahoma, where the agriculture never got much better. The Laffoons were "Arkies" who became "Okies," making the passage with all their possessions in a covered wagon pulled by a brace of mules. When he hit Oklahoma, Ky Laffoon didn't know a chip shot from a cow chip, but not many years later he was a sweet-swinging, big-hitting golf professional who wore cerulean blue sweaters, canary yellow socks with his knickers, and was matching strokes with the finest golfers of his day from coast to coast and even overseas.

"My first pro job," Ky recalls, "was at the Miami Golf Club. I was around 19. My assistant was my 11-year-old cousin, Leonard Ott. I paid Leonard a dollar a day, but he had more money at the end of the year than me. He got his meals and a room over the shop. Didn't cost him anything to live.

"The next year I got the pro job at a club in Joplin and played in my first tournament. It was in Hot Springs, Arkansas, about 350 miles away. It took me two days to get there in an old Ford that couldn't do much uphill. Two days. They had a driving contest before the tournament. Jimmy Thomson and Johnny Rogers, the longest hitters in the game, were there, but I stepped under the ropes and hit a baby dimple ball 300 yards with a hickory-shafted driver and won me a thousand hamburgers."

A thousand *hamburgers?*

"Hamburgers cost a nickel a piece in those days and I always figured money by how many I could buy with what I had."

How ya gonna keep 'im down on the farm after he's seen Hot Springs and hit it up with the stars? No way, as we say today. Hot Springs was the appetizer, California was going to be young Ky's main course. He borrowed $50 from his father and "lit out" for Hollywood to become a movie star—maybe.

With a noble nose, sturdy chin, and high cheekbones, Laffoon was a curiously handsome fellow, a bit in the way of a 1920s Marlon Brando with raven black hair smacked flat with pomade and parted down the middle in the fashion of the day. Nevertheless, "I only got honorable mention from the studios. Truth is, I was too scared to be a movie star. I just wanted to get out and see what else was happening in the world. I played a tournament out there—finished six, one, six, and out of the money. The Depression was beginning to set in about then and I got a job as a rough-neck in the oil fields. Talk about work! After that I decided if I ever got a good job I was going to take care of it."

When he made a reputation as a golfer and some friends in Hollywood, Ky got some movie offers. But by then golf was his game. A natural athlete with a strong, sinewy body, Laffoon did not rely only on given gifts of strength and coordination. He was a thoughtful student of the game. His own student.

"I never learned from anyone," he remembers, "because there was nobody around who knew much. There was all kinds of different theories.

Some guys broke their hands right at the takeaway. Runyan dragged them back from the ball and so on. I made my own swing, with everything working in one piece and all together. Didn't break my wrists until about waist-high, then pronated so they were under the shaft at the top. I always believed in holding the club real firm.

"The biggest problem most golfers have is losing the club at the top of the swing. They have to regrip it coming down and then the thing can go anywhere. That was Hogan's trouble as a young player. Another thing, I took the club straight back and brought it down inside out. Had a loop in my swing, but when I was going good had a six-foot hook. I always say, the eye guides the mind, the mind guides the body. Keep your eye on the ball and hit it with your hands going fast through the ball."

Toney Penna, now a master club designer but in Laffoon's heyday a young touring pro, remembers that Ky was one of the first pros to spend a lot of time on the practice tee. And the late Fred Corcoran, who managed the tour through the 1930s, once told of watching Laffoon practice his swing facing a tree.

"I did that to learn to stay behind the ball and to get it up better."

In 1934 Laffoon had his best competitive year. He won the Park Hill Open, in Denver, with 266, the lowest 72-hole score on a regulation course recorded up to that time. In the Western Open referred to earlier, Ky shot all six of his rounds in the 60s (it was a 36-hole playoff with Cooper) even while losing. He won the Eastern Open by eight shots with a 65–67 finish over the par-71 Sandy Burr course, in Wayland, Massachusetts. For his 22-tournament 1934 season Laffoon had the lowest stroke average—72 and points—on the tour and was second in total prize money to Paul Runyan by $356. Runyan took in $6,761.61 in 21 events.

As further evidence of how good a golf swing Ky Laffoon made for himself, in 1934 he was runner-up in the Canadian Open and 14 years later tied for second in that same event. And in 1950 at age 41, Laffoon tied "Skip" Alexander for the Empire State Open, losing in the playoff.

Yes sir, Ky Laffoon could play some. He won 12 tour events all told. But he never won "big," most likely because of those aspects of his personality that have rendered him a minor character in the annals of the game. True, there was also the matter of poor timing. He came along when the nation had gone bust and the tour barely survived.

"In 1934 they didn't have enough money to put on a tournament in Phoenix and had a pro-am instead. My partner was Barry Goldwater, a young lawyer at the time. We won it. Up in Indianapolis the sponsor ran off with the cash and none of us got paid until the PGA made it good some time later. That was quite a little Depression we had going. The times made you think. We were eating breakfast in L.A. one time, and Byron Nelson wanted some potatoes like I had on my plate. When he found they cost an extra quarter he decided he'd do without. Nowadays they just wonder where all the money's coming from."

It was an era when Byron Nelson, when he became the U.S. Open champion, could be signed by the MacGregor Company for only $900, and Ben Hogan, struggling desperately but with obvious potential, would sign with the same firm for enough to keep him on the circuit another month—$250—Jack Nicklaus's weekly tip money. Thus, in the middle of 1935, while still at the top of his game, Laffoon took a club job at the Northmoor Country Club, outside Chicago. "They offered me everything I asked for, I had two brothers to look after, so I took it. Some days I was giving lessons 10 hours a day."

Still, Ben Hogan, Byron Nelson, Sam Snead, and others scraped through the Hard Times and fulfilled their talent. Laffoon's failure, if it can be called that, had deeper "reasons." He hints at them himself in telling two Hogan stories.

"I was leading a tournament in Alabama once but withdrew to go hunting. There was some good shooting down there. Hogan stuck with it and won the thing."

Another time, in a tour-stop town, Hogan and Ky went to see the movie *Of Mice and Men,* John Steinbeck's moving tale of two poor, itinerant farmhands in the Depression days. One of them, a demented giant who caressed small pet animals to death, intrigued Laffoon, who remembers that as a three-year-old left alone on the farm in Arkansas he passed the time sticking the chickens headfirst on a picket fence and laughing himself into a small heap watching the fowls' bums do a frantic shimmy. Hogan would have none of Steinbeck.

"Ben walked out after a short while. Waited in the lobby for two hours. He said he couldn't stand all that . . ."

Hogan allowed no distractions from his legendary concentration on golf excellence. Laffoon opted to "see what else was happening in the world." Regrets?

"Hogan went fishing and hunting maybe once each in his life. Now he has nothing to do but build golf courses, go to the factory, hit balls. Me and my cousin Leonard Ott went down to visit Ben a few years ago. He couldn't understand what we do with our time. Well, hell, there's a million things to do. I hunt, fish, drink, eat, play golf, play cards, got three dogs and a lot of friends to talk to. But you've got to learn what to do, get your interests when you're young so when you get to be 65 you know what to do with your time."

Laffoon was a Rabelaisian rouster. "I got some terrible cramps outside of Las Vegas once. The doctor examined me and said I shouldn't eat so much. I said I was a golfer and needed food for energy. He said if I didn't eat so much I wouldn't need so much energy. I don't think the man was much of a doctor."

Laffoon learned something about gambling, shilling a few golf matches for the nonpareil hustler, "Titanic" Thompson, before Ky became a known golfing quantity. Laffoon was also the tour's hotel-lobby raconteur, telling stories all night on whatever subject came to mind to whoever would listen. He always drew a crowd, and kept it laughing. Laffoon let his senses be his guide and made up living as he went along.

Almost from the moment he hit the pro circuit Laffoon was said to be part Cherokee. In fact, he is French, Irish, and English. Not a drop of "Injun" in him.

"I was playing up in Boston one summer and was real dark from the sun. *Laffoon* sounds Indian and what with also being out of Oklahoma, having the high cheekbones, and going by the name of Ky, my middle name, which an aunt gave me from someone in her family—my first name is George, which don't sound like much—some young sportswriter asked me if I was Indian. I figured that would make a good story and I said 'sure.' He wrote it up. 'Porky' Oliver started calling me Chief, and it stuck. That makes Rod Curl the *first* Indian in the Masters, not the second."

So the Oklahoma farm boy wanted a few laughs along the way. But the way was paved with a game that can swipe the smile from laughing gas, that requires *some* self-control. And here was where Ky Laffoon "lost it" most of all. Ky was a stormer, a man of Vesuvian rage when it didn't go well. Such was his reputation for temperament that the story of him grinding his wedge on Route 66 was transformed over the years to read that he had tied his putter to the rear bumper of his car and dragged it 1,000 miles across the Panhandle to make the blade pay for its faults. Fact or fiction, it still comes out "colorful."

For a time Laffoon used a driver with a shaft curved like a bow bent to fling an arrow—a weird-looking instrument some thought to be a carefully calculated innovation in club design. It was not *that* calculated.

"Hogan gave me the club up in St. Paul, but it had a hook face and of course I was hooking too much with it. We had some pretty poor clubs to play with in my time. Anyway, I got burned up and banged that driver pretty hard a couple of times. That bowed the shaft, but straightened the face just right. I beat the hook right out of it and played some pretty good golf with it until it finally snapped.

"Yeah, I was always a hothead. Guess it ran in the family. My brother Bill was always walking out on me, getting mad at me for getting mad at golf. One time he was caddying for me in California and had had enough. At the 16th he dropped the bag and walked in. Walter Hagen carried the bag one hole, Dick Arlen, the movie actor, carried it the other.

"That driving contest I told you about in Hot Springs? They had a tournament, too, the South Central Open. I threw a club up into a tree and it stuck. I threw two more up to get the first one down, and they all stayed up there. Then it rained and the three shafts got warped something awful. I only had six or seven sticks all told. Didn't have enough to finish the tournament.

"In that '34 Canadian Open there was a 95-yard par-three. I put it in a bunker and couldn't get the first one out. Got so mad I tried beating the ball through to China. Took a nine and lost to Armour by a shot.

"But mostly it was putting, especially on those U.S. Open greens. They were the only real fast greens we ever played on each year and I couldn't get used to them. Scared me all to hell and gone. What got me was how can a 21-year-old who can see the line miss an eight-footer? It's unnatural. I had a horror of eight-foot putts. I must've spent fifty thousand dollars batting the ball around the cup after missing short ones. You know, backhanding them. Walter Hagen said to me, 'Ky, I can't understand anybody taking so much time on an eight-foot putt, missing it, then backhanding to miss even more.'

"One time, though, I had an eight-footer to win the Cleveland Ten Thousand Dollar Open by two shots. I missed the putt, got hot, and stabbed the next one. That time the thing popped right in the hole. I won by a shot. No telling where I'd of finished if I kept playing hockey with it.

"Yeah, Chief, I could get hot. And I wasn't the only one, you know. Take Lefty Stackhouse! I remember Lefty sitting cross-legged in front of a fire he had going with every wooden-shafted club he had had in his bag. He turned them all into kindling. The guy who loaned him the sticks was standing over Lefty and chewing him out like you never heard before.

"I'll tell you, though, Chief. We could afford to be angry and lose our tempers. It didn't cost enough to stay cool. If we played for a thousand instead of a hundred, we wouldn't have gotten so hot. Same with walking off yardages, the way they do now. We didn't, because it wasn't worth the effort. When you play for peanuts, you got to salvage something for your time. Pride was another thing. I withdrew from a Western Open in South Bend one year because they put the players' parking lot two holes from the clubhouse. That was a long walk. Made you feel like a bum. So I said to hell with it. When I couldn't get mad anymore, I quit the tour."

Ky Laffoon has been living in Springfield, Missouri, for over 20 years now. It is not very far from where his career in golf began. Back to his roots.

"I lived high in my time. Once ate dinner with Al Capone, down in Puerto Rico, hustled Howard Hughes out in California. That was during the bank moratorium and was the only way to get some cash. Got second money there, too. George Von Elm got most of Howard's cash. Hughes always pretended he was hard of hearing—maybe he was—and when I said I'd give him two shots a side he said I said three. But it was always two.

"Anyway, I like it here in Springfield. Give me the simple life. There's all kinds of good fishing, I got a town of 60,000 that don't cost much to live in, a couple of good golf courses and enough players to get a good game. I got a nice fence to keep the dogs in, and all the kitchen gear you need."

He is well fixed financially, although not nearly as rich as he has been thought to be; no oil leases, just some apartment buildings, a house, savings bonds, money in a savings and loan.

"I lived rich, so everybody thought I was. Got all my clothes from the Oxford Company in Chicago."

He is still married to his wife of over 40 years, but there were no children.

"That was planned parenthood. Kids were a lot of trouble for all the traveling we did. A lot of us didn't have any—Hogan, Nelson."

Physically, Laffoon is not at all the svelte 160-pounder of his prime. He weighs 235 pounds now.

"That's only about two pounds a year in the past 35 years. Not so bad."

He is as strong as ever, though. He squeezed my hand to illustrate. The force on my fingers was that of those crushers that render junked cars into square metal pancakes. Ky's forearm is a chunk of granite. His strength, too, was storied.

"I could tear a new deck of cards in half, cellophane and all. Tommy Armour used to make money on it. He'd be playing bridge and drinking in the clubhouse and see me coming. He'd bet whoever was with him $50 that the next man to enter the room could tear up the deck. I'd do it, but he never shared his winnings with me.

"That fellow John Montague, the guy in California who played golf with rakes and shovels? Beat him in an arm-wrestling contest once, but hurt my neck and shot 80. I wrestled Gus Sonnenberg, the champion while we were on the boat going to Australia. Threw him. And Clayton Heafner. Talk about temper! He was ragging Hogan one time and I defended little Ben. Clayt said he'd swallow me whole. I told him he'd have more brains in his stomach than in his head. Clayt never said a word."

Another time, Herman Barron was pestering Laffoon, who was in a hurry to get some practice putts before teeing off. Barron kept kicking his golf balls away. Ky got hot and threw Herman over his head.

"Herman was wearing a white Palm Beach suit and when he landed all the buttons popped off. Damndest thing you ever saw."

In Springfield we ate, drank, talked a lot, and played golf—nine holes at one of Ky's two clubs. His swing of course is not nearly as fluid and loose as it had been. Nor as powerful. His girth is too great, especially through the shoulders and chest. And he is 71 years old. But the man can still play. The course is not Medinah or Merion, Pebble or Shinnecock. But neither is it like the flat, open "bullrings" Ky played in the '30s. A nice little test, and Ky did the nine in a very neat 32—four under par.

"Sure wanted to put a good round on you, Chief. For the press."

The clubs I used for the nine holes came from the trunk of Laffoon's car, the contents of which spoke perhaps as much for Laffoon, and his main time in the sun as all the verbal reminiscence. The pros of his era were vagabonds, "antsy" movers wedded to their automobiles. They spent as much time in them getting from one tour stop to the next as they did on golf courses, in hotel rooms and bars. Their car was a mobile den they attached to each week's "home." It is difficult to break old habits, to not live in the past.

The rear seat of Laffoon's 1977 Cadillac had a rack filled with hanging sportcoats, slacks, shirts. A Men's Shop on wheels. The trunk was a spare closet holding: four sets of golf clubs, two golf bags, numerous pairs of golf and street shoes, two handguns, two bottles of Scotch whiskey, a vibrator ("Does wonders for a sore back"), heating cartridges for cold weather "warmers," the "warmers," a fancy spotlight ("You plug it into the cigarette lighter to catch addresses at night"), many packets of chewing tobacco, cans of sardines, and a jar of peanut butter ("In case you get hungry. You never know").

I never got to the very bottom of the trunk. We had to go play.

JIMMY'S PLACE

(The Wall Street Journal—1993)

When Jimmy Demaret was a young man, Jack Burke, a revered golf teacher and early-day patron of Texas pros, took him to a tournament at Pinehurst, North Carolina, and introduced him around as someone who was going to be the greatest golfer in the world. Burke did not throw praise around lightly, as his son Jackie, Jr., a Hall of Fame tour player, will tell you.

Demaret, though, probably smiled and shrugged it off. That was his way. There's no question Demaret was an athlete proud of his prowess, and a fierce competitor to boot. And he did become one of the best players of his era. But his penchant for fun and games of a more social nature eventually sabotaged the elder Burke's prediction for him.

Many years after he had quit competitive golf, Demaret was asked whether he'd have won more if he'd been more diligent. He replied, "If I hadn't been the way I was, I wouldn't have won anything."

As it was, Demaret won 31 times on the PGA Tour between 1938 and 1967. That's a pretty good record for an inveterate playboy, and one with a curious distinction. While in three of the four "major" championships he was only a sometimes-contender, he won the Masters three times. He was the first to win it that often. What was it about the Masters, or Demaret, that he should have been so successful only in this major championship?

Gene Sarazen, who thought highly of Demaret in most respects, did say of him, "Jimmy was a great golfer, but he tended to give up easily when it wasn't going good." Freddie Haas, Jr., a Demaret contemporary, put it a little differently. "Jimmy was a hot and cold type of player," he said.

The record indicates that Haas had a point: When Demaret won his first two Masters, in 1940 and '47, he was a golfer on a roll. He'd won four tournaments on the '40 winter circuit leading up to Augusta. In '47, he'd won twice prior to his Masters victory, and three more times afterward. In 1950 he won once before the Masters, and once thereafter.

The '50 Masters victory was the only one that was more or less handed to him. Jim Ferrier appeared to have the event locked up with nine holes to play, but went five over par on the last six holes and lost to Demaret by two shots. Sarazen recently recalled being in the locker room on that Sunday afternoon and noticing that Demaret, who had concluded his play with a fine 69 with Ferrier still on the course, was packing to leave the course before the trophy presentation. "Jimmy, where are you going?" Sarazen said. "Take a look at the scoreboard." Demaret saw that Ferrier was making a lot of bogeys, and said, "Guess I'd better stick around." Indeed.

In his other victories at Augusta, Demaret was the man to beat throughout. In 1940 his excellent opening-round 67 was overshadowed by Lloyd Mangrum's record-breaking 64, but Demaret was tied with Mangrum after 36 holes, had the lead by a shot after 54 holes, and with a closing 71 won by four shots. In 1947, Demaret shared the first-round lead with Byron Nelson on a round of 69, was tied for first with Cary Middlecoff after 36 holes, led by three after 54, and ended up winning by two over Nelson. From 1939 through 1950, Demaret's best years as a competitor, he had four top-10 Masters finishes besides his three victories. Yes, he liked playing at Augusta National.

Despite lacking the shot most current assessments say is needed to win at Augusta National—a high ball that flies on a right-to-left trajectory—Demaret still had a game that suited the hallowed ground. "Jimmy always saw the game from left to right," recalls friend Jackie Burke, who with Demaret founded the celebrated Champions Golf Club, in Houston. "He was a phenomenal driver of the ball, never far off line. He teed it real low, and hit the ball close to the ground the way most players of his time did. Also, the greens at Augusta were fast and Jimmy was a phenomenal putter on fast greens because he used a short stroke. Just right for Augusta."

Furthermore, adds Byron Nelson, "In those years, the greens at Augusta were not only fast, they also were very hard. Jimmy played a left-to-right iron shot that landed softly, so he could hold those greens."

From a narrow stance, his feet only inches apart at the heels even with a driver, and with huge hands that belied his modest physique in his prime (he stood five-foot-10 and weighed about 165 pounds then, but got heavier later), Demaret was hitting a controlled, power fade with a weak left-hand grip well before Ben Hogan incorporated those characteristics into his game and made them popular. Hogan may well have gotten the idea from Demaret, whom Hogan liked personally, respected as a player, and often played with in practice rounds and as a partner in four-ball events.

Demaret also was a warm-weather golfer who thrived in the wind. In his first Masters, in 1939, on a pleasant opening day, the Houston native tied for sixth with a round of 72. The next day, however, was dark and rainy and featured hail "the size of robin eggs," and he shot 81. He followed that up with 77–74 to finish well back. Ahh, but in 1940, the temperatures were fine and there were stiff winds almost every day. He went 67–72–70–71, to emerge the victor. And just in time, too, for almost as soon as he finished his last round Augusta National was drenched with a heavy, chilly rain.

Masters week 1947 featured the salubrious Georgia early spring that would warm the soul of the scroogiest of Scrooges. In 1950, the weather was warm enough to bring thoughts of full summer.

But mechanics, technique, and weather can go only so far toward answering the question of Demaret's special relationship with the Masters. Another side of it may be more speculative than spinning cut shots and a safecracker's touch for fast greens, but given Demaret's temperament and taste for life, it's probably valid. Demaret, who grew up the son of a Houston housepainter and was introduced to golf as a caddie, never felt out of place socially at the rich and exclusive Augusta National Golf Club.

On the contrary, "Jimmy had an affinity for Bobby Jones and the aura that was created around Augusta National, the way things were done there," says Burke, Jr. In fact, when Demaret designed the locker room at his and Burke's Champions Club, he modeled it after the understated style of Augusta National's, albeit with a little bit of Texas in the big, sweeping bar where Demaret would hold forth telling stories, concocting practical jokes, singing songs, and quaffing beer.

Ambience is what got Jimmy Demaret's golf game cooking. The U.S. Open was a bit too formal for him—those tight-lipped officials in starched dress shirts, striped ties, and religious approach to the game. The PGA championship was, well, just another weekly convention of his fellow professionals, only with the guys more uptight because a win would make a reputation that could land them a lucrative club job.

What's more, those championships were played at different courses every year, and it would take a day or so to find the homiest bar in town, much less to figure out how to play the course. That last was not Demaret's cup of tea. To be sure, he could "read" a golf course with the best of them, but that took energy better left for partying. "Jimmy could have been as great as anyone if he wanted to be," says Freddie Haas, Jr., "but he wasn't dedicated to that. He wanted to win, but it was *c'est la vie* if he lost. He was distracted by people and life."

Augusta was for Demaret a grown-up version of the college homecoming he'd never had. He knew the course like the back of his massive hands, his favorite watering holes were waiting for him, and if the members of the club that ran the event were on the stuffy side, it was in a subtle, comfortable way—Old South, don't you know. Besides, the Masters was always played around Eastertime and this fed directly into Demaret's incomparable love of, and flair for, colorful clothes.

It's well known that Demaret revolutionized golfwear. Like all his contemporaries, at the outset of his career he wore a dress shirt and tie on the course, woolen pants and leather shoes in drab tones. But not for long. He remarked to this writer, a few years before he died (in 1983 at age 73), that one motivation for adopting the wardrobe for which he became famous was, "Everybody looked like undertakers out there, and the locker rooms stank with all those woolen clothes full of sweat."

He said he got his ideas about color from his father, the housepainter. "It was before they had those electric mixing machines you see in the hardware stores," said Jimmy. "My dad would do his mixing at home, and use the walls of our house to see what he came up with."

The breakthrough in golf clothing came when Demaret was visiting a fabric shop in New York City's garment district in the early 1940s. He saw rolls of vividly colored, wildly printed goods that knocked his eyes out. He said he would like to get some shirts made of that material, and maybe some slacks too. He was told that the fabrics were meant for women's clothing. He said he didn't care, make some up for me. The deed was done, and the pro tour, eventually, went from an undertakers' convention to a pool party. Demaret's sartorial enterprise went beyond a mere fashion statement. The new clothes he "invented" also allowed players to swing their clubs with greater freedom.

But it was the colors that drew everyone's attention, which focused entirely on Demaret because he was initially the only one to dare appear in public in such emblazed hues, and with accessories that included suede or three-tone patent-leather shoes, berets, and other unconventional hats.

He was a dandy, and his outfits were regularly reported as part of a tournament. William Richardson, of the *New York Times,* wrote in 1940: "One of the most picturesque figures the game has ever produced, an easy-going, eye-pleasing fellow who really seems to be enjoying himself in tournament play, Demaret went out today (the final round) as though he were starting out to play a round with no more depending on it than a $5 or $10 nassau, garbed in his usual green ensemble with the brim of his hat turned up in front and down in back to give him a rakish appearance."

At the 1950 Masters, an Associated Press reporter described Demaret in a sidebar devoted to his wardrobe. The headline read: DEMARET, FAVORING PINKS, MUM ON EASTER COSTUME. A few snippets of the report are offered here:

"Dapper Demaret, on opening day, wore a stunning salmon pink sweater . . . Yesterday (Friday), he wore purple pants, purple and red shoes, a knitted white golf shirt with red piping around formfitting sleeves and neckline . . . When he shot 72 today (Saturday) the Blazing Blade sauntered forth in rose pants (old rose, fashion editors would call it) and a neatly matching rose and white shirt featuring a high neckline circling gracefully above a dickey . . . Smiling Jimmy, who selects his wardrobe with as much care as his clubs, wore chartreuse slacks, green and white sweater, light green cap, deep green suede shoes."

For Jimmy Demaret, the Masters was an Easter parade, with golf on the side. No wonder he played so well there.

WALTER HAGEN
BACKSTAGE

(Golf Magazine—1980)

Walter Hagen had "the magic touch." He could make filet mignon out of chopped steak, and he did. One of golf's greatest players and most fabled personalities, Hagen was not quite the way golf historians have painted him.

Certainly, much of the Hagen legend remains intact. His competitive record is unassailable; no one fakes 11 major championships. There also is no question that Hagen had "style." He called his golf shots more than once, did some hard drinking, "chasing," and hobnobbing with royalty. So, too, did he show up late for tee-off times, occasionally in his tuxedo and patent-leather pumps. Yet Hagen definitely played a role in eliminating the caste system by which golf professionals were excluded from clubhouses.

Still, without malice or resentment, Hagen's old mates are wont these days to qualify the man's reputation. For example, Leon Sage, an old hometown (Rochester, New York) pal of Hagen, recalls a party for a newspaperman named Morse. "Morse was retiring to run a chicken farm and in honor of the occasion a chicken was fed some booze. Actually, it was

Sherwood Morse's idea to get the chicken drunk, but Walter got the credit on the story."

Hagen himself, before he died in 1969, was similarly disposed to set his record a bit straighter, once telling writer Charles Price that when he realized the value of his playboy reputation he decided to take advantage of it. "For instance," Price relates, "Hagen said that before he left for the golf course he would ball up his tuxedo and throw it against a wall a few times, then put it on along with a pair of new shoes that pinched a little. He would arrive late, although he had been awake for six or seven hours. With the wrinkled tux and walking poorly, Haig looked as if he had not gotten to bed. Hagen's caddie, Spec Hammond, wore spikes, and on the second hole Walter would change into them."

Noble Miller, another of Hagen's Rochester friends, remembers well how Walter would "stick out that beautiful chin of his and make a tough shot appear much tougher than it really was. He'd take long, slow walks up to the green, dramatize it. Oh, he knew what he was doing in the charisma game."

Historically, Walter Hagen was one of the first athletes to capitalize on his image, enticing the public in much the same manner heavyweight politicians now do. His groundbreaking set the table for the financial feast that has been served up to Arnold Palmer, Johnny Miller, Jack Nicklaus, and others. As Herb Graffis, golf's senior historian-pundit, puts it, "Today's pros should light a candle every day of their lives to the memory of Walter Hagen."

What then was the nature of this man and, perhaps as importantly, the nature of the times in which Hagen flourished?

Walter Hagen's story reflects a classic American success theme, the athlete playing his way out of humble circumstances. He was born in 1892, the son of working-class, first-generation Americans who stuck to Old World notions of security. His father, a blacksmith, advised Walter to learn a trade and thought his boy a "bullhead" for passing up carpentry.

As a youth Hagen was an excellent ice skater. He became a fine fly fisherman and marksman as well, but his first love was baseball, and after a tryout with the Philadelphia Phillies, Hagen, who was ambidextrous, received a very favorable review. That was in the winter of 1914, about five months after he tied for fourth in the second golf tournament he ever entered—the U.S. Open. Still, Hagen gave a baseball career serious thought—until later that same year, when he won the U.S. Open. That settled his athletic future.

His "security," then, was not only his physical gifts for sport, but also the acute understanding of his talent's appeal to those not as well endowed. To this add the instincts and flair of the showman. "Barnum and Bailey rolled into one," says Herb Graffis.

The golf shots Hagen "called" occurred almost invariably when he had a putter in his hands. Harry Cooper, runner-up in the 1927 U.S. Open, remembers Hagen's words as he approached a putt he needed to win the Texas Open at San Antonio's Brackenridge Park Golf Course: "What, me miss this for fifteen hundred bucks?" Hagen then casually holed the 12-footer. It was flamboyance with a calculated hedge, though, for Hagen was by all accounts one of the greatest putters in the game. "Otherwise," attests Gene Sarazen, one of Hagen's fiercest rivals, "Walter was a very conservative golfer, not nearly as bold as people thought. He was not a great hitter of the ball and was wild off the tee. He *had* to make a lot of recoveries. He once advised a friend that to cure his slice he would have to get his stomach out of the way," Sarazen adds, with amusement. "Imagine. I don't think Hagen knew what caused a slice. But then, he never talked about golf in that way. He could never take the game seriously."

As a lad, Hagen caddied at The Country Club of Rochester for such people as George Eastman, founder of Eastman Kodak, and was beguiled by talk of travel and the high life. Standing at the railing, watching club members dance the summer evenings away, he was entranced. Hagen did not resent the rich, he simply wanted a piece of the action. In Walter, Jr.'s, words, "It set Dad's standards. He always wanted a look of success all up and down the line."

Yet with all of his silk shirts and knickers, jeweled cuff links, fine, chauffeured automobiles, and openhanded spending, it is unlikely Hagen was taken for anything other than a "jock" on the make. The Rockefellers, Mellons, Eastmans, et al., were not so obvious. If anything, "The Haig" was doing a satire of the "upper class," and the man on the street, Hagen's audience, loved it.

Hagen also was blessed by the currents of his time. In 1900, Englishman Harry Vardon made a long and highly successful American exhibition tour. His calling card was, "The Greatest Golfer in the World," which he was, and he "sold" precise, no-nonsense, *pure* golf. That was Vardon's nature, and it suited his era. To "grandstand" was to step out of line. Twenty years later, though, after a war produced by the gentry of Old Europe and *won* by the doughboys of democratic America, things were different. It was time for a romp, time to cut the bonds of 19th-century restraint. Golf, the rich man's game, was a particularly apt target, and Walter Hagen was the man with the knife.

In Hagen's style of golf there was none of Vardon's tight perfection. "The Haig" stood at the ball with the wide stance of a baseball slugger, took a loose, rainbow-arc swing, sprayed shots all over the lot, and was constantly flirting with disaster. Neither was there in Hagen the dour, often cranky gravity the Scottish-born pros brought to golf. Hagen never complained about a course—they were one and all "sporty little lay-outs"—and as Leon Sage fondly recalls, "He never had any temper."

The Common Man could identify with Hagen's razzmatazz golf. That he could win while tootin' it up every evening made it all the better. So when this high-flying fellow from the caddie yard became the first American-born golfer to win the British Open (1922), he was anointed. A doughboy had done it again; Hagen could do no wrong.

Possibly the most memorable Hagen quote is, "I don't want to be a millionaire, I just want to live like one." Herb Graffis believes that even this remark was put in Hagen's mouth by Bob Harlow, his manager. Hagen was not an especially witty man, according to his friends—he read little and wrote not at all, except his signature, of which he took great care. He told a story with "expressive hands. It was his presence more than the story itself," says Noble Miller. "He had a high-pitched voice and wasn't exactly handsome, but when he walked into a room everybody stopped talking. Hagen had that *look,* just as Arnold Palmer does."

"Yes," says Leon Sage, "and in the middle of a story if a woman walked into the room that was the end of it. Walter was off."

Everyone concedes that Hagen became a heavy drinker when his playing days were over. However, the truth of his earlier drinking habits did not escape Gene Sarazen. "Walter would party on an exhibition swing, but when an important match was coming up he didn't dissipate. He was a sham drinker a lot of the time." Hagen verified this, once telling Price, "I could beat any sot who ever lived." Price, who spent considerable time with Hagen in the 1950s, recalls Walter telling him how he would order a "triple," get to talking so much he never had more than a sip or two, pour the rest of it into the john, and come back into the room and say, "Can't a man get a drink around here?"

If the gag was noticed, no one was talking. In the Roaring Twenties anything went. And when the sap of that decade ran down into the Depression, who wanted to burst any more balloons? Besides, it was *Hagen.*

After the 1920 U.S. Open at the Inverness Club, Toledo, Ohio, the professional contestants presented the club with a clock on which was inscribed their thanks for the hospitality extended them. The poem, read aloud by Hagen at the presentation, refers to the fact that Inverness allowed the pros full use of its clubhouse facilities. Although this incident has been accepted generally as a precedent, Herb Graffis sheds a different light on Hagen and the "emancipation."

"The 1914 U.S. Open was played at Midlothian Country Club, outside Chicago. Before the tournament the members wondered where the pros were going to hang their coats. Until then they used nails in the back of the pro shop. Since there weren't enough nails, a member suggested room be made in the clubhouse. Other members claimed the pros were not gentlemen. The maverick replied, 'We have as our pro one of the finest gentlemen in the world, George Turnbull.' Everyone agreed, and the pros were allowed in the clubhouse. It seems Hagen took the first step by brashly walking in and using the locker room, and Turnbull made it stick with a word to the members. Hagen received full credit, probably because he won the tournament and because of the reputation he made later."

It was a touchy issue and not reported in the press, but Charles "Chick" Evans, Jr., the great amateur who finished second in that 1914 U.S. Open, confirms Graffis's account. Split the difference. Midlothian let the pros in, limiting them to the locker room. Inverness went the whole route, offering locker room, dining facilities, etc.

The more celebrated Hagen "emancipation" story began to unfold at the 1923 British Open. With the pros banned from the Troon clubhouse, a miffed Hagen drove up in a Rolls-Royce and spread a fancy picnic on the lawn for all the snooty members to see. It was a poignant gesture, but Hagen was kept out anyway.

Some years later, according to Walter Hagen, Jr., it was royalty that once and for all stormed the barrier.

"It was at St. Andrews. Dad and the Prince of Wales had become friends and were out on the town. The 'locals' shut down at 10, and they wanted to continue the evening, so they went over to the clubhouse. The gatekeeper told Edward that his companion was not allowed in. The Prince got angry and said, 'You may be the Royal and Ancient Golf Club this evening, but tomorrow you will only be the ancient golf club if Mr. Hagen cannot join me.' And that was that."

Thus, the real rebel against the social order was its pinnacle personage, the man who would go much farther and give up the throne of

England to marry the woman he loved, a divorced commoner. On the other hand, if Walter Hagen hadn't been with the Prince that evening the pros might have had to wait for Arnold Palmer.

Hagen got a lot of mileage out of his connection with Edward VIII (later the Duke of Windsor). Not only did he conquer the British at *their* game, making golf *ours,* he tickled the soul of his countrymen by crashing Buckingham Palace and addressing the host with brotherly familiarity, supposedly. Hagen told Price he never did this, that the story evolved when they were playing a round of golf and Hagen called to his caddie, who happened to be standing near Edward. "Everyone thought I said Eddie."

So Hagen fudged some, as did the press and others. It worked because he was a legitimate champion and because the folklore was a believable extension of Walter's essential character. And of course, the embellishments on hard truth were harmless. It was fun, the legacy of Walter Hagen with the most impact.

Walter endorsed a few non–golf-related products, but in his heyday the advertising industry as we know it was an infant, just as the pro tour was in its embryonic stage. Hagen had to make most of his "off-course" money on-course. By playing some 2,000 18-hole exhibitions between 1914 and 1941, he earned an estimated $1 million. That's not much by current standards, at least considering the time and work involved. But aside from the fact that it was a substantial sum in those days, the figure is impressive because Hagen did not exhibit for preset fees and expenses paid by other agencies. He barnstormed, playing to whatever size audience he could draw at a buck a head—his standard rate—payable upon entry to the grounds.

More pointedly, "The Haig" did not restrict himself to established golfing country, of which there wasn't that much in the first place. When he went to places, such as Fargo, North Dakota, he had to pull in every living golf fan in the area and more than a few curiosity seekers. Hagen satisfied one and all, by being *and playing* the role of an earthy national celebrity and never slowing down his performance with dry dissertations or debates on the mysteries of what can be a very phlegmatic game. He made golf look fun, and thereby generated interest. No one can say how many persons Hagen inspired to take up golf, but a fair guess is he corralled one for every dollar he made on the exhibition circuit, not counting their sons and daughters.

Walter Hagen seeded the ground from which golf has since sprouted so magnificently. Yet professional golfers as a whole have not picked up where Walter left off. Only in the past few years have the tour pros acknowledged that their role in very large part is that of entertainer. Hagen knew it all along, and performed accordingly. Whether he did it altruistically, for "the good of the game," is a question only he could answer. But even if it were strictly to serve his own ends, he left his mark on golf, and on those with whom he came in contact. This legacy is perhaps best expressed by his friend Leon Sage.

While reminiscing about Hagen, Sage, who is now in his 80s and in poor health, was asked if he could sum up what Walter Hagen meant to him, what Hagen *was*. Somber with the pain of his daily existence, Sage lit up for a moment and said, "With Walter around, everything was always so *lively*."

LEFTY STACKHOUSE IS ALIVE AND WELL AND LIVING IN SEGUIN

(Golf Magazine—1970)

Any man who ever chronicles golf beyond mere statistics writes not of the game if he fails to touch on anger and frustration. And when he does, he will include in his pageant at least one Lefty Stackhouse anecdote or fable. At the mere mention of the name *Stackhouse,* those who knew anything about the American golfing scene of the '30s and '40s will begin to nod slowly and ooze a curious smile. A nod, a smile of . . . incredulity? That's probably the best word, because the feats of golfing temper perpetrated by, and/or attributed to, W. A. Lefty Stackhouse ring of fantasy.

It was Lefty Stackhouse who, after hitting an unfortunate drive, leaped headlong into a thorny bush and refused the aid of fellow travelers, wishing to remain impaled and bleeding, crucified for all to see. It was Stackhouse who missed a short putt, fetched himself a potent rap between the eyes with his putter, and fell stone-cold unconscious to the green. Stackhouse temper is coming off a practice tee, that's a *practice tee,* with every clubhead detached from its shaft. Stackhouse temper. A complete descriptive phrase. Or, Stackhouse equals temper, a precise mathematical equation.

What about all this? Fact or fancy? Stackhouse? The name alone seems contrived, onomatopoeic, its very sound suggesting the sense of violent anger. Was there really a human animal who could reach such heights, or depths, of golfing agony that he would walk into a copse of trees to search out a badly hooked drive, stop before a sturdy oak, and punch its bark with powerful right jabs while shrieking, "Keep your right hand out of the shot?" Indeed there was, and is, such a man. We saw him, talked with him, played some golf with him in Seguin, Texas, home of the world's largest pecan. He's been there for years. He's a small wry man with a somewhat pained, hard look in the eyes and a brow that worry and tension have furrowed deeply. His name *is* Stackhouse and he *did* do a lot of mad, wild, crazy things when the golf fit hit.

What is it that makes grown men so frenzied they'll snap golf clubs in half like lumberjacks crumbling soda crackers? Lefty Stackhouse was part of an era when many men, bitten hard by golf, tried to make a living at it when there was hardly a living to be made out of anything. It was the hard times of the American '30s. Way back then, the covered-wagon pioneers of pro golf who built today's luxury liner were hard-bellied, stony-faced men with piercing eyes searching out the few pieces of meat in a meager stew pot. In a raw struggle for survival, hungry men, really hungry men, react out of a very elemental well of anxiety. There's a keg of black choler down where the beast in us still lives. Tap it with a game like golf, with its inherent trials on human patience, and you'll get golf clubs spouting over the pasture like spears at a jungle hunt.

They've passed a rule now whereby golf pros displaying temper will be fined. But that's like telling an overfed gourmand he'll have to wait a minute for his chocolate mousse. In 1969, the 60th—*60th*—leading money winner made three times as much money as Ben Hogan did in 1940, when Ben was number one. The soup line these days leads to the Waldorf. What's to get so upset about? When they didn't even have a 60th money winner, the pressure of that time drew out a level of character with a kind of color we're not likely to see again—unless there's a Depression.

There was Ivan Gantaz. Ivan would do belly-flop dives into a bunker when it all got to be too much for him. Ivan once missed a short putt, dropped his putter, *then* slugged himself "up beside the haid" with his fists. Asked why he dropped the putter first, he explained that he didn't want to kill himself. There was Indian Ky Laffoon, who cussed the Gods of at least two nations with unparalleled vehemence, after, even before, an errant shot. There was Clayton Heafner, a heavy-browed brute of a man with great pride, who flat walked out of a tournament if his name was mispronounced over a loudspeaker. A younger Sam Snead finished at least one round putting with a two-iron, and Tommy Bolt sometimes didn't even have that much left. If Lefty Stackhouse was the paragon of golfing temper, that's going some. He ran in pretty fast company.

The Heafners, Laffoons, Sneads, Hogans, Bolts, and Stackhouses did not play golf off the largesse of wealthy fathers, did not come out of universities and the middle rung of the economic ladder. Almost to the man they were poor and scratching dry earth for an edible root. They hustled—golf lessons and golfers. They flopped in two-bit cots in tournament towns, borrowed 10 bucks to get to the next stop. Lloyd Mangrum once had to borrow two new golf balls from Craig Wood to play in a Texas tournament. Lloyd won $400 with those "shiners" and never had to borrow another one. Ben Hogan was stickman at a regular evening crap game around Dallas–Fort Worth and used his pay for a shag boy to chase his practice balls during the day. But for every Mangrum or Hogan fit to rise above mean circumstances, there were many men who never quite got on the track, or were derailed somewhere along the line; who stayed angry; who didn't, or couldn't overcome habits and reflexes developed early under strained, humble conditions. Their story is warp to the woof of success.

His full name is Wilburn Artist Stackhouse. The middle name is something to conjure with. Could it be that his father, a laborer in the shapeless, uninspiring oil fields of Oklahoma and Texas, had a dream of something finer for his son? Did he think that maybe, just maybe, a name would help? Perhaps it did, in a way. Lefty has a bit of the creative spirit in him. He was once inspired to make a golf club in the shape of a lightbulb. He molded some wood, flattened and grooved one side into a hitting area, and realized his idea. His pal Jimmy Demaret, ever the wag, called it a "glub." Lefty always had a fine touch for the game and, of course, he was the Picasso-Rembrandt-Goya of fulmination, with a Wagnerian opera thrown in for measure.

He was born in 1909, somewhere in Oklahoma. Just where has never been known. It might have been nowhere in particular—a nondescript wooden dwelling in the middle of those teeter-tottering oil pumps sucking up black juice, the richness of which Lefty never tasted. His stepmother didn't take much to young Lefty. When she left the child stranded beside a desolate road, ostensibly to go for help of some kind, Mr. Stackhouse was prompted to take himself and his boy to the oil fields south of Dallas. Lefty worked for his father as a bucket boy, played a little baseball (a southpaw pitcher, hence the nickname Lefty, that buried the sissified Wilburn, the odd Artist) and eventually learned that some money could be made caddying "over to the local golf course."

Naturally, he began to play golf. His first sticks were just that, branches from mesquite trees. Take a branch with a large knob, shave and plane that knob into a clubhead with face, and you've got yourself a golf stick. His first factory-made was a 9-iron, offered for sale by a local player. Its market value was $1.75, but the seller was asking $4.75. Lefty wanted that 9-iron and "caddied out" the payments. Hard times, hard people.

He began as a left-hander, but, and here's the artistic instinct again, as a man of the town who also played left-handed, lurched and waddled so badly when he swung, looked so "godawful," Lefty decided to go from the leeside. When Harry Cooper came to town for an exhibition and Lefty saw this name professional break open a dozen brand-new balls to *practice* with, then hit them so fine and beautiful, he knew what he wanted to do—become a golf pro. Following his new idol's example, Lefty switched from a cross-handed to a conventional grip, and within six months was the town's amateur champion. All was well. He had direction, a lot of potential, and became a pro. Then, his father died. His stepmother still wanted no part of him, and at age 14, Lefty was very much on his very own.

Is this where and when the temper began? There was no record of Lefty's kind of ferocity in the family line. But maybe they were never tested as Lefty was. It's a solitary business trying to hit a golf ball consistently well. It's man against himself, mostly, and a little familial encouragement doesn't hurt. Lefty Stackhouse, a skinny little bantam, was now standing up to that ball a little lonelier than most people.

But rage is a manifestation of the human personality that springs from many sources. A young, impressionable Lefty, looking for a lead on how to act in the world, often watched a respected judge and a wealthy businessman heave golf clubs and rant in undiluted barrack-ese. Well sure enough, if these two fine upstanding gentlemen could carry on so, then it wasn't all bad, now was it? Then, too, a man draws a little attention to himself when he beats a golf bag into a leathery pulp, and little guys are always trying to seem bigger than they are. Lefty quit school at the fourth grade, a decision he holds to be part of the furious tirades that came. You see, Lefty wanted to hit every golf shot perfectly. Perfectly. When he didn't, he attributed it to stupidity. "If I'da had the education that trains a man's mind for good concentration," says Lefty, "I wouldn't have made so many *stoo*pid mistakes." A rationalization? Of course, but not easy to fault.

Another incident leading to the Stackhouse personality was a trip to play in the Los Angeles Open. Here Lefty saw Walter Hagen, Tommy Armour, and other stars of the time and he was mightily impressed with the fact that these famous shot-makers were shot-takers, too. A man could drink whiskey and play championship golf. Well, how about that! Might give that a try, thought Lefty. And he did. It was a nice way to conviviality, telling jokes, killing time, being "one of the boys." The trouble was, little Lefty couldn't handle the booze. But he kept trying, and so the die was cast and his life fell into a pattern—delirium over a mis-hit golf shot, serum to calm the tremens. As Lefty puts it, if he played a bad round he forgot it in whiskey. But if he played a good one, it called for a celebration. Golf and booze finally blended into a single explosive cocktail. If golf didn't get him, whiskey did, and too often both got together to really sock him.

In a tournament in Hershey, Pennsylvania, Lefty was third going into the last round. The night before the last day, he closed out a bottle of something or other. Ralph Hutchison had advised him to get off the grog, get some sleep, because the next day was a big one. Lefty said he knew it, but was so tense he needed something to put him to sleep. Next day he missed easy birdie putts on the first three holes. He could hardly see the ball, let alone the hole. From the fourth tee he drove out of bounds . . . and out of the money. Some of the best players of his time will tell you that Lefty was a helluva player. He once picked up $650 in a Western Open, another time beat Nelson and Hogan in a pro-am, and Nelson again in an exhibition. He had the stuff, but he got in his own way.

In a Texas tournament he put a ball over a green and against a fence. He tried a ricochet back to the green, but the ball went out of bounds. At that, Lefty took to hammering the fence post with his club like Noah finishing the Ark standing in the first puddles. Lefty didn't know it then, but three men who had been following him were ready to sign him up as head pro at the best club in Dallas. They backed off when Lefty went berserk. When Lefty found out about the missed opportunity, he really blew his stackhouse, practically leveling his motel room.

What the man did with his hands would give a violinist nightmares. He borrowed a Model-T Ford to play a tournament where he could make some badly needed money. Halfway there the car broke down. All the cranking in the world wouldn't turn that engine over. Totally exasperated, Lefty tossed the crank into the windshield, then used the grille for his personal punching bag, smashing the metal until it looked like a piece of pop art. Giving a lesson once, he got angry at his pupil, who wasn't perfect either, and shook his hand violently. It swelled up badly. A doctor later pulled a chunk of glass out of the hand that had been lodged there for years—from a time when Lefty had put it through a car window.

Lefty didn't break one club, he broke sets. He once talked the Wilson Co. into giving Betty Jameson a set of clubs, borrowed them from Betty, and broke every one of them. Once he was five or six up after nine holes of a match, and his opponent wanted to quit. Lefty pep-talked him into going on. The fellow got hot, and by the 17th hole had Lefty all even. He hit a shot close to the hole, Lefty missed the green from the trees, and the match went to the other guy. Lefty then methodically broke every club in the bag over a tree stump. Yet another set, borrowed from a friend, ended up kindling. He bought some new ones to replace them, explaining that the others, wooden-shafted, had gotten warped on the way home. Too close to the train's radiator, or something like that. If all the clubs Lefty floated in rivers, creeks, and ponds were stretched across the Red Sea, Moses would never have had to part it.

One of the most celebrated Stackhouse incidents happened in Knoxville, Tennessee. It was during World War II. There were 20 prizes offered, and only 18 players. All a man had to do was finish and he got something. Fred Corcoran, who was running the tour then, had gotten Sergeant York, the famous World War I hero who lived nearby, to present the prize money, which was paid in war bonds. One version of the story has it that Lefty was on the final green with a short putt to finish up. But he was so bombed on booze he kept falling down, couldn't stand up long enough to make the tap-in. Sergeant York, who had never been on a golf course, and evidently a little naive otherwise, watched Lefty tumbling and staggering, then remarked to Corcoran that he had "no idea golf was such a strenuous game."

Lefty puts it this way. He had been nipping the waters all day, and was very "un-dry" when he came to the ninth hole. Corcoran then reminded Lefty that a lot of young kids were following him, and the impression he was making on them wasn't the most desirable. Fred suggested that Lefty take a little nap in the clubhouse, then finish up the back nine later. This Lefty did, but when he awoke it was black night. In either case, though, Lefty finished out of the money. Only Stackhouse could have managed that.

Stackhouse stories over the years have been, well, embellished. But then, a certain amount of apocrypha is the stuff of folklore. More than once people have come up to Lefty to reminisce. "Hey Stack, 'member down in Florida when you-all turned ever' club in the bag to pretzels, ate the cover off a golf ball, bit the leg o' your caddy, then charged a sleeping alligator?" Of course, Lefty had never been in Florida in his whole life, but he didn't say anything. He didn't want to embarrass the fellow. Fact is, Lefty doesn't mind all the exaggeration. As slim and specious as it may be, Lefty has a claim to fame, which is one more than most people have.

If you're an old-fashioned, hard-nosed puritan with no tolerance for the frailties of man, Lefty Stackhouse was just a foul-tempered, unregenerated drunkard. A bum. A golf bum, no less. Dismissed! But every man who has ever known him has liked him and continues to. The only person Lefty ever hurt was Lefty. He's what he's always been, a friendly, generous, outgoing man who has never made an enemy in his life. At least nine young boys from Seguin, including Shelley Mayfield and Buck Luce, got their first pro jobs through Lefty's help. Perhaps because of his small size and pugnacious, but totally honest manner, kids have always been drawn to him. When he was in AA, he sat down with Tommy Bolt, who was having some drink problems that threatened his tournament career, and evangelized "Thunder" about the evils of drink, the silliness of getting mad. It's a scene that sparks the imagination—something like one bull telling another to walk easy in a china shop. But Bolt was close to tears, and promised to go straight. He did. Lefty helped Betty Jameson and Babe Zaharias with their games, and has been instrumental in the growth of the Pan-American Golf Association, a Mexican-American group in an area where the Mexican population is an important social entity.

Lefty's doing all right now. He runs the public course, Starcke Park, in Seguin. His wife, Evelyn, known to all as "Dutch," had some property and there's some security. If he were to be remembered at all, he would like it to be for some of the good things he has done for golf. But Stackhouse will always stand for temper. That aberration, when it reaches the extremes to which Lefty took it, becomes terribly fascinating. We derive some kind of secret pleasure out of a man getting as mad as Lefty did. Maybe it's a vicarious release from our own tensions, since there is not a soul among us who wouldn't like to fly off on the wings of vi-tooperation now and then. Lefty Stackhouse has done it for us. He's served as our clown, a funny-sad Emmett Kelly of golf. What an act. It hasn't been topped yet.

WHEN YOU STOP TO THINK ABOUT IT...

(Golf Magazine—1972)

It is said that any man can win a U.S. Open . . . once. Which is to say further that the biggest, toughest, most demanding championship in the game is not always won by the best player, or even one of the better players. It doesn't happen often, but now and again a golfer will put it all together better than he truly knows how . . . and with sublime timing. The record book of Open champions is then inscribed with such names as Sam Parks, Tony Manero, or Jack Fleck. It happens.

To win two U.S. Opens, however, is another matter. For a man to beat the big heat of this particular competitive furnace more than once, it must be more than a fluke, even should those two victories be the only ones of his career—which they never are. Once lucky, twice *good*. To the point, there are no Tony Maneros or Sam Parkses in this crowd. Look it up. It's in the book.

To win U.S. Opens back to back is yet another matter. One of a rather high order. Someone has recalled that through a recent stretch of U.S. Opens, four defending champions did not make the 36-hole cut. An interesting statistic. I won't dwell on it much here except to say that this championship, perhaps more than any other, has a way of taking the toll of golfers with the very best credentials. The statistic includes Julius Boros, Ken Venturi, and Jack Nicklaus.

Indeed, to win back-to-back Opens is so rare an accomplishment that only three men in the more or less modern era of golf (from the late '20s to the present) have turned the trick. Each, you would have to say, if everything intimated so far is right, must be forever-remembered "immortals." Yet only two are: the late Bobby Jones and Ben Hogan. The third is little more than a curiosity—a name with which few of today's golfing fans are familiar and which those from his own time offhandedly recollect with vague remembrances like: "Oh, the guy who combed his hair before putting." Or: "Yeah, yeah . . . big, good-looking guy. Really had it for a while there." The "guy's" name is Ralph Guldahl. He won the U.S. Open in 1937 and 1938.

As noted, two-time winners of the Open do not stop there. Ralph Guldahl also won a Masters tournament ('39), three Western Opens ('37, '38, '39), a tournament today that was, in Guldahl's time, a championship almost equal to the U.S. Open in formidability and prestige, and a few ordinary tournaments on the relatively abbreviated tour of his day. In brief, Ralph Guldahl's accomplishments could hardly be considered a fluke. The fluke, you might say, was that his competitive brilliance was so brief.

Guldahl was born in November of 1911. He turned pro at 18 years of age, won his first Western Open at 25, his first U.S. Open at 26. In 1939, at 28, he won the Masters. Later in 1939 he won the Greensboro Open and something called the Dapper Dan Open. After that . . . nothing. Not yet 30 years old, at an age when you could expect at least 10 years of even better golf than he had already played, he came up flat empty. The man could really and truly play—and then he couldn't play at all. Herbert Warren Wind recalls asking Sam Snead what had happened to Guldahl's game. Sam and Ralph traveled together occasionally and were often partners in best-ball and two-ball tournaments. Sam said it started sounding as though Guldahl was hitting the ball with a bag of mush. The click was gone. Sam had looked closely at his friend's swing, but he couldn't *see* anything different. He only *heard* something different. The uncrack of doom. That something—that something special—was gone. Almost literally overnight, the long, straight tee shots turned into slices. Slices! The six-iron shots began coming up 30 feet short instead of 2 feet past. Putts started breaking away just below the hole, instead of curling in from the high side.

Where did his game go? And why?

Could it be that at age 28 Ralph Guldahl had used up his quota of championship energy? Physically this would not seem to be so. He was in the car accident in Chicago that killed George Payton, Jr., a young pro of tremendous promise. But there was no Hogan near-tragedy for Guldahl. He was shaken up, bruised. But nothing serious. A big, tall man, his limbs were straight and sound. No withered left arm, like Ed Furgol's. Perhaps his back hurt from time to time, but all golfers' backs do, eventually. Guldahl himself says, among other things, that it was "a matter of getting heavier . . . and laying off the game during the World War II years." Maybe, but that doesn't sound terribly convincing.

It is said that, even while making his great run of championship golf, Guldahl was not memorable. He never hit any spectacular shots or made any late-round "charges." Oh, there was one. On the final nine of the '39 Masters he knew he needed a 34 to tie Snead, who had already completed the 72 holes with a final-round 68, and on the par-five 13th, from a sidehill lie, Guldahl cut a wood shot from a hook stance to within eight feet, got the eagle, and whipped Sam. But the general consensus of his style was as Jimmy Demaret puts it: "Ralph played a lot like Bobby Locke. He hit the same shot every time." A little draw. Or was it a little fade? So he hit one little draw—or fade—after another and when the scores were totaled up, Guldahl had the lowest one. That's all. Next case.

Another pro of his time says: "Guldahl could win 20 tournaments in a row and no one would know him." *Consistency* was always very much a part of Ralph Guldahl's vocabulary. Still is. Consistency! A virtue with a dull ring. Joe Dey, Jr., recalls Guldahl as being "the original slow player." Like all "slow" players, Guldahl would prefer the word *methodical*.

To spend time with Ralph Guldahl, as this writer did recently, is to be in the company of a courteous, gentle man with a strangely high-pitched, embarrassed giggle of a laugh. He talks of tears coming to his eyes when he watched Ben Hogan try to putt in recent years. Guldahl has the distant, private reserve about him of many high achievers, yet it seems not to derive from a deep inner confidence. Somehow you feel you're *not* in the presence of someone of substantial professional accomplishment. His mien, carriage, manner, is that of a man who never convinced himself that he was as good as he was. A highly subjective evaluation, but so be it.

Those who played with and against him say Guldahl was always a loner. He admits to it himself. He went his own way—stayed pretty much to himself. By virtue of his outstanding golf, he did have the limelight. But when his golfing genius left him, he slid back, without too much of a fight, into the shadows. Perhaps that is where he always wanted to be.

Guldahl is a first-generation American, born of parents who came to Dallas, Texas, from Oslo, Norway. Steady, hardworking people, his folks were. His father was employed with the Continental Gin Company for 25 or 30 years. His younger brother spent his life in the U.S. Postal Service. Consistency.

Ralph was the second son, a generally unattended position in family hierarchies. Second sons tend to "go their own way" because no one tells them to go *any* way in particular. He lost all but 25 percent of his hearing in one ear at age 11 and was near death from the ailment that left this sense defective. Sometimes a person "turns off" because he *is* turned off. He was always tall, but rather stooped and round-shouldered. Was this posture developed out of a sense of shame? It was not uncommon for tall children of his generation to scrunch up to be like the majority. When it was fairly sure that his game was gone, he was quoted as saying, when asked what he thought happened, that he was "basically lazy" and, also, he simply became "bored" with it all. Was this a rationale drawn from the well of characteristic Scandinavian stoic fatalism?

While all of this is obviously very speculative, from knowing something of his personal background we may have an answer, or at least a clue to the short fuse of greatness that lit Ralph Guldahl's golfing career. Every man is the product of his genes, family environment, and other such forces over which he has no absolute control. And while, for a time, he may override these forces, he almost inevitably returns to his basic mold.

Then again, there may be another answer or clue—again very speculative, but having a quality with which all of us can identify. In its narrow, sports-oriented context, the story of Ralph Guldahl's abrupt fall from golfing grace touches on the age-old conflict, or question, or argument between instinct (intuitive behavior) and reason (scientific method). Sound a trifle high-flown? Far out? *Intellectual,* God forbid? Wait! The thing revolves around a very simple hypothesis. Like, do you try to figure out if you should stand a little closer to the ball at address so you can make a more upright backswing and thus strike the ball with a more descending arc with the irons, or should you just put that there ball up on a peg, take a holt of the stick, rare back, pummel the thing, and hope for the best? Now we've all hassled with that one, haven't we?

Myself, Ralph, and his wife, Laverne Maydelle, sat together in the Guldahl home. It's a moderately sized place amid others like it, tucked up on a small hill in one of the multitude of "towns" that make up the city of Los Angeles. It's only a few miles from the Braemar CC, in Tarzana, California, where Ralph has been golf director for the last 10 years. The interior of the house is all Laverne Maydelle. Imitation gold leaf is stuck at random on the fireplace screen. Voluptuous, curved, velveteen lamp shades are elaborated with thick ribbons. The sofa is plushy soft and also of curving design. Pomeranian dogs, little bits of coiffed canine, yip and yap. Ralph Guldahl, in his plain brown wing-tip shoes, solid dark brown V-neck sweater and solid dark brown conventionally cut trousers, sits in 1930s American Quasi-Sybaritic surroundings looking as out of place as a vacationing Boston dry goods salesman in a Tennessee Williams stage set. Laverne Maydelle does much of the talking—in the style of a west Texas Scarlett O'Hara. Apparently something of a tease as a young girl, she tells of when Ralph came courtin' and asked for her hand in marriage just days before he was to leave to take an assistant pro job at Franklin Hills, in Detroit. She said she answered coyly: "I wonder who I'll be married to when you get back?" Like maybe Ralph's older brother, a "wild boy" and her first boyfriend. Then she tells of how Ralph was near tears and how she "gave in" the day before "Guldy" was to leave, and they were wed— she at 16, he at 19. And she talked a lot about her being a mixture of English, Scotch, Spanish, American Indian, and even a little bit of Gypsy, the latter accounting for her love of gambling and astrology, and her "abil- ity" to divine future events. Laverne talked about their only son, Ralph, Jr., who tried professional golf but was erratic—inconsistent—and, being a handsome boy, "like his father," played in some Hollywood movies (bit parts in shoot-'em-ups), and how her half-Indian, half-Irish father, a San Angelo, Texas, lawyer, practiced until he was 82 and once appeared on the old Groucho Marx TV show. Laverne talked a lot.

Ralph sat like all men who have lived a long time with a garrulous woman. Put him in a spin, stick a phonograph needle into his epidermis, and out of his pores will pour a verbatim rendition of Laverne Maydelle's monologue. He stifled yawns, nodded perfunctorily, dutifully, at the right cues, and generally sat through it all in a state of benign torpor.

Then Laverne Maydelle said, "When he sat down to write that book of instruction—that's when he lost his game."

Ralph didn't straighten like a bolt at the remark, because Ralph Guldahl doesn't move that way. But he shifted in his chair with percepti- ble uneasiness. The glaze came off his eyes. A sensitive nerve had been struck. Struck again, because the remark was not a new one. He had heard it many, many times since 1939, but it was one he seemed unable to let drown in the rest of his wife's verbal waterfall.

"Ah," he said, "I just got too heavy and laid off the game too long and hurt my back."

The thing is, Ralph Guldahl, when at the top of his game, didn't think much about what he was doing with the golf club. Like most kids of his time, growing up around the Tenison Park municipal course in Dallas, Guldahl revered the then-renowned Harry Cooper. But he said to me, "I don't remember ever learning to play golf. It just came from playing all the time."

George Fazio, a perceptive golf man with a classic swing, developed out of continuous experimentation and thought, remembers that when he and Hogan and Nelson and Mangrum and all the others were young and talking technique, Guldahl had nothing to contribute.

"How would you play a shot out of that fluffy grass, Ralph?"

"Why, I'd just take the club for the distance and hit it."

Obviously, without thinking much about it, Guldahl would hit the shot well. When he had it. He began playing golf at age 11. In high school he captained the golf team and once won the Texas State High School championship with rounds of 65–71. He was 16. He never practiced much, only enough to loosen up before playing. The only thing he ever considered doing—being—was professional golf. He missed his high school graduation ceremony when it conflicted with the Texas Open, which he entered as a professional. He tied for 11th and received a check for $87.50. Later that year he qualified for the U.S. Open at Interlachen, where Bobby Jones won the third part of his Grand Slam. It was 1930 and Guldahl was, at 19, the youngest player in that Open field. He finished in a tie for 15th with a 308.

The rest of his record, at least the most important parts, we already know. It was all there on an ever-improving scale, from high school days through 1939. There was no need to analyze, and analyze he didn't. It wasn't his nature. Ralph Guldahl pretty much took things as they came.

In 1939 he was a star and stars in golf are always asked to write books on how they "do it," with the intention of helping all the folks "out there" play a little better . . . and to make a little money, which is always nice. So Ralph Guldahl contracted to write a book of golf instruction. Being an honest, conscientious man, he wasn't going to turn the assignment over to a "ghost," who would sit down with him, take a lot of notes, then go into a back room somewhere and begin typing. Ralph was going to write it himself. After all, it was his book.

So he holed up in hotel rooms, watched himself in mirrors and on film, and for the first time in his life gave serious, analytical thought to what he had been doing with a golf club all this time. The book is one of those in which you flip through the pages and the still photos become a motion picture of Guldahl swinging a club. It sold for two dollars. It came out in 1939, the last year in which Guldahl was ever a factor in professional tournament golf.

Instinct against reason. Ben Hogan, as it's been said many times before, *made* a golf swing. He started out a wild, natural hooker of the ball. If he had let it be—played the damn thing—golf would not have had one of its greatest players . . . and technicians. Hogan thought about every position he wanted his body and the club to be in at every point in the swing. Then, with unmatched hours of practice, he put thought into action.

Men like Hogan, or more recently, Gary Player, will tell you that any man who does not know what he's doing every time he hits a golf shot will eventually fail. George Fazio, from the same school of thought, remarks that Guldahl "didn't know enough about the swing to come back."

The majority of opinion seems to be in favor of reason—the scientific method. There is much evidence to support it. It might also be said, though, at least in the case of Ralph Guldahl, that when science intrudes on intuition, given that the intuition is good, it fails.

"Given that the intuition is good." There's the catch. How many have it . . . good? Not many, it would appear. But should those who do fiddle with fate?

JOHNNY MILLER
MADE IT
BIG BEFORE HE
EVER WON

(Golf Digest—1973)

J ohnny Miller has put backspin on the wheel of fortune. He personifies a new twist in professional sport. Until a few years ago a pro golfer first proved he had the stuff of champions by winning a major championship, or at least a lot of tournaments. *Then,* with the fame that came, he cashed in on what the golf pros call "off-course" money—endorsements to us. Even Arnold Palmer, the supreme exemplar of personality merchandising, did a large quantity of victorious playing before he parlayed a nervous pants hitch, a neat nasal twitch, and an emotive grimace into a small corporation worthy of conglomeration.

Switch! Prior to Johnny Miller's stunning victory in the 1973 U.S. Open he was already collecting some $150,000 a year from endorsement contracts with a dozen business firms. Not only had he never won a major title up to that time, he had won only two ordinary tour events in four years.

How does such a munificent windfall come about? The genesis is in Arnold Palmer. Johnny Miller represents a sophistication of the process of selling charisma—image. First, you gauge the tenor of the times. We are smack in the era of pure Up Front. People who pay substantial money for a golfer's image do not require a total winner. That's old-fashioned. They simply want exposure.

Johnny Miller was—is—just the ticket. He has a graceful, powerful golf swing. He is Tallness, Slimness, Blondness, Youthfulness. He looks good in clothes. He is precisely the right combination of middle-class American humility and self-confidence. He speaks well without being profound. Possibly most vital of all, he has the flair, or luck, of superb timing.

Miller first splashed onto the national golf scene with a fine performance as an amateur in the 1966 U.S. Open. He was up with the leaders all the way, and anytime an amateur makes a run at a U.S. Open it's a story. He got a lot of notice, most noticeably on television, to which was added a pairing with Arnold Palmer himself. To top off that caper, he chipped a ball into the cup—all on prime time. He made an exciting dash at the 1971 Masters, faltering on the home holes but while doing so displaying a daring spirit in trying for a big second shot to reach a par-five in two. Again, on prime time. He had a round of 61 in a Phoenix Open. A 61, even in Arizona, makes news. When he hit a disastrous shank, the all-too-human error was on a finishing hole at the Bing Crosby Pro-Am, which gets one of golf's biggest television audiences. Interestingly enough, his two victories before the '73 Open—the Heritage Classic and Southern Open—went relatively unheralded.

All of which is to say, a performer can kill 'em in Kansas and never get out of the wheat fields, but even if he bombs on Broadway he's a star . . . because he's on Broadway. So Johnny Miller became a very salable commodity without an important victory. Yet for all the various intrinsics in Miller's makeup, his package had to be put together. If that sounds like Miller was a box of cornflakes, so be it. Packaging is what it is.

The packager of Johnny Miller is his business manager, a fellow Mormon named Ed Barner whose firm, Uni-Managers, International, represents a number of other pros, including Billy Casper, Jerry Heard, Sam and J.C. Snead. Some people see the business manager as a remora clinging to the underbelly of the shark and feeding off its hard-earned crumbs, an attitude toward 10-percenters going back as far as the munitions middlemen of the Napoleonic Wars. Barner, in fact, takes 20 percent of all his players earn, including tournament prize money. That last sticks sharpest in the craws of his man-eaters. The off-course money a manager deals for is one thing, but golf pros detest giving away part of what they themselves dig out of the turf.

Barner justifies his cut, as all agents do, on the grounds of providing convenience and business expertise. While the pros roam the fairways in search of birdies, he single-mindedly pursues their financial well-being. Barner is a smooth-skinned, tall man in his 30s with a background in communications and show business. He has a degree from Brigham Young University, where Miller went to school, and he's worked as a radio and television announcer. Barner fairly rhapsodizes his rationale for taking a huge piece of his players' action:

"We book the players' rooms in advance, make all their travel arrangements, handle their taxes and legal suits, book exhibitions. Their minds are free to win more on the tour. We send out letters with a brochure to every ad agency billing over a million dollars a year. We tell them of our players' availability as *figurative* business partners who, by way of endorsement, will work for the betterment of a company's product; for a round of golf with six to 10 executives who won't forget the experience. I don't like to quote numbers, but Jerry Heard hasn't won a tournament in over a year and we're making him off-course more than double what his two wins in 1972 were worth. We got Lanny Wadkins into a land development deal, long term, that is phenomenal. We booked Sam Snead into 16 exhibitions at a big number. We . . ."

Hold on! What about Johnny Miller? Did you do anything to create this image of his that sells so well?

"He was always a good dresser," said Barner. "We take no credit there, although a few years ago we worked out a deal with Palm Beach clothes where Johnny would wear their line of striped slacks. They wanted to sell slacks, striped slacks, and Johnny looks good in them. He's tall. They gave him pants and some money. But when the Sears deal worked out, Palm Beach was very good about letting us out of the commitment."

How about image making?

"We insist that he signs his autographs as Johnny, which has a more familiar, friendlier ring. John is kind of cold, not as affectionate as Johnny. He likes John, so when he signs his name he separates the *ny* from the rest. We also advised him to sign autographs whenever he could. We keep reminding him to say thank you. Golf pros are not always prone to say that. We also wanted him to have his hair styled. He wasn't too crazy about that, especially when we found a barber in L.A. who did the right job but charged $25. Johnny still reminds me of that $25.

"We wanted to improve his public-speaking ability and had him sit down a few times with Mark Evans, a broadcasting executive in Washington,

D.C. Mark taught Johnny some of the tricks, inflection, emphasis, that kind of thing. Then we sent Johnny to some speaking engagements for practice. We get our players' teeth capped, or rearranged, if needed. Remember Jerry Heard? Had a big gap between his two front teeth when he first went out on tour. Jim Simons's front teeth projected out a little. Fixed that.

"Johnny has been with us his entire professional career. We knew we had a product that would sell, and all the time we were gearing him up to be ready for delivery. Before the '73 Open he was contracted to MacGregor, whose equipment he uses. He was with Hughes Airwest, Ford Motor Co., and Palmetto Dunes, the resort on Hilton Head Island, which gave him the use of a home down there for an occasional break from the tour. He was with Sears-Roebuck and Simmons Mattress Co. He had three contracts with Japanese firms—Del Monte tomato juice packers there, Sangyo, which makes golf accessories, and Asahei Kasei, which makes golf shirts. That last one is worth 30 grand a year. Japan is very big on golf, as you know; particularly anything that has to do with American golf. He had a couple of golf camps; one in Park City, Utah, another in association with the American Leadership Study Group, which runs the camp in St. Andrews, Scotland. He had a couple of small contracts, one with Flexi-Grip, the other with a golf magazine."

If Barner takes credit for some big accounts which may or may not have come to Miller without managerial assistance, the fact remains Barner's firm is administering them.

Each of Miller's multiyear contracts ("We never sign for one year only," says Barner) was negotiated with the explicit understanding that Johnny would play the tour regularly, anywhere from 20 to 25 tournaments. He had to stand still for promotional photography and television commercials, and make periodic appearances at corporate functions, such as playing 18 holes with a gaggle of buyers from Butte or sellers from Spokane, but he did not necessarily have to win on tour. The contracts, however, had bonus and escalator clauses predicated on Johnny's winning a major championship. When he flashed home with his remarkable 63 at Oakmont in June, his contracts immediately and automatically increased in overall value by close to 60 percent. He was "geared up for delivery." The Open victory, naturally, opened more doors to the off-course money bank, but to all intents and purposes, Johnny Miller had already made out.

That Miller was eventually able to win a Big One is a credit to him. It can be a risky business for an athlete to put the cart before the horse, or any modern equivalent thereof. A man can become a celebrity without any real achievement, a kind of star without portfolio, make a lot of money, and forget what he originally set out to do—become the best at his game.

There was a recent instance of a tall, handsome, smooth-swinging young man named Bruce Fleisher, who won the national Amateur title and little else. Before hitting one golf shot for money he engaged a manager, worked up endorsement contracts, and developed his own symbol (*à la* Jack's golden bear etc.), a clenched fist with the two-finger vee upraised to show he was in with the youth movement. Bruce went so far as to conjure up a reputation as the Joe Namath of golf with the teenyboppers. He had no use for the "longhairs," but wanted to attract the kids, and he figured everyone loved a lover, even one on the verge of marriage. Then he failed to get his player's card first time out. All that dressing and no salad. He finally got on the tour, but has been mostly a "rabbit."

Johnny Miller, of course, presents the opposite side. But did Miller ever think that too much too soon could have been the demise of a fully realized golf talent?

"I'll say this," said Miller, "it can go either way. You can lose your desire to win, if you're making a good living without it. Or you can use the financial security to become a winner. It's up to the individual. Lee Trevino might be playing better, or winning more tournaments anyway, if he didn't do so much off-course stuff. But you've got to make it when you can. He has what I call *doing things* contracts. He has to have his body in a lot of places. That's been my thing, too, but now with the Open victory maybe that can be cut back. Like Nicklaus, who mostly sells only his name.

"You know, it can also get boring if you win the tournament every week. You know what I mean?

"Money is only important if you don't have it, and if I had to depend solely on what I make on the tour I would really be worried. I'd probably play like a lot of guys on the tour. You know, lay a shot up safe instead of going for it so you make sure of getting into the top 60 and getting an exemption. With my contracts, before the year starts I know I am okay financially and can play the tour like it was for two-dollar nassaus."

THE
TWO SIDES OF NICK FALDO

(Golf World—1997)

The hug Nick Faldo gave Greg Norman on the 18th green at the conclusion of last year's Masters was one of the warmest gestures ever seen in golf. No matter that the hugger and the huggee were evasive about what was said between them during that embrace. The hug was enough, and beyond mere good sportsmanship. It said much about empathy, sympathy, the depth of human feelings. That the hug was clearly initiated by Faldo made it surprising to many. Here was a champion athlete whose public image was that of an icy, emotionless, totally self-absorbed mechanic at work—Robo-Pro. So sharply etched was that image, you might wonder if the hug was not so much thoughtful as thought out, that it was a preconceived act. "Oh no," says Faldo, taken slightly aback at that suggestion. "You don't plan something like that."

Indeed, the hug was spontaneous. And a reflection of another—or *the other*—side of Faldo that has emerged since he came to the United States more than two years ago to play most of his competitive golf. And it's that side that may get in the way of his quest for golf's Holy Grail.

When Faldo made the decision to concentrate his efforts on the U.S. PGA Tour, he said it was for professional reasons. The quality of the courses and practice facilities, the high competitive level and its depth, he felt, would put him over the hump. He would jump from being one of the best players of his own era to one of the best all-time. He has not gotten there, yet. There have been only three victories to date—the '95 Doral-Ryder and '97 Nissan Opens in addition to the '96 Masters. When he wins, he wins well, and it has only been a couple of years, but in the gaps between his superb, winning golf he has been, by the standards to which he must be held, rather ordinary, almost run of the mill. By comparison, when Jack Nicklaus didn't win, he was very often very much in contention, especially in the majors. Not so, Faldo. How come?

It appears that Faldo has gotten something from his American Journey that he may not have anticipated. He's loosened up. He's a long way from California Cool; it's more in the way of Maine Mellow. But it is different, and prompts the question, Can He Who Has Made It This Far as a Grim Grinder Go Farther as a More Convivial One? It's not as if you can tell at a glance, from a distance, this transformation in the public Faldo. On the golf course, in competition, he still goes about his business with production-line precision. He actually keeps a physical distance from the others in his pairings and makes no idle conversation with anyone. He speaks only to his caddie, Fanny Sunesson, and oddly, they chatter constantly. Faldo plays most if not all his practice rounds as a single. Just he and Fanny, who along with providing yardages and swing checks and putting alignments is also an overprotective nanny keeping fans and interlopers with notepads from her charge.

On the practice tee Faldo is just as self-absorbed, cranking out one shot after another. However, there was an instant on the range at last month's Doral-Ryder when a touch of the *other* Faldo emerged. He was hitting from the far left side of the range. Just ahead and to the left of his spot was a practice bunker. A player circled behind Faldo to get to the bunker, and in passing asked, in a joking manner, if he was safe hitting from it. Faldo nodded easily and said of course he was. He then took a full swing with a driver and cold-topped a ball, which skittered past the edge of the trap. A small bit of fun, but given Faldo's reputation for sternness, a departure. A hint of the *other* Faldo emergent.

The perception of Faldo as the quintessential stiff-upper-lip "Brit down from Cambridge" and all that, is not at all on the mark. Hang around him for a bit, listen closely, and you catch the tone of his middle-working-class background, and a lot of Beatle-ish send-up of stuffy pretension, intellectual and otherwise. Asked at a recent press conference if he felt he had a "spiritual affinity" with Ben Hogan, Faldo rustled restlessly in his chair and muttered an arch, "Oh, here we go again." His off-the-cuff asides reflect someone with a quick mind, a sharp sense of humor, a flair for language, and a tart tongue that is often wickedly irreverent. If subtle is your taste, Faldo is your man. Nothing as blunt as Norman's "I played like s—" for him. When David Feherty mistakenly called Faldo's girlfriend, Brenna Cepelak, "Brenda" during the on-camera interview following Faldo's Nissan Open win last month, Faldo called Feherty a "plonker." One British journalist who heard that could hardly believe his ears. *Plonker* is British slang for a part of the male anatomy. "A brilliant word," says Faldo, with a giddy relish. And one that gets the job done, even if you don't know what it means.

It is a given that Faldo's lighter mood these days has much to do with his being free of the constant and incredibly nasty intrusiveness of the British tabloids on his private life. It got particularly crude when Faldo broke up his marriage and began traveling and living with Cepelak. Perhaps in moving to the U.S., he also had in mind that here the customers for that sort of yellow journalism are into Oprah's weight, Elvis sightings, and three-headed children born in remote parts of Macedonia, not professional golfers. So far. And also that the "straight" American sports media does not dwell much (in print, anyway) on an athlete's sexual and marital peccadilloes. To be sure, there are the occasional references to all that at media conferences, and at the mere mention Faldo immediately drops a steel curtain around himself and freezes. However, in a less public forum he is not loath to put the scab-press trashing in perspective, concluding with a Faldo-ian slice of wry. "It's strange to me how human beings can do what they do to others of their kind," he says. "Do they go home at night and say to their wives, 'Had a good day, luv, really bashed this Faldo fellow. Editor loved it.' 'That's nice, dear. Some supper?'"

Faldo's American Journey has served to put him at ease in another way. He is fastidious to a fault—a neat freak who trims his fingernails only once a week, on Monday—and the consistency of American life as he experiences it suits Faldo's need for order. Be he in Los Angeles or Miami, Chicago or Houston, the hotel rooms, courtesy cars, food, television programs, etc., are predictable. "I started in the early days of the European tour," says Faldo, "when you had to get a cab to the course and the driver didn't know what golf was let alone where the course was. So it's kind of nice to be spoiled in the U.S. Everything is so well organized, so you can just get on with it [the golf]."

Much has been made of Faldo as a Hogan clone. There are definitely aspects of Faldo's way about golf that compare with those of the "Wee Ice Mon." Despite his fit, powerful body, Faldo has never overpowered a golf course. Though he just recently made a grip change in order to find some more distance, Faldo, like Hogan, is a fairways-and-greens golfer. And there are other similarities. The work ethic, of course—the inexhaustible mental and physical energy for practice. The capacity for intense concentration. And an obsessive secrecy concerning golf methods.

Asked how he tamps his emotions, how he manages to stay so calm on the course, he says, "Oh, I have some tricks." Asked what might they be, he turns coy: "Well, I'm not divulging them to anyone."

The Hogan parallel doesn't go much deeper than the golf itself, which may keep Faldo from reaching Hogan's level as a champion. Faldo is far more emotional than Hogan ever let on to be. Hogan bawling warm tears upon winning a big championship, as Faldo did moments after sealing his last British Open victory? Unimaginable. Or Hogan giving Sam Snead a big hug after Sam blew a U.S. Open? Forget it.

Hogan had no hobbies, no interests outside of golf. Faldo is a devotee of pop stars Phil Collins and Elton John, attends their concerts, collects their CDs. He goes to the movies, is very fond of fishing, and gets wonderfully animated, rhapsodic even, describing a fishing vacation he took in New Zealand. You needed a crowbar to get Hogan out of Fort Worth. Faldo says there is a lot of the world he still wants to see, and he takes something away from his travels. At Doral, two Oriental men requested he take a picture with each of them. Faldo acceded, and each held his hand for the photo. Faldo asked them if they were Thai. They were. Men holding hands for a photograph is a Thai custom. Faldo said a word or two to them, in Thai. Then, as he walked off, the rogue humor rose up in him. "Glad they weren't from San Francisco," he said, "or they'd have grabbed my bum."

Hogan was asked once if, as a tournament pro, he ever considered himself an entertainer. He responded immediately, and with typically abrupt finality—"No." Faldo allows there is an entertainment quotient in what he does for a living, and goes along with it by occasionally "having some bits for the crowd." At Doral last March, one such "bit" included agreeing to pose for a snapshot with a fan's wife, and their infant twins who were sprawled out in a double carriage. Entertainment quotient aside, this particular request may also have been granted because of its specific nature. Kids were involved. There was a poignant moment during the bit when Faldo tweaked the cheeks of the toddlers. It was not a mere gesture. Faldo sorely misses his three children.

There were always lengthy periods when Faldo was away from home, but now those breaks are much longer and there is a different tone to them with the "official" separation and impending divorce of Faldo and his second wife, Gill. The children live most of the time with their mother, in Nick's old home in Florida, so the kids can see their dad more often. Significantly, Faldo has done the same thing in England—bought a house very near the old homestead. To be near the kids.

Ben Hogan made a decision early in his career not to have children. He said it would be unfair to them, because he would be an absentee father. His golf came first . . . and last. Faldo, perhaps in part because he was an only child, has chosen to produce a family (and, as often happens with an only child, a larger family than he had) and still work relentlessly at his golf. Nothing unusual in that. Most tour pros have children, some quite a few, and Jack Nicklaus has proven beyond a doubt that a big family does not necessarily stand in the way of great achievement in golf.

But there is more to it than having or not having children. There is the marriage itself. Marriage is no easy proposition for anyone, but the problems are often magnified and have a peculiar character by one partner being a world-class golfer. Golf is a demanding mistress. It takes much of the time and attention of the golfer, not only on the course but off. Many professional golfers have said, in so many words, that they are, *they must,* be selfish when it comes to their career. Which is to say, the golfer of the house needs to feel tranquil in his private life. In other words, at the risk of sounding antifeminist, the spouse has to be . . . amenable. It is not a matter of ego massaging, but being willing and able to stay the course despite periods, sometimes long ones, of loneliness. No one knows for sure how any marriage actually works, other than their own, but from all that we can tell those partnerships of the game's great players—Hogan, Nicklaus, Palmer, Watson, Casper—have at least been constant. No doubt some bargains were struck, but one way or the other the marriages stuck. That they did had much to do with the success of the players.

Faldo is doing, or trying to do it, differently. By a lot. He is attempting to perform a risky balancing act. He is grabbing for the gold ring in golf from a precarious perch on the slippery pole of personal upheaval. It's not the first time. In 1985, he completely overhauled a test-proven golf swing, a monumental career move that has been thoroughly documented. But what was not as well known was that at the same time he was working out the new mechanics with his coach, David Leadbetter, Faldo was breaking up his first marriage and, before it was officially dissolved, starting what would become the next one.

He has done the same thing again, but with even more involvement. Children. Just at that point in his career when he says he wants to make the ultimate effort to place himself historically at the pinnacle of his profession, he leaves his marriage and takes up with an American woman who is half his age. It is his doing. By all reliable accounts, Gill Faldo was and remains devoted to her estranged husband. It seems odd that a man who plays his game so close to the vest should be such a big risk-taker in his personal life. Maybe Faldo needs the turmoil to stimulate his golf.

In any case, someone like Faldo, who apparently is trying to satisfy two human urges—one for emotional or sensual satisfaction, the other for high professional attainment that he knows very well requires stability and calm—has to be very good at compartmentalizing his life. He has shown a capacity for keeping career and *the other* separate, but in the weeks before he won last year's Masters Faldo received a lot of hate mail taking him apart for leaving his wife and children for Cepelak. And yet, he went out and played superb, major-winning golf—albeit, with a little help from Norman.

Then again, as already noted, he didn't do much of anything after winning the '96 Masters, and did even less in the two years leading up to last year's bizarre Sunday in Georgia. At the press conference that Sunday evening, Faldo was queried about the relatively listless golf he had been playing until then, and why he was again in high form. Had he made some swing changes? Faldo sloughed the question with, "Oh, I just got back to *natural* golf," the word *natural* loaded with his brand of sarcasm.

The fact is, it was a period of time when he was going through a wrenching breakup of his family. Hence, the ordinary golf. Period. There is something of the Jekyll and Hyde in the Faldo story. On the golf course he is a narrow-eyed, fang-toothed assassin. He is extremely competitive, with an ever-watchful eye on his opponents. Asked whether he noticed anything to indicate Norman was feeling the pressure during that last round at Augusta, Faldo replied, "Yes, he began gripping and regripping his club more, and taking a lot more time over the ball." Did it make a difference to you? "Oh, yes," he said, "it gave me a boost knowing he was getting tight."

Faldo wants to achieve enduring fame as a great champion. He has a keen sense of history, and knows better than anyone that the '96 Masters will always be known as the one Norman lost. Faldo also knows that he can win three more Masters, another British Open or two, and maybe a PGA, but that to be considered in the same class as Hagen, Sarazen, Hogan, Nicklaus, Palmer, and Player, he must win a U.S. Open. Faldo is in excellent physical condition. He works out regularly, and proudly shows off his washboard abs. But he is 40 years old. And he's using up a lot of emotional energy with his personal life.

Off the course, Faldo is a man with a range of interests, and certainly one with a passion for living. Never mind surface appearances. The so-called Robo-Pro is only so called. The man is human—perhaps all too. Problem is, the nongolf side is intruding on the golf side. The separation of church and state has not been all that effective. Given Faldo's superb golf technique, sheer talent, and enormous willpower he just may be able to have his cake and eat it, too. If he can pull it off he'll be one of the rare ones who have.

TOMMY BOLT
IS ALIVE AND WELL
AND LIVING IN
CRYSTAL SPRINGS

(Sports Illustrated GolfPlus—2001)

Okay! Is it true that you, "Terrible" Tommy Bolt, withdrew from a Houston Open while waiting in a downpour to play your approach, because, you said, you were wearing clothes worth more than you could win?

"That is true, yessir. Why stay out there and ruin all those good clothes when you're only going to win 50 or 100 dollars."

Is it also true, Tommy "Thunder" Bolt, that in Philadelphia one summer you hit a totally pure 4-iron to a two-tier green, the ball landing on the lower level and, as you planned, adroitly hopping onto the upper deck and jerking to a stop a couple of feet from the stob, but because this work of art received not a single response from the gallery you said to your caddie, "Let me ask you, boy, is that a gallery behind that green or an oil painting?" and when your caddie confirmed it was not an oil painting, you said, "Well, let me tell you something, boy, if these folks don't appreciate Ole Tom then go pick that ball up because Ole Tom is going home." And you withdrew?

"I never said go pick that ball up. I withdrew from a lot of 'em, but I don't remember that one."

The memory lapse is excusable. In his 25 years on the PGA Tour (1946–71) Tommy Bolt withdrew from a lot of tournaments. He threw even more clubs. The photograph of him rearing back to heave his driver during the 1960 US Open, his face contorted with rage, is archival.

"I wasn't the only one out there who threw clubs," says 84-year old Tommy Bolt, two-time Ryder Cupper, winner of 15 PGA Tour events including the 1958 US Open, at Southern Hills, in Tulsa, site of this year's national championship. "When Arnold Palmer started on the tour, he didn't know which way to throw 'em. Winnie [Palmer's wife] was always going back to retrieve 'em. I said, 'Arnold, throw 'em ahead of us, and we'll pick 'em up on the way. Hell, man, anybody who hasn't thrown a club isn't serious about the game.'"

To be sure. Temper is to the golfing nervous system what lava is to Vesuvius, and Bolt was no where near the only one out there who stormed off the premises in mid-round, swore magniloquently, buried, bent, and broke clubs. But Bolt became the archetype of golf rage, because he did it with a certain panache. When Ed Furgol, the '54 US Open champion, catapulted his irons into the turf past the hosel he was the picture of a man furious not only at golf but the world. When beefy Clayton Heafner withdrew from a tournament just before hitting his opening drive, because the announcer mispronounced his name, no one minded his departure because Heafner's perpetually squinched beet-red face reminded everyone of their last case of cramps. To get current, when it doesn't go right for Craig Stadler he just looks like a petulant fatty denied his second piece of pie.

Tommy Bolt, though, was a cartoon of Man Angry at Golf. Tall, with a Marine Corp.-erect posture, Bolt had a short-stepped, foot-sliding swagger. His head was held head high and tilted back, which accentuated the jut of his prognathous chin. His teeth were in a Kirk Douglas cement-lock that didn't widen a millimeter when the soily language spewed—seeped— forth. Add to it his dress—impeccable, expensive, and definitely stylized. No rumpled mound of material formed at the top of his shoes, and every outfit with its own pair of color coordinated shoes. Bolt was not into Day-Glo, but neither was he one for your basic browns, blues and whites.

His antics, combined with his distinctive outfits (costumes?), made Bolt's tantrums fun to watch. It was vaudeville, or burlesque. And in the spirit of the latter's traditional "take it off" chant, the gallery would try to stir Bolt into his act. It wasn't hard to do.

"In Hartford one year Tommy was being ragged by the gallery. He finally had enough, and after marking his ball on a par-three hole he did a slow 360 all the way around the green cursing the crowd as he went."—Gene Littler.

Ask contemporaries for thoughts on Bolt, and the first response is a warm chuckle followed inevitably by stories.

"We all enjoyed him. There was no meanness in him, and he came up with so many funny lines."—Mike Souchak.

His way with a phrase was another component in the Bolt oeuvre that separated him from the other temperamentals.

"In Mobile one year the course didn't have much grass on it, and was soaking wet from steady rain. Someone asked Tommy if he had misread a green. He said, 'How in hell can you read mud.'"—Jack Tuthill, former tour manager.

"We're walking to the first tee in the Club Pro, in Phoenix, and it's starting to rain. Tommy says, 'As soon as I lose the crease on these pants, I'm out of here.'"—Bob Rosburg.

Then there is the one about his age being misprinted in the Detroit Free Press, making him 49 not 39. When told by the paper's reporter that it was just a typographical error, Bolt said, "It was like hell. It was a perfect 4 and a perfect 9."

Where did you get that flair for drollery, Mr. Bolt? "When I was a kid selling newspapers around Shreveport, you did whatever you needed to get that nickel in your pocket. Those were hard times. If a guy said he couldn't read, I'd say he didn't have to, he could just smell the paper. It was just a bunch of bullshit, anyway."

The comeback may say more about Bolt than that he just had a quick wit.

Bolt was a much better player than he's been credited for. Fifteen wins is impressive for someone who didn't go on tour until he was 27. And he won on big courses. Bolt's first pro victory was the North & South Open, on Pinehurst Number 2. He won the Los Angeles Open, at Riviera, the Colonial on its superior layout; and of course, the US Open, which he led wire to wire. "I birdied the very first hole, and when I picked the ball out of the hole I said to myself, 'I wonder whose going to finish second.'"

"His Open victory was a masterpiece. It was a real hard course, it was real hot, and it was a very good field. That was some score he shot there." (283 - +3) —Bob Rosburg.

What's more, at age 55, in the suffocating heat of south Florida in July, Bolt was tied with Jack Nicklaus for the lead after 63 holes in the 1971 PGA Championship. He birdied the 10th—"I may have been leading at that point"—but bogeyed the 17th and finished sole third.

Of the seven rounds of 60 shot on the Tour between 1951 and 1957 (the magic low number in those days, and another wasn't shot until 1990), five were on hardpan Texas "bullrings," another on a short resort track in Virginia. The one other was on a formidable layout in the northeast—Wethersfield CC, in Connecticut—which is where Bolt shot his.

Finally, there was the six-hole playoff for the second Legends of Golf tournament. Bolt and Roberto DeVicenzo got into a birdie duel that Bolt further enlivened, when, after he topped a second straight DeVicenzo birdie putt, pistol-pointed a "take-that" finger at his rival. On the next hole, DeVicenzo returned the gesture when he birdied on top of Bolt. It was all in good spirits, and was good theater along with excellent golf—DeVicenzo (and partner, Julius Boros) won on the sixth extra hole with a sixth straight birdie. The tournament itself sprung the notion of a senior tour, and it was effectively jump-started by Bolt and DeVicenzo. They proved the old guys could still play, and to boot had plenty of spirit left.

"[Ben]Hogan told me he thought Bolt was the finest ballstriker he'd ever seen. He also told me not to tell him he said so."—Jack Tuthill.

"In a tournament in Milwaukee once, on a long par-three, the first day I hit a 2-iron on the green. Bolt hits a driver on the green. Next day, same hole same conditions, I hit a 2-iron again on the green, and so does Bolt. I ask him how come a driver yesterday, a 2-iron today? He says, 'I just didn't feel as strong yesterday.'" —Dave Hill.

Big league talent with an artistic sensibility, not to say temperament, and a touch of anal retentive helps explain the temper. "I was a perfectionist," says Bolt. "If things didn't go just right, I was frustrated. I like everything in order. Like I dress, that's the way I want to play golf."

"He just hated to not pull off the beautiful shot he had in mind. He walked off the course with more chances to finish third or fourth or fifth, because that didn't mean as much to him as playing pretty. Hogan was always fussing at him to just go out and play, forget the bad ones. But Tom couldn't do it. It had to be right artistically."—Mike Souchak.

Then the temper hurt his game? He would have won more had he been cool?

"I think he used his temper to his advantage. It took his mind off the game and kept him from choking. He'd get mad, and that would rivet his mind to the job."—Jackie Burke, Jr.

"The thought that he couldn't deal with imperfection is on the mark, but he also developed a reputation for his temper and felt he had to keep it up. He was a true entertainer, he loved being on stage."—Billy Casper.

"I got a little ham in me," admits Bolt. "I want people to see me hit good shots. I'm a John Barrymore, man. I'm an actor."

*"When he won the US Open, in the locker room just before the presenta-
tion ceremony I congratulated him, and he said, 'Mouse, you watch old Tom. I'm
going to walk down those stairs so slow they're going to lay a two-stroke penalty
on me.' There's this long flight of stairs from the clubhouse down to the 18th green
at Southern Hills, and sure enough he almost walked sideways keeping all those
blue blazers waiting for him. He was making an entrance."*—Bob Toski.

Bolt is ambivalent about his reputation for fulmination. He says it has
been blown out of proportion (as do his old tour pals). It's as if it's the only
thing that he is known for. Actually, it pretty much is. He admitted it himself, when, a few years ago he thanked a press group for writing "all those
stories about me that weren't true, but if you didn't nobody would know
who I am."

What that says about the kind of world we live in is informative.
Exceptional talent is not always its own reward. Bolt needed caricature to
secure a place in his game's songbook.

*"He would have won 30 tournaments if he didn't have a temper. But after
awhile it was his calling card, and he began to play on it. It was a way to get attention, which was hard to do when Hogan and Snead were the stars of the day."*
—Bob Goalby.

He played the card well. Perhaps too well. Bolt lives with his wife,
Mary Lou, rent-free in a home within the upscale Black Diamond Ranch
residential community, in Crystal River, Florida. He earns it by playing
golf with potential home buyers, hanging around the clubhouse shaking
hands, telling stories, being a grand old golf pro famous for his temper
tantrums. Bolt also owns a 600 acre farm in Arkansas on which he has
raised cattle, and where his only child, 42-year-old Tommy, lives with his
wife and two children. He has contracted to play Razor clubs, which he
will use on the Grand Masters super-senior circuit recently organized by
the PGA Tour to compensate for the lack of a pension plan for pros from
his era—four tournaments, with each player guaranteed no less than
$12,500 per event. Bolt also does some corporate outings, and when he
was offered $50,000 for his US Open gold medal he responded, "I ain't
rich, but I ain't poor. I'll hang on to it."

He says he reads the Bible every evening, and is no longer the hard
drinker he was. "I drank my share, but nowadays I just have a glass of wine
with dinner."

So life is good for Tommy Bolt. Only one thing is missing, a place in
the PGA Hall of Fame. Bolt is anxious to be voted in, feeling this would
recognize his talent at golf, finally, not his temper. His chances are long,

though, and lengthening. At last count he had only 19 of the 65 percent of the votes needed, and no one has gained votes as each year goes by.

Why won't he make it? Veteran golf writer, Furman Bisher, may have the read on it. When asked if Bolt belongs in the HOF, Bisher, said: *"Well, his swing sure should be."*

Which suggests that the reputation for temper he cultivated to get his game noticed continues to have a reverse effect. And, too, when it comes to the sanctification of sports stars, "bad boys," even if they really ain't, aren't allowed in. It's the image thing.

THE RISE
OF THE
TIGER

(The Golden Era of Golf—2001)

The race issue didn't disappear, never to be heard from again, after Lee Elder became the first black golfer to play in the Masters tournament, in 1975. In a 1979 interview with a *New York Times* sportswriter, on the eve of his defense of the Westchester Classic, Elder said blacks were still struggling for equality in "a sport that continues to feel uncomfortable about black players . . . It still hasn't changed enough. I overlook a lot of racial things I should be more forward about." His wife, Rose, no wallflower, expanded on her husband's remark: "The prejudice thing is still very real. You'll find some bigots in nearly every gallery. Their favorite expression is, 'Hit it, nigger.' Or somebody will yell, 'What are you doing in a white man's game?'"

And yet, the player who became the most dominant in golf worldwide at the end of the 20th century was (is) Eldrick "Tiger" Woods. Strictly speaking, Woods is a mix of various racial strains. His mother is half Thai, a quarter Chinese, a quarter white. His father has a touch of white, a good bit of Native American and Chinese, and half black African blood.

Which brings to mind an opinion once expressed by Cliff Roberts, the cofounder of the Masters tournament, and who resisted inviting blacks to play in his tournament only until public pressure became too great. Roberts said: "Marriage between members of different races was a mistake," and that, "mixed breeds were the most worthless of all in every respect." Against such wrong-mindedness, Tiger Woods stands tall and straight, lithe and strong. He is articulate, intelligent, and the next great golf champion.

However, when Woods first joined the PGA Tour, at the age of 21, he was reluctant to inject himself into the race issue, making the point that he is multi-ethnic. Nonetheless, to most Americans if there's a drop of black in you, you are black. Woods surely understood that, and after his first year on the PGA Tour, when he became one of the highest-profile athletes in sport, he began to get more involved in programs to bring inner-city kids, in particular African-Americans, into golf. Some of his first efforts were ill advised, though, especially two television commercials made by Woods's most visible and richest corporate retainer, Nike. In one advertisement, Woods said on camera that he still had trouble getting on certain golf courses because of his color. This was sharply criticized and very soon withdrawn, because no one believed it for a minute. The second commercial was set in a tenement-lined city neighborhood showing mainly black children standing on rooftops with sets of golf clubs at their side, and walking through a busy Harlem street with a bag of clubs over their shoulder on the way to a golf course. It was pie-in-the-sky, a case of a corporation attempting to declare a social reality that didn't exist, or certainly didn't yet, while trying to locate a new market for its footwear.

Soon after, the Tiger Woods Foundation was established to promote realistic efforts to get minority youngsters into golf. This added on to, and began to help, already existing organizations that had been working toward the same end. The American Golf Corporation, which operates hundreds of municipally owned public courses around the country on a lease basis, many of them inner-city sites, makes its facilities available for as little as one dollar and sometimes free. Tiger Woods and American Golf contracted for five years to produce at least five clinics at various American Golf facilities around the country. Woods has shown sincere interest in these clinics, which he will not do at private clubs but only at inner-city public courses. He is relaxed, doesn't rush, and thoughtfully puts each youngster's hands correctly on the grip, checks out the stance, and is thoroughly engaged. He has received high marks for his work in this area.

On the other hand, some of the magic went out of the Senior PGA Tour in the 1990s because the junior circuit (PGA Tour) became much more interesting than it had been for a while. Within a four-year period a new group of young players arrived with exceptional ability and fresh competitive energy. They included Phil Mickelson, Justin Leonard, David Duval, and especially Tiger Woods. Woods in a number of ways is the synthesis of all that has happened in American golf over the past 100 years, which is to say, almost its entire history. There is, first off, his ethnic background. Woods personifies American's immigrant history—he is an Ellis Island in golf shoes—and by all means Jesse Jackson's Rainbow Coalition.

Leaving aside his natural gifts for golf, Woods has profited from the wealth of information about swing mechanics that over the last half century has been uncovered or rediscovered and, more to the point, so widely disseminated. It all is exhibited in his symmetrically attractive, and sound swing. There is in Woods's swing action nothing unusual, such as Hogan's pronated flat plane, or Nicklaus's flying right elbow. Woods has used a sports psychologist since his late teens to act as an objective sounding board for any doubts he may harbor. And he has become a model of the benefits of modern weight training and flexibility exercises.

An important addition to the advances in swing mechanics and dealing with the psychology of golf, Woods (and his peers) plays with the best golf ball and the strongest and most reliable shafts the game has ever had. He also plays week in and week out on strains of golf grasses developed over the past 25 years that give perfect lies and incredibly smooth greens, both of which providing infinitely more predictable results than ever before.

All of this is synergized in a young man with what appears to be an intrinsic genius for athletic timing, intelligence, an unmistakable urge to be a champion of champions, and faculties of concentration that let him perform at his very best when he needs to be the very best. In the end, this capacity overrides all the modern technology and horticulture. The stuff of a great champion is not exactly quantifiable, not in any scientific way at least. Woods has it, whatever that *it* means.

Woods followed up a superlative amateur golf career—featuring an NCAA individual championship while he was at Stanford University, and an unprecedented three consecutive U.S. Amateur championship victories—with a swift start in professional golf. He won two of his first six tournaments, and in 1997 swept the Masters as no one ever had before. He won by 12 strokes, at 18 under par. All of which generated an exceptionally high level of future expectations. But things being the way they are in the instant-everything postmodern world, the future expectations didn't materialize fast enough for the golf public . . . or perhaps its story-hungry media. When Woods didn't win another major title until the 1999 PGA championship questions arose, or were arisen, about the potential assigned him. Perhaps he didn't have it, after all. Never mind that during the hiatus between major victories he won six tournaments on the PGA Tour, had six top ten finishes in the majors, and won over $6 million. We should all suffer such slumps.

Nonetheless, Woods himself thought he was not living up his notices and with his coach, Claude "Butch" Harmon, he went about making some important changes in his swing. What needed improving? He could be wild with a driver, especially when the situation really needed accuracy and length—such as in the U.S. Open. Another glaring problem was his tendency to overshoot the greens with short-iron approaches. From 100 to 140 yards he didn't seem able to translate the distance properly to swing and touch. This nullified his distance advantage with the driver. His putting was erratic, too, in the six- to sixteen-foot range. He was either very good or just mediocre, and mediocre doesn't cut it at his level.

Harmon had his man shorten his backswing to gain better control of both accuracy and distance. He also changed the angle of his wrists in the backswing, cupping them more. And he slowed his exceptionally fast, almost violent hip turn in the downswing. It all took a little over a year to work out, and jell. As improved ball striking often does, his putting became steadier, with bursts of brilliance. Finally, Woods came out in 2000 some twenty pounds heavier; he had bulked up with a program of weight train- ing and flexibility exercises. The spindly kid with the superfast swing was history, replaced by a big, broad-chested 180-pounder with enormous power and much improved control of his shots. The payoff was a huge 1999 season that carried into 2000—nine victories in the United States, five of them in a row. To have made these adjustments when already doing so well is the mark of Woods's dedication to his craft and the extent of his self-confidence. He felt he could make rather major technique changes and still be competitive in the process. He was right.

At the same time that he was taking care of his game, Woods also decided to improve off-course situations that had become troublesome. He released the veteran caddie who had been with him through the early triumphs, in part at least on the grounds that the caddie had himself become a minor celebrity and was publicly playing the role. He forgot who the real star was, and that the star often resents sharing the spotlight with aides. Woods also sacked the International Management Group agent who had wheeled his first very lucrative endorsement deals.

In his first four years as a pro—1996–2000—Tiger Woods has had a truly phenomenal passage through time and has continued his pace into the new century. He made comprehensive changes in his swing technique, traveled thousands of miles overseas to compete and do hands-on clinics with inner-city kids, and all the while defeat the cream of the game's professionals in the highest competitions. In 2000 he broke every U.S. Open record on the books in winning by an unheard-of 15 strokes, at Pebble Beach. A month later he won the British Open by eight strokes, and a month after that he won the PGA championship in a stirring shoot-out with little-known but inspired Bob May.

One of the fascinating effects of Woods's preeminence is, when he doesn't win a tournament every week, or at least every other week, he is considered to be in a slump. Never mind that when he isn't winning he's finishing in the top ten, or five, or two. Such was the case after his 2000 PGA championship victory. The "slump" continued through the early part of 2001, and then was "snapped" with what is becoming a Woodsian run of superb championship golf.

In the Bay Hill Classic, a mini-major in view of the high-quality field and outstanding golf course, Woods closed with a truly outstanding birdie on the tough last hole to edge Phil Mickelson. He took advantage of a good bit of luck, his pulled drive hitting a spectator and staying on trampled rough where he could make a full swing. The approach was still not that easy, in that the pin was tucked in the right corner of the green, guarded by a bunker and water. Did Woods try to cut the ball in from left to right and avoid the trouble in front? Not at all. He simply blasted a 6-iron right at the hole, and finished some six to eight feet from the cup. He needed the putt to win, and he made it. Stunning golf in the choice of second shot, the ability to pull it off, then making a putt to take it all.

He followed that victory with another the following week, in the Players championship, the unofficial fifth major. Here he was simply steadier than those who got into contention, or, as is more and more the case, they were intimidated by Woods's presence.

The two victories in a row prepped Woods for the Masters, but good. He won it by two over David Duval, and created an argument. Did his Masters victory constitute a Grand Slam, being he now held all four of the major championships, starting with the 2000 U.S. Open? Purists said the Slam must be achieved in the same season. Others said it didn't make any difference, he had them all at once. One way or the other, he is is the first to do so, and everyone expects he will also be the first to win them in a single season. It seems there is nothing Woods can't do in golf.

And all of it done with remarkable poise, especially for someone only halfway to 50 years of age. Quite a saga being written by a young man who stands as the ultimate expression of the golden era of American golf.

METHODS
&
MORES

NIGHTMARES!

(Golf Magazine—1979)

Chi-Chi Rodriguez stood on the 18th tee at Augusta National Golf Club convinced he had a lock on the Masters. With a two-stroke lead and only the last hole left to play, a dream was about to come true. But it didn't, because Chi-Chi woke up.

It was a dream, one that Chi-Chi has had many times and from which he always awakes at precisely the same moment—just before he hits the ball. Jerry McGee has an almost identical and recurrent dream, except he gets closer to a conclusion: He reaches the 18th green at Augusta National and needs two putts to nail down the victory. Then, as Jerry puts it, "The alarm goes off."

These nightmarish dreams are but two examples indicating that if playing golf for real is not frustrating enough, it can be worse during that time when we are supposedly resting from the game's trials and tribulations. Actually, extensive research over the past 25 years on the physiology of sleep has convincingly shown that while our bodies are sleeping our brains function at almost full steam, and primarily in the form of dreams. Applied science aside, dreams have been the source of much contemplation since the dawn of civilization (at least), and beginning with Sigmund Freud's pioneer work, *The Interpretation of Dreams,* at the turn of the 20th century, what we dream and why has become an industry within the industry of psychoanalysis.

Athletes do not dream any more than do "ordinary" people, but perhaps because games playing tends to focus so sharply on essential human conflicts and desires, athletes' dreams evoke greater interest. Which probably accounts for Artemidorus of Daldis, a second-century A.D. Greek writer, devoting a large portion of his treatise on dreams, "Oneirocriticon," to athletes. For example, Artemidorus recounts an episode in which a sprinter, the night before he was to compete in the Imperial Games in Rome, dreamed he became blind. The next day he won the race, and the dream, as Artemidorus interpreted it, foretold the victory, because the leader in a race, like a blind man, cannot see his rivals.

That seems to be a fairly valid interpretation, but on the whole any reading of a dream is tricky—highly subjective and dependent on considerable personal, private, background information, the kind of stuff this writer is not equipped professionally to obtain. However, from the research done here on golfers' dreams, a general pattern can be seen. To wit, golfers' dreams are most apt to be ones of dark portents, imminent disaster, anxiety-provoking incidents, frustration; and since I spoke for the most part with quite successful players, the pattern is not reserved, as might be expected, for "hackers." Consider Ben Hogan, who in a moment of self-revelation, told of a dream he had and his reaction to it, which is typical of this fiercely competitive perfectionist.

"I once dreamed I was going to make 18 holes in one in a single round," Ben said. "I got 17, and on the 18th my drive lipped out. I got mad as hell."

Dave Stockton suggested, after hearing the Rodriguez-McGee dreams mentioned earlier, "Maybe it's because they've never won a major championship." Yet Tom Watson, who has won a few big ones (so far), said he has golf dreams all the time and in them he is always in "impossible situations." Asked for an example, he stopped short and with a pained expression said he didn't want to talk further about his golf dreams.

Others were not so "tight" as Tom on the subject. Al Geiberger, for instance, relates a truly fantastic dream he once had. He is playing in the Masters and in his hotel room is waiting for his wife to get ready. She is very slow, and Al leaves without her. At the course, Al's tee-off time is approaching, his wife is still not at the course, so he sends his caddie back to get her, giving him his shirt to use as a pass to get back onto the grounds. With his tee-off time moments away, Geiberger has no caddie, no clubs, and *no pants*. Instead, he is wearing bermuda short pajamas, the fly of which has no buttons. Standing on the first tee now, every time he addresses the ball he becomes indecently exposed and must cover himself. He does this very calmly, believing no one notices his difficulty. Finally, he hits his drive, a sky-ball that goes 50 yards forward. End of dream.

Carl Jung, a colleague of Freud's who studied dreams extensively and integrated them deeply into his psychoanalytic system, said that dreams are a kind of safety valve, a release from the relatively restrictive behavior imposed on us by society. In dreams we are free to indulge in fantasy, in imaginings often suppressed while we are awake. Golfers, apparently, are particularly prone to this if only because they (we) are into a game best played by internalizing the emotions. It is a lonely game that demands much self-control, and no negative thoughts. In golf dreams, though, we can unleash terrors and potential crises that must not be articulated on a real golf course.

Thus, Dave Marr dreams he is at the U.S. Open, is called to the first tee, but doesn't have a club—his caddie has not arrived. "I'm looking back at the USGA official," Dave recalls, "one of those stern guys wearing gray and dark blue, and I'm worried he's going to put two strokes on me for slow play, or delay. I see a can on the tee with a handle sticking out of it that is actually the small end of a ham. I decide I'll use this for a club, but now I can't find a level lie on the tee. I'm paired with my buddies, Bob Goalby and Mason Rudolph, and they're pulling for me, but I can't for the life of me find a level spot. And the USGA man is frowning. It never gets resolved. The dream ends at that point."

Most golfers' dreams uncovered for this piece are not nearly as overtly bizarre as Al Geiberger's pajama game or perhaps Dave Marr's ham-on-a-slope act. Neither are they quite so puzzling to understand.

Terry Diehl and Carol Mann both have recurring dreams of being in a dark forest. For Carol, there is not only the scariness of the place, but an out of bounds that drops off into a bottomless void. Terry is lost in his woods, cannot find his way out, and cannot be found. "I'm wandering around bumping against trees and stumbling into deep pits."

Jerry McGee often dreams of losing his driver and wedge in an airport. So does David Graham.

In Frank Beard's most recurrent golf dream he has great difficulty getting his golf glove on. It is much too small, and when he finally does squeeze it on it is so tight he cannot hold the club properly. One of my own golf dreams has a similar theme. The grip of my club is very fat and it is impossible for me to get my hands together on it. A friend speculates that this dream is saying that the dreamer's real grip is unsound. I've been checking that out.

That many golfers have dreams with a similar motif, only the details being different, is one of the more intriguing (and in a way comforting) revelations that surfaced while nosing around on the subject. For example, another of my own recurring golf dreams, the one that inspired this article, puts me in a very small room with an important shot to play. But I cannot take the club back because the wall is too close behind.

Frank Beard is similarly stymied, by a hedge directly behind him. John Mahaffey has a gallery at his back that won't move, and Jerry Heard is in a deep hole no bigger around than himself. Big, tall George Archer dreams he is in a phone booth. Billy Harmon, youngest son of one-time Masters winner Claude Harmon, often dreams there is a brick wall restricting his backswing—"usually at Pebble Beach, for some reason." A friend of Billy's, when he was considering playing the pro tour, often dreamed he had to play his big shot out of a kitchen. "The refrigerator, stove, tables and chairs, and whatnot are in my way. I can't make my swing." It may be significant that this fellow decided against the tour, opting instead to sell insurance. Could it be his dream was telling him he had a much better shot at three squares a day in a kitchen than on the pro circuit?

In any case, so many golfers having the above dream motif or theme illustrates what Carl Jung called a collective, or archetypal, image. That is, it symbolizes one of the game's elemental dilemmas. Is there anything more unnerving for *all* golfers in *real live* action than being up against a tree or fence or back edge of a bunker and unable to get the club started back properly, or at all? If you cannot turn on the ignition you may as well stay in bed . . . if you can take the nightmares.

Charles Price, *Golf* magazine's colorfully thoughtful contributing editor who as an amateur once took a run at the pro tour, also dreams of being in a small room with an important shot to play. Charlie can take the club back, but he has to hit the ball through an extremely narrow doorway.

"I can't get myself angled right to do it," says Charlie. "I can't set up. I'm playing with Sam Snead, by the way, and he did it. Got the ball through the doorway. Naturally. In the dream I'm yelling at Sam, 'How'd you do it, how'd you do it?' And, 'Wait for me, wait for me!' When I told Sam about the dream, he said if it ever happens he'd wait for me."

In his study of dreams, Carl Jung also theorized that in our sleep we are capable of conjuring up analogies between our personal, modern-day "problems" and ancient myths of which we have no conscious knowledge.

A fascinating case in point comes from Jerry Heard, the lively Californian making a fine comeback on the tour after a back injury. Jerry has a recurring dream in which he is hitting an iron shot to a green set on the side of a steeply sloped mountain. The ball gets up onto the green, but keeps rolling back down the mountain to his feet.

"There's no way I can keep the ball on that green," says Jerry. "It is brown and hard, which makes it worse. I keep trying to figure a way to make the ball stay."

I asked Jerry if he had ever heard of the myth of Sisyphus, which comes from ancient Greek mythology and has been used in recent times by the French writer-philosopher Albert Camus to symbolize the fate of mankind. Heard, who was hitting practice balls, said he had not heard of it. I told him about Sisyphus, king of Corinth, who, for having insulted Zeus, God of the Gods, was condemned to the eternal punishment of pushing a heavy rock to the top of a high mountain. When he got the rock to the peak, it went rolling down the other side, and Sisyphus had to go back to work.

Jerry Heard nodded, said, "That's it, baby," then went back to hitting golf balls. For real. And in his dreams.

THE
TEACHING
SPIRIT

(Golf Journal—1978)

In our endless search for The Secret to what we sometimes like to pretend is a mere game, we have all, at one time or another, been led down strange, unfulfilling paths by gurus whose powers lay more in a beguiling delivery than in the worth of their ideas. Promising heaven on earth is not restricted to deodorant commercials.

On the other hand, there are golf teachers who may be loaded to the gills with true wisdom, but who transmit little or none of it because of a teaching manner as stimulating as congealed oatmeal. The ideal, obviously, is the middle ground—a teacher teaching good stuff in a captivatingly convincing style.

Not an easy combination to find, that. So, on the personal premise that more budding golf careers have been discouraged by dull academics than by silver-tongued hypnotists, my own inclination is toward the latter. If I am guilty here of opting for image over substance, which many believe to be the bane of modern society, so be it. Golf may be more than a game, but it is not world politics, either.

In my view, golf is a game of feel more than of rigid mechanical stan-dards. The latter, of course, is our usual frame of reference—position of the hands, angle of takeaway, etc., etc., etc. In the end, though, the physical motions we settle on are almost invariably the ones that *feel* best. Why else do we see such vast variety of contortions among players both bad *and* good? Nicklaus invented his own swing, Palmer was hardly a classicist, and I dare anyone to play well trying to swing as Hogan did. Or consider Miller Barber, who earns a fine living Out There with an action resem-bling an enthusiastic lumberjack's. (On second thought, don't consider Miller Barber.)

But enough of this philosophy, absorbing though it may be. The point is that should you fall into the clutches of a golf teacher whose psalm turns out to be pscrewy, so long as he leaves you with the spirit to carry on the quest for The Word, that is enough.

My own teacher, for but one brief lesson, was Alex Morrison. That name will be familiar only to those who have been around golf a long time or are steeped in the game's more arcane lore. Alex Morrison is not likely to be installed in any of the many golf halls of fame. He was a golf pro, but never at any of the more celebrated clubs (or at any club, for that matter), and he was never a member of the PGA. Neither did Alex play competitive golf, at least on any reportable level. His brother, Fred, the winner of a tour event or two in the 1920s, was the "player" in the fami-ly. And yet, Alex Morrison is something of a legend in golf instruction.

This was the result of a combination of things. Alex wrote much of his golf instruction for *The American Golfer* at a time (the 1920s) when Grantland Rice was the editor and the magazine was at the zenith of its well-deserved popularity. He also had a golf studio, in Midtown Manhattan, where he taught many notable persons with access to the pub-lic ear—actors, politicians, and the like. Besides that, he played the vaude-ville circuit in the heyday of that dear departed entertainment medium, giving a combination of golf instruction and exhibition (hitting cotton balls into the audience) in an act complemented by a traditional comedy routine. In short, Morrison had exposure on a number of key stages at a time when golf in America was a fascinating curiosity. None of the above guarantees legend, but Alex did (and does) have something to say about the golf swing, and he said (says) it with a certain style, which (in case you have forgotten) is what we are here to talk about.

In 1969, I was an associate editor with *Golf* magazine, assigned to handle much of the instruction content. I was ever on the lookout for new ways, or old ones recalled, to explain the royal and ancient conundrum, and Morrison's name came to my attention. It rang a small bell. It was only a faint ring, but with that paper maw demanding its monthly fill of "how to," I was in no position to wait for Big Ben's gong. On a trip to the West Coast, I arranged to meet with Alex and work out some instruction articles.

In one respect, I then found myself in the most frustrating editorial job in my experience. Perhaps it was because of my *lack* of experience, with my post–World War II Chicago street language background trying to deal with a manner of written expression born in late-Victorian primers. In any case, the articles that came from Alex were, to me, written in a convoluted, obtuse, barely comprehensible prose. Putting them into a form I thought best for my readers took a good many agonizing days, punctuated with any number of expensive phone calls to California for clarifications. (I'm ahead of the story, but on purpose.) Alex Morrison in the flesh had a gift for instruction; but it could not be duplicated, at least in my judgment, via his written words. (To this day, Alex has not forgiven me for what I did to his copy. Maybe he shouldn't.)

Anyway, we met in Riverside, California, where he still lives. He had retired in body, but not in mind. The rooms in his small, tree-shaded bungalow on Fifth Street were crowded with the heavy, dark wood furniture stylish on the eastern seaboard in his salad days. The warm but somber ambience of the place was perfectly suited to deep theoretical thinking. As far as I could tell, that is precisely what Alex Morrison did most of the time. He spent his days in his shadowy Faustian chambers, contemplating the golf swing in its many parts: as a whole, as an aesthetic expression, as a phenomenon of physical engineering. His lifework. A serious man not given to much light banter, he was totally absorbed in his subject. Whenever I tried to make conversation of any other kind, Alex gave it very short shrift and then returned to backswing, pivot, pronation, supination, and all the rest.

I believe Alex sensed very quickly that he was not quite getting through to me (my brows felt as furrowed as the old sand bunkers at Oakmont). So, after a half hour or so of this monologue on golf swing theory, he suggested we go out to a golf course where I could hit some balls. By practical application, he thought, he might better get his ideas through to me.

On the practice tee of the Victoria Country Club, I hit a few shots. Alex was talking all the while, much in the vein of his earlier discourse, but I heard little. I hadn't played in some time and was concentrating on simply holding on to the club. Then he asked me what my main problem was. I could have expounded for a couple of hours, but I settled for my tendency to hit iron shots fat, particularly under pressure.

Instantly, Alex was a different man. Confronted with a specific, *real* problem, he left his ivory tower and became specific, concrete—and more than a little excited.

The reason I hit behind the ball, he said, was that my hands were behind it at address. I told him I was aware of that, but that I had never been able to put my hands forward and at the same time keep the club-face square to the target; if my hands were ahead in the conventionally correct way, when I squared the clubface it looked shut. I didn't like that look, had no confidence I could get the ball airborne that way. Therefore, I did what I did—hands back, clubface laid open.

"Well, put your hands ahead," Alex said, "and leave the clubface the way it looks best to you. Laid back, if that's the word."

"But the ball will start right and go more right," I said.

"Try it and see," he countered.

I did. The ball did not go right. It went straight, with a slight draw, even. And most important, it was struck crisply; not fat. Still, I was skeptical. I told Alex it was an accident. Also, he was suggesting something contrary to classical technique.

"And is the way you're compensating classical?" Alex asked, with a distinct note of disdain.

"No, but . . ." Alex would not let me finish. He became aggressively determined to make me believe. "Hit another," he commanded.

I did. The ball, not the ground, was hit first, and it went straight.

"Another!"

I did as told. Same result. With each shot I expected the ball to shoot right. None did. Beautiful! A revelation!

Alex explained: "The force created in the downswing is going to square the face at impact. Unless," he added thoughtfully, "you let yourself get too rigid and don't allow a natural flow in your swing."

With that, he instructed me to let the club swing back very loosely. I did it. So loosely, in fact, that the shaft banged against my neck. I winced.

"That's all right," Alex said with enthusiasm (after all, it wasn't *his* neck). "Bounce it off every time. It'll teach you to be flexible."

I took a number of practice swings, each time caroming the club painfully off my neck. "It's starting to hurt, Alex."

"Never mind that. Keep it up."

I obeyed. I had to obey, because I was in his thrall. There was no denying him, no stopping him. He was an engine going full tilt. After a while he ordered me onto the course to play a few holes and use the new "action." (Forget all the mechanics now. Here comes the part of the story that means the most.)

There were no caddies around, nor, in the excitement of the moment, no time to get a pull cart or power cart. I went to pick up my bag, but Alex would not let me touch it. My job was to play, he told me, and he lifted the sack, one of those big trunkish ones, onto his shoulder. On his other shoulder he put his camera equipment, another heavy bag (Alex used a bulky vintage press camera). It was not right for him to lug such a load, I felt. I reckoned him to be in his mid- to late 60s and he seemed a trifle out of shape, noticeably heavy through the middle. He would not hear of it. He headed for the first tee, and there was nothing to do but follow.

Before each shot, Alex sternly reminded me of the position of my hands and made me bounce the club off my neck during practice swings. I played nine holes, hitting shots of uncommon (for me) crispness and accuracy. With each, Alex was beside himself with delight. I myself was so exhilarated I hardly noticed that as we came to the final hole, he was beginning to waver under the weight of my clubs and his cameras. His steps were labored, his breath came heavily. Yet, as obdurately insistent as a caste-born lackey to his sahib, Alex would not let me take my clubs, not even for the last 20 yards. He just kept exhorting me to play on.

If he had a heart attack on that last fairway, I am convinced, Alex would have been compensated by my (and his) success. His face was aglow. It was the red of exertion in part, no doubt, but mostly it was a look of supreme, blissful satisfaction. You know that look when you see it.

A couple of days after that lesson from Alex Morrison I developed a terrible ache in my neck that lasted for two weeks. When I told my wife where it came from she was finally and irrevocably convinced that golfers are totally mad. (She doesn't play, of course.) Then, when Alex's copy began coming in, there was that monstrous editing job. All this was a small price to pay.

Since then I have often lapsed into the old bad habit at address. And, naturally, I have allowed many another swing theory and aberration to intrude on my golfing peace of mind. (Indeed, I have only recently found a solution to keeping the face square and the hands ahead that belies Alex's advice—it has to do with the left-hand grip and seems to work without battering my neck.) Whenever things go astray, though, and I feel an urge to slouch off to Quitsville, I recall that look on Alex Morrison's face and his undiluted fervor for my cause. The vision is more than enough to restore my energy, my Will to Seek The Answer (or at least, An Answer). Somehow, not to keep on trying would be to profane a holy spirit. I've got enough problems already without taking on something like that.

ARE YOU TOO SMART TO WIN?

(Golf Magazine—1980)

Next to the idiotic, the dull unimaginative mind is best for golf."

Does that provocative comment from Sir Walter Gridley Simpson's book *The Art of Golf* reflect the haughty attitude of worldly persons toward "dumb jocks"? Or was the author, writing in 1892, offering a "how-to" lesson?

Lord Byron Nelson recalls an adage that made the rounds during his heyday on the pro circuit: "It isn't necessary to be dumb, but it sure helps." And Tom Watson, who is lording it over today's tour, remarks, "Yes, you want to be, in a sense, dumb to play well. You can get into it better."

Can it be? *Must* one be dull-witted, unimaginative, *dumb* to be a champion? Conversely, can one be too "smart" to be a winner?

Maybe so.

Bobby Jones once wrote, "To play subconsciously considerably lessens the nerve strain of competition. More than that, it is usually the most effective way to play when the swing is in the groove."

That, undoubtedly, is what Nelson and Watson mean by "dumb," a state of mind in which all sentient thought is subordinated to the here-and-now business of hitting the ball. In our era, this form of dumbness has become known as "tunnel vision." And this tunnel vision is indeed a major asset for golfers.

George Fazio, the quondam touring pro now designing golf courses, tells of being paired with Ben Hogan in the 1948 U.S. Open and holing a 4-iron shot on a par-four. At the end of the round Fazio found that Hogan, keeping George's card, had not marked the card where "Faz" made the deuce. It took a few hours to convince Hogan to enter the score. He never saw Fazio's shot and clearly did not recognize the accompanying gallery roar. Ultimate tunnel vision.

Hogan, of course, is no dummy, and neither is Hubert Green when he says, "I cannot remember any shots I've played or anything I've said during a round *when I've played well.*" Ironically, in fact, this dumbness to the outside is actually a reflection of the intense concentration inside the golfer. He is working his brain overtime—but on a very limited subject.

Golf, great golf at least, seems to require this full measure of psychic energy. As Dr. C. W. Bailey wrote in *The Brain and Golf,* "Golf is a demanding mistress and cannot endure a rival."

But just in case the mind does wander, a good dose of the game will bring it back into line. "Excessive golf dwarfs the intellect," Lord Simpson wrote. Watson puts it this way. "Hours of beating balls and playing and thinking golf can develop a deep concentration and shut off the rest of the world."

In this vein Watson has become a somewhat less interesting personality. When the Stanford graduate in psychology first came on tour, he was willing to discuss mental aspects of his bout with the choke factor. He spoke out in support for George McGovern's candidacy for president, which took some extra cogitation if only because he was going against heavy grain, and made a lot of eye contact in conversation. Now he is distant, more often gazing past people; he believes chatty journalists should be kept out of the locker room at the Masters and while he did flash a bit of his innate intellectual vigor in responding to this inquiry, he prefaced it with a restless, "What is all this stuff?"

If Watson has dulled some as a personality, he has proven that being "dumb" or, more properly, numb to outside influences by sustained attention to golf, does indeed work—like a million bucks.

On the other hand, while Tom Watson was with a single-minded thrust of mental (and physical) energy climbing to the top of his profession, his contemporary, Ben Crenshaw, was cultivating deep interests in golf history, literature and architecture, and ornithology. Ben not only collects classic books on golf by Lord Simpson, Arnold Haultain, Bernard Darwin, and other "heavy" writers, he reads them, on the eve of tournament rounds. He planned to pass up the November–December 1979 Far East tournament circuit to be at the side of course builder Pete Dye, who is building a new course in the United States. Ben wants to learn about golf course design, an art almost as consuming as playing the game. When Crenshaw plays a tour stop in North Carolina he trains his binoculars on the eastern bluebird; in Napa, California, on the acorn woodpecker.

Is it significant in view of all this extracurricular activity that Crenshaw, who was supposed to become the new King of Golf, has yet to win a major title? That despite a fine record on the tour he has not, by his own admission, fulfilled his high promise for greatness as a player? When asked, Crenshaw nodded thoughtfully and conceded. "Interests outside of golf definitely detract from the attention the game needs."

Then, one *can* be too "smart" or "imaginative" to be a golf champion, if these words are defined broadly, as acquiring more than superficial knowledge of a variety of subjects or simply being more responsive to the multitude of mental stimuli in a civilized environment.

Without demeaning the pros or doubting their raw intelligence, one may say that nearly all the great champions of golf's modern era *during the process of reaching and then playing in their primes* were by all accounts men of rather narrow intellectual breadth or curiosity. Only Bobby Jones, who studied literature at Harvard and passed the law bar while becoming good enough to win the Grand Slam, would be the exception to this rule. "Imagination is a serious handicap," says Frank Hannigan, the terse, incisive golf *savant* of the United States Golf Association. "Jones's greatest accomplishment was being able to win with it."

Many excellent, accomplished golfers, and hundreds who have passed through the game's time-space continuum making no mark at all, could hit golf shots every bit as good as Hogan, Nicklaus, or Player. They just didn't hit them as often, and not because of swing mechanics, which were susceptible to breaking down under pressure. Tommy Bolt and Tom Weiskopf come readily to mind.

Then Ben Hogan, et al., dominated because they could better screw their minds to the sticking place, right? Did the Hogans get a better shake of the genetic dice, being presented at birth with brainworks enabling a higher degree of sustained attention? That's a tough question to answer, but we do have a few clues.

Studies of the brain tell us that the right half, or hemisphere, manages visual/spatial tasks, organizes and processes data in terms of *wholes*. The brain's left hemisphere is the more analytical, imaginative side specializing in details and a *verbal* processing of information. From this can it be said the great golf champions have better-developed right brain hemispheres, and that the lesser players are too left-hemispheric?

No doubt the best take something from each side. Jack Nicklaus visualizes whole golf shots very well, but is no slouch at details. After all, it was Jack who first began, or at least popularized, stepping off yardages and referring to written notes on the golf course.

But assuming both sides work equally well, what other mental strengths—or weaknesses—will help a golfer become a champion?

Jesse Haddock, golf coach at Wake Forest University, types golfers as engineers or naturals. "You can't be entirely scientific, though," warns Gardner Dickinson (another university graduate in psychology before becoming a tour pro), "because science doesn't have any *feel* to it."

Then, give us mostly an ordered, logical engineer's mentality, spiced with some artistic audacity and a flexible eye for form. Naturally, the omnipotent Nicklaus pops up. For all Jack's pharmaceutical precision (his father was a druggist), and perhaps Teutonic grandiosity, when he does get into trouble he has, you might say, a Gallic gift for creating imaginative shots to get back into line.

Ben Crenshaw combines the tenacity of Ben Hogan and the nonchalance of Walter Hagen. Gene Littler expresses this as "giving a damn, but not giving a damn. It's a fine line." Writer Charles Price prescribes some musical inclination. "The perfect golf mind is one that composes a concerto in three movements; not a symphony," says Price, "because the smaller piece requires a more disciplined imagination."

"A golf champion cannot be fatalistic," says Ed Sneed. "You do have some control over your destiny in golf." Willfulness, then, must be a component of the perfect golf mind. And if you are not born with it, produce it.

Gardner Dickinson remembers some advice Horton Smith, first winner of the Masters, gave him: that to create a positive attitude you must lie to yourself, more or less. "Horton said to exaggerate the length of putts you've made—turn a 14-footer into a 40-footer. And Sam Snead,"

Dickinson continues, "never blamed himself personally for a poor shot. He'd lay it off on a spike mark, a camera click, a sudden gust of wind. There's something to say for that. Self-deprecation never helped anyone."

Dr. Bailey agrees: "If we can persuade ourselves that we are in good form we may have confidence and act that part suggested to us with success." Which is what the *new* "mind technique" merchants are telling us in more technical language.

No one has yet discovered which genes produce tenacity, mendacity or perspicacity, so we must conclude our speculations with environmental influences, of which a tad more is known. For instance, evidence has been gathered to the effect that firstborn and only children are more successful, in no little part because of the close attention given to their aspirations. And that the poorer classes striving toward upward mobility have an edge. Marilyn Ferguson, author of *The Brain Revolution,* reveals that a research team shocked infant laboratory rats, expecting to produce greater emotionality and poor learning habits, but "to their astonishment found that stressed animals were superior to the unstressed by almost every measurement. Rats reared in a quiet, sheltered environment developed into jittery animals unable to cope with normal surroundings."

These social and environmental factors lead us to the ultimate question, "If a perfect golf mind could be cloned and then raised under ideal conditions, what would that mind and those conditions be like?" Try this: The perfect golf mind will result if a player is a firstborn or only child reared by a family struggling to make ends meet in or around a good-sized city, feeds on his mother's milk while listening to the shorter works of Mozart, Beethoven, the Beatles, or Elton John, is treated kindly when he complains, and then is made to walk off the meal and fold his own diapers.

Later, he will not so much receive formal education as become overly inquisitive about why he hits a poor shot or cannot make a classic swing, but he will get enough education so, as Al Geiberger says of Tom Watson, he "knows how to use his smarts" and to play "dumb."

CHIPS AND PUTTS: NOTES ON THE ART OF SCORING

(Diversion—1978)

Let's assume that when you play golf you are trying to make the best score possible. Obviously? Not necessarily. Golfers are inclined to seek sole satisfaction in creating "classic" shots—balls struck dead center on the clubface that rise dramatically, float majestically for a moment, then descend as softly as a butterfly with sore feet. There is much to say for this approach, but it is mostly in the way of rationalization; e.g. "I may have lost the match, but I proved I could hit a golf ball perfectly at least once."

One or a couple of really fine drives or 4-iron shots can ease a lot of golf pain, but I maintain that the greater pleasure in golf comes from cumulative achievement, which, strange as it may seem, is more obtainable than a single classic stroke. Recalling Jack Nicklaus's five-birdie finish to win the Jackie Gleason–Inverrary tournament last February, Jack's big victory smile appeared in no way dampened by the reality of his having slopped the ball around quite a bit. All was saved, though, by his holing a 90-foot chip shot and a couple of lengthy, snaky putts. Entirely stylish he was not, but to coin a phrase, style is the residue of knack, or the last refuge of the knackless. Whatever. Now back to our presumption—playing to win.

While it is always desirable to hit classic golf shots, and we must never give up trying, the average golfer simply is not going to hit very many. Even those few he does catch right are no guarantee of overall success. The scrambler—he who can slice a drive into a thicket, chunk the next one into a bunker, poof the sand shot onto the fringe of the green, and then run the putt into the cup, and, as the saying goes, turn chicken gizzards into goose pâté—makes his own truth. The way to do this, of course, is by following Nicklaus's Inverrary example, with superior work around the greens. And here, average golfers of the world, you *can,* you *must* take refuge, for you have just about as good a chance as Jack Nicklaus.

How's that? The ordinary duffer performing on the level of Jack Nicklaus? Yes, which is another reason golf is so fascinating a game. No hacker can hope to win a single point from Jimmy Connors, or play any part of a baseball game the way Pete Rose does. But he can chip and putt with golf's premier players. First of all, chipping and putting do not require the physical strength and fluidity, nor the complicated machinations of the full-body swing that the majority of golf does. As far as I can tell, the few fundamentals for chipping and putting advanced by golf teachers have not sold very well. In terms of mechanics, these are the most individualistic, idiosyncratic parts of the golf game. Styles of address and stroke are as varied as the range of putter designs. And no less effective, one over another. In short, chipping and putting live by the touch system, that is, a developed feel for the shots. This feel is obtained merely by doing it a lot. If the average golfer, therefore, spends whatever practice time he can afford on nothing but chipping and putting, he is going to become relatively adept at them. Such ability brings better 18-hole scores and a far better chance of defeating considerably better players from tee to green—what might be called the David-beats-Goliath syndrome.

As you may have guessed, the above wisdom has not been handed down from some ivory tower. Ex-peerience, mon. When I was 15 and only three years a golfer, I entered a Chicago junior golf tournament. With a score in the low 80s I managed to qualify for match play, an eventuality I must not have expected because I hadn't considered having to travel home that evening and return early the next morning. This was no small problem, as I lived on Chicago's far North Side and the course was in a distant suburb south of the city. I did not drive a car, of course, and in fact had taken my first train ride (the Illinois Central) to get to the course in the first place. I was a naif, in many respects.

A club member nevertheless arranged for me to stay overnight in a room in the clubhouse. Stuck in this place, I had nothing to do after dinner except chip and putt on the practice green. Which I did, for maybe three hours, quitting not because I could no longer see the ball, but because the mosquitoes were bringing me all too close to anemia. The mosquito welts eventually disappeared, but not a wonderful touch for chipping and putting, as my first-round opponent would learn the next morning. He was some five years older and far more experienced than I. He played on a college team and wore two-tone golf shoes. He hit booming drives, long and hooking, to my slithering slices, and took divots with his irons *after* ball contact. In all, my play from tee to green was on the order of Jackson Pollock gone berserk on a four-mile canvas; dribs and drabs of scattered "paint" everywhere.

But when I came onto or within ten yards of each green I was a Leonardo of precision, a Goya of grand form . . . and a Tintoretto working in red. And my opponent became gradually more apoplectic, as I made my pâté with a deft nick of a wedge or 8-iron and a silken stroke of my putter, righting all my wrongs and sending him muttering off to the next tee to again try to bomb away my pestiferous strafing. He didn't, and the muttering grew to raging vituperation, which only lessened his chances of winning. He would not shake my hand when the match ended, and I was the victor. He was not a good sport, but in a way, I can forgive him.

I must say that in the year immediately following that victory, I fell into the quest for the perfect golf swing and the well-powered drive and iron shot. But after all, I was a kid and kids believe good form and hard hitting are marks of manhood. Okay, but with middle age upon me and those notions tempered by time and wisdom, the lesson I learned at 15 on that practice green has not been forgotten. I fully expect my future opponents will be reminded of it, too.

ONE FOR THE YIPPER

(Golf Magazine—1982)

When you address a short putt by placing the blade behind the ball and feel as if you've stuck it in a sea of quick-set epoxy, and when at last you manage to get the club in motion the forward stroke feels as if you're touching a hot iron with your finger, then, brother, you have the yips.

Yips have been the bane of golfers since the beginning of golfing time, scarier, more unspeakable and universal than even the shanks.

The term *yips* is probably derived from that hot-iron flinch, which can be so rapid that you hit the ball twice with a single "stroke." Other traumas beside the glue-stuck putter may precede this so-called flinch, or twitch, or jab. There is hand trembling, a deadening of the arms as if shot with novocaine, shaking knees, a dread hollowness in the stomach, short, gaspy breathing. These are not dramatic fictions, but the documented experiences of such eminent golfing persons as Harry Vardon, Sam Snead, Ben Hogan, and Bobby Jones, who once said his yips gave him "the most incredible sensation" he had ever known.

The trembles, the gasps are external manifestations of the yips. But what has happened within the nervous system to cause the malady? Do the nerve ends actually deaden, or fray or wear away with age? Professor Bob Rotella, a sports psychologist at the University of Virginia, has an explanation that not only sounds plausible, but is supported by scientific evidence. It is the premise on which much of this article is based.

Rotella says yippers are victims of a response to fear that formed in man quite a few million years ago. It is known as the fight-or-flight syndrome, which works in a couple of basic ways.

Situation: Little Pithecanthropus, who has not yet learned to use sticks and stones to defend himself, leaves his cave one morning to hunt some breakfast. A couple of miles down the road he runs into a big, toothy marsupial lion growling with its own hunger. Pithecanthropus says to himself, "I'm afraid!" This intellectual revelation signals his body to react. A lot of blood moves to fill the deeper, larger muscles so if Pithecanthropus chooses either to fight the lion or flee from it, he will be as strong and/or swift as possible. What's more, because much of the blood filling those muscles with strength comes from more surface areas of the body, should Pithecanthropus be cut while fighting or fleeing there is less chance he will bleed to death. A wonderful reflexive phenomenon, the fight-or-flight syndrome.

Now, the blood diverted to the big muscles comes from a number of places. The stomach, for one, which is why we get that sudden hollowness there when facing a touchy two-footer. And also, says Rotella, "It is why for years we have been telling athletes not to eat much before a game. Blood is needed to break down the food, and if there is not enough, the food burdens performance."

The blood in fright also leaves the toes and fingers. This pertains most to golfers and yips. With less blood in the fingers it is harder to feel the clubhead and the desensitized golfer finds it difficult to start the club back, not to mention making a smooth, controlled forward stroke. The nerves are not so much deadened as simply cold, relatively speaking, according to a device Rotella uses in biofeedback training. This device measures the temperature of the hands under both relaxed and stressful situations.

Which brings to mind a habit of Bobby Locke, one of golf's great putters. As he walked between shots Locke shook his hands at his sides, surely to keep the blood circulating in his fingers.

That golfers lose sensitivity in the fingers would explain why yips seem to attack mostly when they putt. They can manage to hit full shots without a fine touch. Indeed, they may tend to swing too fully under pressure because of those full-blooded bigger muscles.

Rotella, who with Linda Bunker has written a book entitled *Mind Mastery for Golf,* outlines another physical response to fear: "Hormones are secreted from the brain when we interpret a situation to be stressful. This causes a constriction of the muscles around the chest and throat. Rapid and shallow breathing results, and if this gets severe enough you can choke to death.

"This is where the term *choking* comes into athletics. The only cases I know of this actually happening is with drowning victims. Many will self-suffocate from lack of oxygen rather than water in the lungs. They die from the fear of drowning."

It is unlikely any putt will be so fearful that a golfer will suffocate over it. On the other hand, any shortage of oxygen is going to dampen his efficiency.

Modern man can do without the fight-or-flight syndrome, now that we have everything from nuclear bombs to Mace to fend off the lions, but it has not yet leached out of our system. Some athletes might find it useful—weight lifters, say, or National Football League linemen—but evolution does not discriminate among players of different games, so golfers, who depend more on feel and touch than brute force, are stuck for the time being. Thus, the golfer must find ways to counteract nature, to beat the yips down if not altogether out.

This is not at all impossible. THE YIPS CAN BE ZAPPED!

Fear of missing putts comes from having missed putts. Golfers are notoriously negative historians, remembering the disastrous shots, theirs *and those of others,* far out of proportion to the good or even passable ones. Golfers fear they are going to write more bad history, and by yipping fulfill the prophecy.

Worse yet, too many golfers take too much responsibility for their acts. It has been shown that not all golf balls dropped by hand down a chute and rolled at exactly the same speed over a controlled path to a cup, go in the hole.

"We tend to blame ourselves too much when a missed putt could very well have been caused by a bump in the green," says Al Geiberger. "It might also help to avoid the do-or-die attitude, that every putt must be made; it causes far too much tension."

In short, golfers may be overly sold on the much-touted self-reliance and individuality of golf; a little fatalism may not be a bad thing, at least in curing the yips.

Still, golfers are heavily inclined to look for solutions through mechanics, over which they have the greatest degree of control. Fair enough. While admittedly golf's technical component can be overemphasized, technique is still the most practical way to cure the yips.

One mechanical approach cited by many is to develop a set routine before addressing a putt, what Raymond Floyd calls putting "by the numbers."

"My yips were a nightmare from in close. I got very reluctant from two feet," says Floyd. "I got out of it by working up a pattern for putting. A count system. Get the line, one; set up at the ball, two; one more look at the line, three; hit it, four. You don't get long lags between numbers because the nature of making a count doesn't let you. After a while you just count subconsciously."

Rotella takes the point a bit farther. "A routine programs not only the physical motion, but the mental processes, which helps in concentration. When you are concentrating, you don't think about choking, missing, or even those you have missed. It is like coming home to your favorite chair. You've been there before, feel easy in it, and so you read, think, and perform better."

A routine also seems to speed up your pace of play, a good thing in itself for avoiding yips. "The longer you stand there, the harder it gets," says Gene Sarazen. "What happens is," says Tommy Bolt, "the longer you take the more you think of ways to miss a putt, and the more tense you get."

No one is able to explain why golfers don't think more of ways *to make* a putt the longer they stand over it.

Another common cure for the yips is to make a change in your mechanics, sometimes a quite radical one. As Geiberger points out, "From years of doing something the same way you can get bored or inattentive and develop 'hang-ups.' By changing a method, you can occasionally become fresher and more alert. You might even try putting left-handed for a while, at least on the practice green."

Which brings up Ben Hogan. When Hogan was suffering from the yips in public during his last few years of national competition ("I could get the putter through if I ever got it back," said Ben, "but that was the problem. I would stand there and shake and it wouldn't move. People were saying, 'For Godsake hit it,' and I would say the same thing."), he received many letters offering help. One was from a champion trapshooter who said he had once gotten to where he could not pull the trigger. He switched to shooting left-handed or fingered, and after a year won the national championship, left-fingered.

Hogan did not pick up on the trapshooter's cure by making a big change in his putting style, but he might well have. His contemporary, Sam Snead, who referred to his well-known yips as the "yickies," went to the sidesaddle stance on the greens and put some 10 years on his remarkable career.

Art Wall, Jr., got over his yips once by going to cross-handed putting. "I did that because it is so good from six feet or less," says Wall. "When I regained my confidence and made a lot of putts, I went back to the conventional grip"—and continued to make them.

Bruce Lietzke switched and stayed. According to fellow tour players who knew Lietzke when he was at the University of Houston, his mediocre collegiate record was due primarily to the fact that "he was only an ordinary putter and prone to the yips." When he turned pro, Lietzke went cross-handed and has had a superior record.

Johnny Miller advises closing your eyes when you stroke the putt, so you're not intimidated by the ball. "That's a funky way out," says Miller. "A more normal way is to keep your eye on a mark other than the ball. When I won the British Open I was concentrating on the path of my right hand. I didn't even see the ball most of the time."

More than a few players advocate avoiding concentration on the ball when putting. "Pick a spot, a blade of grass about an inch in front of the ball, no farther," says Dave Stockton. "Watch the ball roll over that spot. If the spot is on the proper line, the ball will fall."

Ken Venturi believes in concentrating on the putter blade. "Without moving my head, I track the blade with my eyes. I also think this method helps get me out of the 'must-make' syndrome."

Indeed, if a National Yips Home-Remedy Contest was held, it would take a year to hear all the entries:

"Play all putts as though they were straight in" (Tom Kite). "Tempo and acceleration. Don't quit on the ball" (Hubert Green). "Keep the left wrist going through it" (John Mahaffey). "Before a crucial putt take a number of practice strokes whipping the putter back and forth as fast as you can. The buggy-whipping produces a nice light touch" (JoAnne Carner). "My friend Harold 'Jug' McSpaden got an old hickory-shafted mallet putter and weighted it down with 20 ounces of lead. Then he gripped it as tightly as possible and dug the nail of his right thumb into the grip. He practiced this way for hours, hanging on with the left hand, hitting it with the right, and overcame the yips" (Byron Nelson).

Billy Casper, the health-food entrepreneur, says he is selling a vita-min- and mineral-stoked food supplement that will cure, or keep you from getting, the yips. Billy's Neo-Life Stress 30 Pak has capsules and tablets containing, among many things, seven different vitamins, soybean extract, selenium yeast, and desiccated ox bile.

All these cures sound fine, but they may only work for the advocate of each. It seems Rotella's physiological explanation of the yips offers a foundation upon which a general golfing audience can find help. For instance, it makes sense according to "fight-or-flight" to squeeze the grip a little tighter when under pressure. You activate what blood is left in the fingers, and get *some* head feel. Tom Watson is a "white-knuckler" in this way, and Jimmy Demaret and Louise Suggs found it effective when they were winning big on their respective tournament circuits.

Then again, you may want to take the hands out of the action as much as possible and become an upper-body or arms-and-shoulders put-ter making use of those blood-filled bigger muscles. Many have tried this. Leo Diegel, for example, was a brilliant golfer from tee to green during the Hagen-Sarazen era, but a nervous man who many thought had termi-nal yips. Diegel adopted a strange-looking position that became famous: his elbows held akimbo so the forearms were parallel to the ground, his head sunk low toward the ball. He looked like a bat hanging from a rafter, but his hands could not be at all active in the stroke, and Diegel putted well enough to win back-to-back PGA championships (1928–'29).

Geiberger's friend, Wheeler Farrish, went the Diegel route, but with his own odd twist. "He gripped the club the way you would a butter churn," Geiberger explained. "Both hands held the club full-fingered, with the right hand twisted way around to the left, the left hand way around to the right. The only way he could move the club was with his shoulders. Everybody laughed at him, but Wheeler won the amateur part of the Crosby tournament two years in a row with his butter churn."

Diegel and Farrish are somewhat bizarre examples of the arm-shoul-der putting method. Ben Crenshaw is a prime example of how it works in a "classical" motif. As we know, Ben is a very fine putter and has shown no signs of yipping.

There may also be circumstances brought to the golf course that a person may not realize could cause yips. For example, a national magazine study recently noted that because dentists work many hours a day in close proximity to people, some tend to discourage hugging and kissing with their family. They need some physical space after eight hours belly-to-shoulder with patients. By the same token then, is it not conceivable that dentists might get the yips on a golf course because they go from one form of very close, careful work to another?

Finally, there is the widely held notion that yips come with age. Or, a variation on this theme, the "You-Can-Go-to-the-Well-Only-So-Many-Times Theory," which Hogan delineates.

"I know several 75-year-old men who are very good putters. But had they been playing golf tournaments for 20 years, well, the drop of water on the rock is going to wear a hole in it, you see. Those fellows haven't been under intense pressure all this time."

Actually, both of these theories seem to be myths. For one thing, many young golfers have had the yips. Twenty-five-year-old Bernhard Langer, the fine German pro, for instance. Mark O'Meara, in his second year on tour, claims that he had a case of the yips while playing college golf a couple of years ago. "Yips can make you a very good iron player," says O'Meara. "I had the yips for about six months and hit the ball great from tee to green. I *had* to. But I was so bad on the greens that at one point I started chipping my long putts. Chipped one in, too. The coach said I was hurting the team by complaining so much about my yips, so I agreed not to say another word. I think that helped. I also went from a heavy to a lighter putter."

And Dr. Richard Coop, an educational psychologist with a special interest in sports, tells of a young high school golf champion who played his first match for the University of North Carolina on a Grandfather Mountain course with very slick and rolling greens.

"He four-putted a lot that day," said Coop, "and from then on he couldn't draw it back. He would double-hit, and knock six-footers seven feet past the hole, a feat fairly common among yippers."

"If older golfers get the yips more often than younger golfers, it is probably because they have let themselves get out of physical shape," says Professor Rotella.

"When people get into their 50s," Rotella continues, "it is not uncommon to lose some circulation in their extremities—toes and fingers—and only exercise is going to stimulate some flow. The trouble is, people let themselves become run down. They've been working hard to make a career and raise a family; they often eat too much, are tired, maybe a little lazy, and their bodies get out of tone. My guess is that the 75-year-olds Ben Hogan was talking about as being good putters were probably in top physical condition."

Rotella further suggests that older golfers victimize themselves even more by accepting the idea that yips come with age.

"Yips is not an old-folks disease," says that professor. "If people *think* it is, then it will be, but it has not yet been proven to be so."

Well and good, but man does not live by science alone. There is also an incorrigible humanism within our hearts, as Bob Goalby suggests.

"When you're older you just don't get as many birdie chances," says Goalby. "You feel as though time were running out, you get anxious and yip it. It's also interesting that we older guys are apt to force our games when playing with the younger players, but are much cooler playing among ourselves."

Speaking of cooling the yips, Al Geiberger says his mother developed a putting style that fooled a lot of people. "She always putts up on the toes of her left foot and whistling. Everyone thinks she is so cool and casual. But I know it's her way to beat the yips."

GAMESMANSHIP

(Golf Magazine—1980)

During his first season on the PGA Tour Jerry McGee ran into an established player who put a sting on him. It was the old paralysis by analysis caper.

McGee had shot a 68 in the first round of a tour event, while the veteran with whom he was paired struggled to a 73. Afterward, Jerry went to the practice range to wind down a bit and keep up his muscle memory.

"I was hitting balls and pretty deep in concentration," McGee recalls. "About halfway through the bag, though, I realized someone was watching me. It was the old pro I had played with that day. I was surprised. Here was a man who had won a couple of tournaments and a lot of money and he was studying me, a rookie. I said something to that effect and he said, real slow and serious, 'That was a super round you played today and I'm kind of curious to see if that grip of yours has anything to do with it.' He didn't explain himself any more. I hadn't been thinking much about my grip, but I did all that night and the next morning. And not to my advantage.

"I started the second round with three straight bogeys. The pro didn't say anything. He just went along making pars, and between the third green and fourth tee it struck me that that guy did a number on me the evening before. So while we were waiting to play the fourth I went up to him and asked, very slow and serious, like any kid talking to an elder statesman, 'Sir, at impact do you breathe in or out?'

"Well, let me tell you, the old pro had a helluva time after that. He made a mess of bogeys and after he putted out on 18 he came walking toward me pointing a finger, his face all red, and said, 'You little SOB, you got back at me!' We became kind of good friends after that."

Gamesmanship: one competitor trying to get an extra, psychological edge on another, get him thinking more—or less—than is good for him. It is as much a part of sport as the swinging of clubs and bats or the tossing of balls. It adds a touch of spice to the play that most of us seem to enjoy, when we are not the victims. And yet, some golfers hesitate to admit it goes on. Because golf has a gentlemanly tradition, the purist apparently thinks trickery is unfair, if not a downright cheat.

Perhaps the most famous instance of gamesmanship, if it was that, came on the last green of an 18-hole playoff for the 1947 U.S. Open. Sam Snead was over his ball ready to stroke a short putt for a par when his opponent, Lew Worsham, decided to call for a measurement to see who was actually away. Worsham had a par putt of almost the same length. Snead backed off; officials came out with a tape measure and found that Snead was 30 inches out, Worsham 28½ inches. Nearly five minutes elapsed, and when Snead finally got to putt, he missed. Worsham holed out to win the championship.

Was Sam foxed by a wily Worsham? Lew's response to this has always been a Mona Lisa smile. And Snead has never allowed that he was taken by a trick. That may be Sam's pride "speaking," but in the years since he has never avoided Lew. Neither have golf fans heaped calumny on Worsham, who has enjoyed a long and successful professional career at fine, upstanding clubs. Nor was Lee Trevino reviled for the gag he played on Jack Nicklaus moments before the two began their playoff for the 1971 U.S. Open. Trevino lobbed a toy snake at Jack's feet. Everyone laughed, including Nicklaus. The tension was broken. Did Lee consciously try to upset Jack's vaunted concentration? Was that a factor in Lee's subsequent victory? Maybe.

Gamesmanship has two modes. The kind that is unequivocally "dirty pool" has a golfer with white shoes standing close enough to an opponent so the latter can see those gleaming boots. Then just as the other fellow takes the putter back, he crosses his feet. Or the loose-change gambit: rattling coins in your pocket, while supposedly trying to find a tee, when the opponent is in the middle of his downswing.

There are more subtle "dirty tricks." During the final round of a recent Milwaukee Open, Ed Sneed was leading the pack. While waiting to play an approach shot, his playing partner, who was a close second, said to Ed, whose wife was expecting their first child, "You can really use the money with that new baby that's coming."

"If he was one of my pals," Ed notes, "I wouldn't have minded. But he wasn't—isn't—and besides, he's not the type to make such extracurricular remarks on the course."

Attempts to disturb a player's rhythm go two ways, by rushing the play or, as in the Worsham-Snead episode, by slowing the pace. Bruce Devlin tells of the latter happening to him when he was making a strong rush to win the Masters. In the middle of his final round, Devlin had a touchy bunker shot from about 35 feet. His partner was on the green, but "away."

"He was close to the lead, of course," Bruce relates, "but having trouble. He took a good bit of time on his first putt, which was okay, but after he hit it about five feet past he decided he wanted to putt out. I didn't say anything, and again he took a lot of time. He rolled that one four feet past, but again didn't mark. He kept putting, and very slowly. He missed the third putt and finally tapped in, but by that time I was steaming. I must have waited eight or nine minutes to play from the sand. I got it out about six feet from the cup and missed the putt. That finished me."

Art Wall tells of a similar incident during a playoff. He remembers his opponent, who had the honor, "taking an inordinate amount of time" to play his tee shot on a par three. "It was much more time than he needed," says Wall. "He knew the course extremely well and club selection was no great problem. I knew what he was doing, and for a very successful touring pro I thought it was an awful thing to do."

All the above is the stuff of poor sportsmanship, and no one appreciates it—except the perpetrator. On the other hand, when Walter Hagen pulled the "Peek-a-Boo, Too-Bad-for-You" ruse, it was an acceptable mode of gamesmanship.

Gene Sarazen believes Hagen was the first master of this ploy. On a shot of the same distance as an opponent who Walter noticed looking in his bag for club selection ideas, Hagen would pull out a 3-iron, let's say.

The peeker, first to play, would follow that lead and after he knocked his ball 20 yards over the green, Hagen would go down to the 5-iron he planned to hit all along and win the hole. Gotcha!

A wrinkle on this is the one in which you hit first with the 3-iron but take something off the shot—hit the 3-iron to 5-iron distance. By hiding the "soft" shot in a big-swing motion (like a baseball pitcher with a good change-up move), you can fool the peeker into going full-bore with his 3-iron and, again, winding up in the "tulies" beyond the green.

This scam, of course, takes more than a little skill, touch and club control. E. J. "Dutch" Harrison, a tall, loose-jointed shot-maker of the old school, was one of the best at it. Indeed, when older touring pros reminisce about gamesmanship, Harrison's name is mentioned often.

Harrison camouflaged a shrewd mind under an easy southern country-boy charm. "E. J. killed 'em with compliments," Bob Toski remembers. "'My oh my, what a wonderful golf swing you have there my friend,' he would say; or, 'That's the finest little ole putting stroke the game has ever known. Knock 'er in there, chief.'" Many a golfer was lulled—and gulled—by Harrison, the "Arkansas Traveler."

Some golf romantics would like to see a return to more match-play competitions if only because gamesmanship tends to raise its head more often in this format.

As it is, there seems to be little hanky-panky on today's rather sterile tour. Gibby Gilbert says, "There better not be any out here or there'll be a lot of dead bodies lying around. We're playing for too much dough." Andy Bean doesn't know of any gamesmanship "out there," but concedes he may be "just a little naive." Jerry Heard believes there might be some among the younger tour players, but not among the established pros "because they respect each other's games and professionalism." Ed Sneed, for one, would not quite agree.

Be it malicious or merely sly, gamesmanship must be dealt with. Clayton Heafner, a big man and one not known for indirect diplomacy, issued a simple warning to one coin jiggler: "Keep your hands out of your pocket when I'm playing, mister."

That pro paired with Bruce Devlin surely did not four-putt to keep Bruce waiting; and it is possible he took so much time because he was trying to gather his composure with his roof caving in. Same with the slowpoke Art Wall came up against. Yet Bruce and Art *thought* they were being stung, and that was enough. As Toney Penna remarks in acknowledging that psychological warfare existed during his tour days, "If you knew a guy could be rattled, you owned him." And he was fair game.

In any case, in gamesmanship it takes two to tango. Look into the other fellow's bag to see what he is hitting, and you open yourself up to a sting. "A guy might try to *help* you by advising you to watch your shadow to check out a swing move," Gardner Dickinson comments, "but shadows are distorted and you could end up swinging like a cripple. You have to take that stuff with a grain of salt, or ignore it." To which Bob Hamilton, 1944 PGA champion who as a kid was a shill for "Titanic" Thompson, the fabled hustler, adds, "You could mark your ball on a green and ask the other fella if the coin is in his line and you might confuse his read of the putt . . . if he pays attention to you."

A sports cliché has it that the best players do their most effective "talking" with their equipment, with their talent. As someone has said, the best gamesmanship is knocking a lot of shots close to the hole. No doubt, but it is equally doubtless that the ability and the competitive record of a champion produces a psychological effect on opponents that can be considered another form of gamesmanship, to wit, intimidation, which can be effected by one's mere presence and occasionally enhanced by the "silent treatment."

One illustration comes via Eliot Asinof, a close observer of sport who has written such books as *Eight Men Out* and *Seven Days to Sunday.* Asinof tells of following the threesome of Wally Armstrong, Lee Trevino, and Jack Nicklaus in a round of the Doral Open. Armstrong was leading the field at the start of the day, but was, of course, the minor actor in this group. That was to be expected. However, Asinof noticed that for almost the entire round Trevino and Nicklaus said not a word to Armstrong, even during lulls when Trevino was cracking jokes. "It was as if the kid didn't even exist out there," says Asinof. Armstrong did not play well and by the 16th hole had lost his lead, and then some. On this hole he bunkered his approach and as Trevino walked by the pit he uttered his first words to Armstrong: "Long day kid, huh?"

Do champions consciously shut out opponents? Are they aware of their impact as star performers and personalities on lesser players? Of course, and what more conclusive example could there be than Ben Hogan, who was known among his tour contemporaries as "Blue Blades," a symbolic reference to the old Gillette product and Hogan's forbidding, razor-sharp look and overall manner when at his golf.

Bruce Devlin relates that a few years ago he was having a conversation with Hogan, during which Ben recalled his playoff with Jack Fleck for the 1955 U.S. Open. "On an early hole," said Devlin, "Fleck missed the green wide to the right and had a tough pitch over a bunker from thick rough. Hogan was on the green in two, about 20 feet from the hole. It took a while to clear the gallery and whatnot before Fleck could play from that stuff. He was being careful otherwise. He finally got the ball on the green about 60 feet from the cup, and was still out. As he was walking onto the green he passed Hogan and said to Ben, 'Sorry to keep you waiting.' Hogan replied, 'That's all right, we've got nothing else to do today.'"

Hogan told Devlin he didn't think that was the decisive factor in his losing to Fleck, but he did say he realized at the very moment he uttered his simple, civil remark to Fleck that he had given up an important edge he had going in, the icy, almost inhuman exterior that always sent an extra shiver of fear through the hearts of his foes.

Gamesmanship is a sword with many edges, none of them dull.

THE
GODS OF
PUTTING

(Golf Tips—1993)

Some of the best putters I've ever seen in over 40 years around the old Scotsgame have had the oddest strokes. Odd, that is, in relation to what passes for classic or sound or pure as those words are defined by the technique mavens. Bad they aren't, because those odd strokes got the ball in the hole regularly. More importantly, they holed out when they positively, absolutely, unquestionably had to.

Take for instance my old caddie pal, Charley Bud Whitehead. Over the putt he looked like someone with a permanent muscular disability. His head was tilted to the left because he was right-eye dominant—I guess. His foot stance was closed so he appeared to aim to the right of his target, but his shoulders were open—aimed left of the line. He had a very distinctive far-forward press. He took the club back to the inside and swung it outward in the downstroke then back down the line of putt. Sometimes the blade went to the left after contact, sometimes to the right, sometimes it chased after the ball. And he made everything. Everything. Had? Made? Has! Makes! We had a caddie reunion a couple of months ago, and I played

with Charley Bud and he was still holing them with the same gooney . . .
stroke? And chuckling as always when we purists as always made fun of it.
    Or Bobby Locke, the legendary South African blade-master. His
stroke was not unlike Charley Bud's. Make that vice versa. Locke came
first. Locke aimed right of the hole with his entire body, looked at the cup
over his left shoulder, took the blade so far inside it nearly brushed his
knickers. He then swung the blade around to get it going down the line
of putt. Everyone said he hooked his putts, and that's how it looked. But
he was just coming to square from very far inside. If he brought the blade
straight to the ball from the back of his backstroke, he'd have hit it 20 feet
right of the target. By the way, Locke made an interesting remark once,
during a long-ago interview. Asked how he played breaking putts he said,
"All putts are straight putts." Which is to say, you figure out where the ball
will begin to turn, and aim for that spot. Which makes it a straight putt.
Good notion.
    Billy Casper stood conventionally at the ball, but put his left hand up
against his left thigh, which he used as a kind of block against the hand
breaking down, or over. The stroke itself was a wristy short pop, no smooth
flow back and through à la Crenshaw. And Billy made more than Ben has,
or ever will.
    Point being, if you want to make putts you will. Want transcends
technique. It has to because, for one thing, the entire putting stroke is too
short. The main thing is to have the blade square to your target line when
you hit the ball. And that's not too difficult, since you only pull it back a
few inches. If you want to make that happen, because you want to make
putts, you will.
    Of course, everybody wants to make putts so I'm talking about
degrees of want. But first it should be said that even masters of the putting
art miss putts. Paul Runyan once calculated that putts from 12 feet and in
are makable. After that, the odds on making a putt from 13 to 50 or 80
feet are the same. That sounds a bit off, but Runyan is a very smart man
about golf and made a great study of putting. For another thing, you can
run balls by hand down a chute toward a hole, each going the very same
distance on exactly the same line and at exactly the same speed, and some
will go in and some won't. Why? A ball may be just a tad out of round.
Maybe a snit of uneven grass popped up. Or the God of Putting decided
it wasn't that one's turn. Oh yes, there's a God of Putting. I'm convinced.
    The thing is, the Lockes and Caspers and Nicklauses realize that
they're not going to make them all, even those from 12 feet and in, and

they accept it. That's why you never see them get angry when a putt does-n't fall. Stunned, but never angry, because they expect to make everything despite the God of Putting. Which is why they make more than others. Because they very much want to. What makes their want different from the rest? For one thing, more scope to their thinking about golf.

It's commonplace in golf that superlong hitters are usually either very poor or simply indifferent putters. Same with most good, and in some cases even great shot-makers, those who can play brilliant approaches from any distance or angle, from any kind of lie, to soft greens, hard greens, whatever. Reason being, these people expend all their psychic energy on the long ball or the superb iron shot and when they pull it off are satisfied with that alone. Putting doesn't interest them. It's understandable. To hit a huge drive—high, straight, and far—or to nip a 6-iron out of a tight lie, the ball cutting just enough to get into a pin set behind a bunker, takes so much more actual physical effort and skill, and is infinitely more satisfying aesthetically than merely standing dead still over a ball sitting on ruglike grass and tapping it with a simple, flat-faced putter.

Moe Norman, the fabled Canadian pro who many experts say is one of the two greatest shot-makers in golf history, Ben Hogan being the other, put this notion in the perspective I'm getting at. I asked why he didn't seem to pay much attention to putting, and as a result was quite ordinary in that department. He replied: "An office secretary who never played golf before can knock in a 20-foot putt the first time she tries. But she'll never, never be able to hit a 212-yard 2-iron onto a green." Right. And that's why Ben Hogan once suggested a scoring system in which putting was not worth as much as hitting a green with a 2-iron. The latter should be worth a full stroke and a six-foot putt a quarter of a stroke. Something like that. No one was about to buy that idea, so what Hogan finally did was learn how to hit his approaches 12 feet or less from the hole. He knew about the putting odds, of course.

Last December there was the big-money tournament in Jamaica, in which Nick Faldo and Greg Norman got into a playoff. On the hole where it was decided, Faldo hit a fine approach that covered the flag and ended up on the back fringe about 15 feet from the cup. Norman had driven into a fairway bunker, but hit a magnificent shot from there to with-in three feet of the hole. Clearly, Faldo would have to make his putt to stay alive. Then again, maybe he understands the notion being proposed here, that players such as Norman, a man proud of his power and ability to make difficult shots from a distance, was apt not to attend with due diligence to his three-foot birdie putt. In any case, Faldo had to make his putt. And as you may recall, he did just that. A 15-footer—3 feet over the Runyan Calculation—smack in the hole. After which, Norman hit a weak putt that fell below the hole. End of story.

So as not to be too hard on Norman, he was no doubt shaken by Faldo's ringer. And his putt did have a bit of break in it. Surely he wanted to make the putt, which was now for a halve. But the manner in which he missed, on the low side, not even touching the hole, suggested the work of someone so pleased with his ability to knock it stiff from a fairway bunker that the rest of the job was too boring, not challenging enough. He may even have felt, deep in the recesses of his soul, that he shouldn't have had to make it. Not after that great iron shot.

Therein lies the difference between the truly great players, of which Faldo is one, and the merely very good ones. They are complete golfers. They go the whole route, leave no stone unturned. Such an attitude takes an extra dimension of character. The equation includes a wanting that transcends the obvious delights of great shot-making, and a willingness to accept the need for the comparatively mundane business of rolling a ball gently along the ground. There was no greater example of that combination, in my experience, than Jack Nicklaus in the third round of the 1972 British Open. As it happened, Nicklaus did not win that championship, but never mind. To set the scene.

Nicklaus had already won the Masters and U.S. Open, and was now making what would be his greatest run at the magical modern-day Grand Slam. The British was to be Number Three. Everyone felt sure that if he managed to win it, the fourth and final leg, the PGA championship, would be his for the taking. Nicklaus decided on a conservative game plan for the Muirfield Golf Club in Scotland, but on a dry and very fast course Lee Trevino and Tony Jacklin bolted boldly ahead. After three rounds Jack was six back of Trevino, five behind Jacklin. In the final round, Nicklaus decided to take the gloves off and have an aggressive go at the course and history. He used his driver off tees where he had been using a 1- or 2-iron. It paid off. He reeled off one birdie after another with short pitches and even chip-shot approaches. By the 11th hole he had actually taken the lead, making up a huge deficit against two of the best players in the game.

At the 11th, Nicklaus had a six-foot putt for yet another birdie. He went through his routine as meticulously as always. And also characteristically, he stood over his putt for what seemed hours—as though he was in a trance. But before he took the blade back there was a tremendous gallery roar from two holes back, where Trevino and Jacklin were playing. Muirfield is a compact layout, none of the holes are as far from the others as on most courses, and the reverberations from the ninth green were loud and clear in volume and meaning. It was the unmistakable shout of an eagle. Indeed, Trevino had done just that.

Nicklaus stepped away from his ball, and went through his entire routine once again. As he stood over his ball, yet another roar came from the ninth, an even louder one, for this was for the eagle of Great Britain's own Tony Jacklin. This time Nicklaus stepped back and issued a response: "Whew!" he whewed, shaking his head in amazement. One would think that after these two disruptions, Nicklaus might be shaken enough to lose his composure and the sureness of his stroke. Indeed, one could excuse him if he failed with his six-footer. But no. He went once more through his routine, stood over the ball for a millennium, then stroked it into the heart of the hole. It was a marvel, it was the ultimate expression of someone who would not be denied his will, his wanting.

I would go so far as to say that if, after those two putts by Trevino and Jacklin the sun plummeted beyond the horizon and it became pitch black, Nicklaus would still have made the putt. I had seen that happen, more than once, and paid the price. Charley Bud did it all the time. No lighted matches were necessary as we played our 54th hole of the day, at 9:30 in the evening. No car lights required. If it was a putt to win it all in the dark, Charley Bud found the even darker bottom of the hole.

ROOTS

(Golf Magazine—1977)

Thomas Wolfe wrote that we can't go home again, meaning that once we reach adulthood we must look out for ourselves; shed the security and values of our parents. That may be true in some ways. But as far as our golf life goes, it can be said that we never do leave home, that we take it with us wherever we happen to tee it up. By *home* is meant the golf course on which we first learned to play. The influence of the home course. Ben Crenshaw believes his recurring problem with tee-shot accuracy is a reflection of the course on which he grew up. "It was so wide open I could hit it anywhere. So I never learned to control my drives the way I'd like to. I wish I had grown up on a tight course."

Given his income despite a sometimes errant driver, one cannot feel too badly for Crenshaw. The point of his remark, however, illustrates how much the environment of the initial learning experience can influence subsequent style and performance, even for a lifetime. This holds in all walks of life, but in games playing it is especially pertinent to golf because no two courses are alike the way all baseball diamonds, basketball and tennis courts, and football fields are. You can usually tell a golfer by what sort of course he has eaten—or been eaten by.

The cradle in which we flail around, getting our first golf nourish-
ment, can have a negative influence, a positive one, or both. To wit, when
Ben Crenshaw snaps a big hooking drive into the "trash," more often than
not his putter puts him back in the game. He is one of the best putters
around because the greens at his golf cradle, the Country Club of Austin,
were bumpy. He had to learn to roll the ball. Thus, says Ben, "It was easy
when I got to the good ones [greens]."

What kind of golf course would be best on which to learn the game
to the fullest? From the following comments of a number of touring pros
on the influence of their home courses, a consensus develops. At the same
time, we get some insights that can make watching the pros in action a bit
more interesting. For example, the next time you see Hubert Green at the
clubhouse turn with a chance to win and he has a couple of tight-driving
holes to maneuver through, consider that as a youth he played more than
1,000 formative rounds of golf on the narrow, heavily wooded Birming-
ham Country Club "track." "This made me a better driver," says Green. "I
learned position golf and more finesse off the tee."

And when Tom Watson misses a green with an approach or has a slippery putt, such as the 12-footer he made on the 17th at Augusta National
to seal his 1977 Masters victory, know that in such circumstances Watson
harks back in mind and body to his kid days around the Kansas City
Country Club. "The course was long and the greens very small. For both
reasons I missed a lot of greens. Chipping and putting were really necessary
for me to score. I practiced those two things more than my long game."

A bet on Johnny Miller is pretty good almost anytime, but is especially
enhanced on windless days. The San Francisco and Olympic Club courses
on which Miller grew up are enclosed by trees, a factor he is sure helped
him to develop his fine big swing and unhurried rhythm. "All those trees
blocked most of the wind, and I didn't have to fight that. When you play in
the wind regularly, like in Texas, you tend to make a quicker, shorter swing
and hit the ball lower. At home I could hit the ball high, which is what you
need on most of the tour courses now, and especially at the Masters."

Lee Elder will attest to Miller's comments, as will anyone who has
ever come out of Texas. Elder's first golf was on the Tenison Memorial
Municipal Golf Course in Dallas, where not only was the wind a constant
companion, the ground was something on the order of an interstate.
"That's why my approach shots have a generally low trajectory, I hit so
many punch shots. And I have trouble playing to elevated greens and playing off soft turf, where I take too much divot." When Elder goes to hilly

Augusta National, or wherever the greens are raised, he sets the lie of his irons more upright for a more vertical swing that helps produce loft on his approach shots.

Rather than adjust their equipment for special occasions, such Texas-bred pros as Jimmy Demaret and Lee Trevino developed basic cut-shot swings. Demaret, with his huge but most flexible hands, could pinch the ball off the interstate slab and spin it back before it found an exit. But the swing manipulations of a Demaret, or even Trevino, are less necessary nowadays because, as Johnny Miller rightly notes, most tour courses are watered so well. Indeed, the grasses are getting so lush that we are hearing more and more about "flyers," those shots that tend to squirt off line and/or go too far when blades of grass get between clubface and ball at impact. That may be one reason why Lanny Wadkins is making such a splendid comeback following serious illness. Wadkins says that down around Richmond, Virginia, where he grew up, the golf course grass is a mixture of blue, rye, bermuda and whatever else might creep in. In Wadkins's word, the fairways were not "pure," and he had to learn how to play flyer lies.

The superb long-iron and sand trap play that marked Julius Boros's illustrious career was earned the hard way: "Where I learned to play in Connecticut there were a lot of bunkers and long par-threes. Before I sharpened up my long-iron game I was in the sand a few times." Of course, motivation to learn is no small factor and if the golf cradle does not have enough of the proper instructional "toys" they must be searched out. For instance, Jerry McGee: "I played a nine-hole course in New Lexington, Ohio, that didn't have a single bunker. I had to go elsewhere just to practice bunker shots. Now I'm an excellent trap player."

But there is more to a golf course than such specifics as grass texture, width of fairways, and so on. On the course just outside Johannesburg, South Africa, where Gary Player got his golf feet wet, there was "very little, practically zero play during the week. I was able to practice all day long as a youngster in complete privacy." Add overall climate, too. Johnny Miller believes the mildness of the San Francisco–area weather allowed him to play all day without great strain: "It doesn't take it out of you the way heavy heat does." And if Dave Stockton, standing in the middle of an ironing-board-flat Arizona fairway, seems very sure of which club to use, don't be surprised: "I grew up next door to Arrowhead Country Club, in San Bernardino. It was very flat. You could stand at one end of it and see all 18 holes. This made me a good judge of distance on flat courses."

Stockton touches on the element of feel in golf, for even though he, as do all the touring pros, steps off the distances and can tell you he has 137 yards, two feet, four inches to the pin, in making the shot there must still be a sense of familiarity with terrain. This writer recalls how very much at home Lee Trevino of Texas felt in the 1971 U.S. Open at Merion Golf Club on Philadelphia's mainline. It had nothing to do with Trevino's social background, to be sure, only that Merion's normally plush bluegrass that June was fairly tight and dry—just the kind of ground on which Lee was raised. It was even turning Texas brown, and Trevino was in clover, so to speak. On the tee of one par-three, he said: "Hey pard, watch me spin this little dude in there." He heeled up a node of turf, propped his ball on it, and with a 4-iron beat out a smashing clothesline of a shot that had the holding action of epoxy. Lee beat Nicklaus in a playoff for that Open and, germane to the theme of this article, also beat Jack out of the 1972 British Open, played on a Muirfield links baked hard by an unusually arid summer. Which might suggest to betting persons that when two of the best golfers in the world are at the top of their games, go with the one who is most "at home."

Speaking of Nicklaus in this regard, those with rather long memories will remember that in Jack's first winter tour as a pro he was nowhere near as impressive as everyone expected he would be. The 1962 winter circuit began with the Los Angeles Open, then played at Rancho Park, one of the most heavily played public courses in the world; and it looks it. Rancho is a rabbit farm full of scrapes next to the manorial lawn of a Scioto Country Club, Jack's home course. Nicklaus was well down the money list at Rancho, and through March, playing on a number of other short-playing hardpan tour courses, seemed to be struggling. Rookie jitters? Not likely, considering his past record and that in '62 he would win the U.S. Open and finish third on that season's total earnings roster. Jack himself alluded to the answer to his slow start in a subtle but unmistakable way. In 1963 he did not play at Rancho. In fact, he did not play another Los Angeles Open until it moved to grassy Riviera Country Club. Furthermore, he did then and has almost invariably passed up tour events played on the seared earth of Arizona or elsewhere.

The above is in no way meant to denigrate the enormous talent of Jack Nicklaus, golfer. Only a fool would be so foolish. It is only to say how smart Jack has been in handling his career and in being able by virtue of his ability to pick the places he knows he has the best chance for top performance. Most tour pros play anywhere because they don't make enough money in one, three, or five places. Jack, by and large, goes where the courses have the lusher grasses on which he built his swing and are longer in length and more architecturally demanding to favor his power and exceptionally keen mind for strategic golf. Jack concurs. Asked what type of course he thinks best on which to learn the game, he generalized at first: "It should have some length, but some need for precision, too. Small greens. And it should definitely be a thinking man's course. Scioto is all that. The course at Merion would also be a good one for beginners" (under normal playing conditions, we presume).

A consensus seems to have emerged. The ideal golf course on which to prepare for all the complexities that crop up in the game will have narrow fairways, mostly tree-lined but with some rough. A few of them will be hilly, a few flat. It will have some bentgrass, some hardpan. There will be a few fairway bunkers, a profusion of traps around the greens. The greens will be generally raised, relatively small, and slightly undulating; make nine of them bumpy, nine glassy smooth. Wind will be around some corners, calm around others, and the mean temperature will be 72 degrees (figure your own Celsius). And it will be as populated by people as a booze bust for Moslems.

You may have just such a layout already, but it is not likely, and to build one would not be feasible, according to Jack Nicklaus the golf architect, because "no one could afford it." In the end, then, we take what we can get for our golf cradle and go from there. If you are a Charles Coody you are happy there is anything at all. He grew up in a west Texas town of 5,000 people. The rocky, flat nine-holer in Stamford on which Coody picked up grip stance and punch shot was the only one within 20 miles. "It wasn't the best golf course in the world," says Coody, "but we played every day from sunup to dark and I'm just thankful we had it."

Finally, there is the ultimate romanticism of Juan Chi-Chi Rodriquez. He got into golf as a caddie at the Berwynd Golf Club in Puerto Rico. A poor kid, his future opened up at Berwynd. Chi-Chi would earn much-needed money and learn to play so well he became, by the standards of his economic background alone, a wealthy man. Berwynd could have been a Merion or a Rancho Park and it wouldn't have made any real difference. To this day, when his game goes off, Rodriquez leaves the tour and returns to Berwynd. "I just sit around out there thinking about how I used to hustle bags and got to where I could shoot 68 regularly, and think of where I came from and where I've gotten to because of golf. Then I go back on the tour with my spirits high. I begin to play well again."

Which seems to say, among other things, that one *can* go home again—and probably should once in a while.

TEMPER!!!

(Golf Digest—1967)

O ne of the first times I threw a club came after I'd made a 3-iron shot that was supposed to carry a bunker and land on the green. Instead it kept its preordained engagement with the sand. I flung the club as if it were a javelin toward my bag, which was standing nearby in a cart. The grip end of the club hit an edge of the bag, which, in turn, hurled it back in my direction. The iron end struck me dead in the nose, and flushed forth a torrent of blood that dripped—cunningly—onto the white portions of my golf shoes.

But I played on. I walked the next two holes with my nose pointed to the sky and a handkerchief clamped tightly aboard.

Golf, I confess, is my favorite medium for expressing the doubt and discontent that smolder inside from time to time. I know that many other golfers have the same fatal weakness. Poker is supposed to be the one game that brings out the real nature of a man. But golf does it so much better.

Off the course a man may speak softly to shrieking women and bawling children, smile patiently at cabbies fleeting by him in the rain, or stanch the flow of blood from a shaving nick with an unemotional "tsk-

tsk." But put a golf club in his hand, and a slice in his swing, and the same man—if he's like me—becomes a raging bull, a maelstrom of invective, a tempest in a tee box.

For a man of such nature, a single bad bounce or one blown putt may be enough to set off an uncontrollable blaze of emotions. A period of edgy expectation begins for his fellow players, who automatically brace themselves to witness one of the many bizarre forms that a bad temper can assume.

Take Lefty Stackhouse, for example. The name alone suggests the heat of a boiling inferno. Once during a round of golf that was clearly getting the better of him, Lefty played a tee shot that twisted off the fairway. After viewing his ball's line of flight, he spun around, noticed a cluster of thorny bushes behind the teeing area, and suddenly made a sprinter's lunge for the shrubbery. A few yards from his target he leaped and fell sprawling into the mass of thick and pointed foliage, face first. There he lay as one of his stunned fellow golfers approached and extended a hand. Stackhouse told his mate to leave him alone, that he wanted to stay right where he was. Propped on a bed of needles like an Indian fakir, Lefty had decided to suffer the pangs of outrageous golf in the most direct fashion available.

But Lefty's action was mere caprice compared to other displays of the ancient art of self-exasperation. Take the case of the man who had been hooking the ball all day. No matter what steps he took to correct himself, shot after shot would take an abrupt 90-degree turn to the left and dart like a frightened deer into thick woodland. The tortured man kept the peace until the final hole when, from the 18th tee, he sent another angling blazer into a copse of oaks. Quietly, too quietly, he shuffled into the timber to locate his ball. But no sooner had he reached the trees than he gave up searching and instead placed himself in front of a sturdy oak. Then, like a boxer working over the big bag, he began punching the tree with straight rights from the shoulder. Mighty blows they were, too, worthy of many of today's heavyweights. With every punch the golfer screamed in strained tones, "Keep your right hand out of the shot"—whap—"keep your right . . ." Needless to say, after debarking the oak the tormented man was able to keep his right hand well out of shots. For over a month.

My first experience with turbulence of this sort occurred as a caddie in the late '40s. At that time I encountered a man named Ky Laffoon, an old pro with a reputation as a player of caliber, and as a man of thunderous temperament. Having just finished a round of caddying one day, I returned to the caddie shack and heard that fabled Mr. Laffoon was on the course. I rushed to the 15th tee, and sure enough, there he was, a stockily built man with disdain written across his brown-red face, which resembled a soft apple too long on the stalls. Preparing to tee off, Laffoon pulled a driver from his bag. His club had the strangest shaft I had ever seen. It was so curved that it looked more like a bow to fire arrows than a club to strike golf balls. He teed up his ball and after a few harsh words to the world at large brought up a tremendous volume of tobacco juice and spat it generously on the head of the club, inundating the worn wooden surface with a shiny coat of tan-brown liquid—for "good luck," he muttered. Tobacco juice or no, he hit a flamboyant slice that headed toward some thick rough near a fence. As soon as the ball began to slice, Laffoon began marching after it, rending the air with a veritable waterfall of sulfurous abuse. His delivery was marvelous. The stream of hot verbal acid flowed as the waters tumbling over Niagara, pouring from his tongue with an easy smoothness that could only derive from years of accomplished contumely. But more astonishing was his bending of the driver shaft as he walked until it looked like a U-turn symbol. Finally he held the club to his eye, looked down the shaft, and remarked that now it was just about the way he liked it.

Also as a caddie, I once had the pleasure of carrying the bag of a very fine professional, Ed Furgol. I worked for him for two weeks, during which time he was competing in the late George S. May's All-American and World Championships at Tam O'Shanter near Chicago. Furgol was then a regular on the PGA circuit, probably reason enough to be high-strung, and by nature he had strong reactions to the misfortunes that befall all golfers. He was, and still is, a wonderful player. He went on to win the U.S. Open in 1954, and is now a much-mellowed man on the course. But he once had a temper, and I think it cost him a lot of money during those two weeks at Tam O'Shanter. In those days Ed reacted with a beautifully controlled system of club throwing. After finishing high on his follow-through, as was his style, he would hold still, watch the flight of the ball, and, if it was not to his liking, simply thrust the still-lifted iron clubhead downward into the turf.

The club would descend like a steel arrow shot from a mighty catapult; the clubhead would slice through the turf almost soundlessly, driving into the sod hosel-deep. To extricate the article, I had to place my feet solidly and pull with all my strength. With each uprooted club came clods of dirt and grass. For two full weeks I was yanking out clubs and dutifully cleaning every groove. After 18 holes of this, I would feel, and look, like a dirt farmer.

Temper generally comes to the surface in violent displays of displea-
sure. But it can develop quietly, too. Like the time Skip Alexander finished
putting on the 18th, again at Tam O'Shanter. Skip was a quiet, well-man-
nered gentleman from the South. He rarely said a word, and when he did
it was in a slow, easy drawl that could never offend anyone. Yet he was also
susceptible to the extreme demands of inner rage.

As noted, Skip had finished putting—three-putting—on 18. It wasn't
a good round for him, but at the moment one would never have known.
After his third putt Skip lifted the ball out of the hole, casually tossed it
toward the gallery, and began walking easily toward the scorer's table. On
the way he took hold of his putter, a huge hand on each end, and without further ado, without uttering a word, with absolute aplomb, and only
stopping an instant, he snapped the shaft in two. The crack of timber woke
the people to Alexander's mood. Skip then calmly stuffed the pieces of
putter into the long pocket of his bag and strolled over to sign his card.
Nary a word from him. No pomp, no ostentation. He had had a private
argument with his putter, found he didn't like it anymore, and so he broke
it. That was all.

Temper is often a brief flurry, but not always. During my college days
I watched what may well be the most extended stretch of sustained anger
that ever graced a golf course. The perpetrator was known as Harry the
Moose, a powerful, athletic man with a broad, bronzed, seamed face. A gentleman in every respect, he was a fine person. But he had this weakness.

The great upheaval took place during a 36-hole tournament in
Peoria, Illinois. Harry had entered himself and me, but our entries had
somehow disappeared. The result was that we had no starting time. Upon
arriving we were told to tee off after the last scheduled pairings of the day.
We did, and the first round was a good one for Harry. He had a 69 and
emerged as one of the leaders.

For the second day, we had a choice: tee off last again, or go off
first, at 5:45 A.M. Normally Harry's eyes never really unlidded until
around noon, but perhaps because he was nervous, or anxious, he chose
the dawn patrol.

Of course Harry had been peeved at being overlooked by the schedule makers in the first place, but the 69 helped ease his attitude, and the
next morning we squished through the dew to the first tee. Harry the
Moose promptly sent a squeaking duck-hook into the rough, a little bunt
that seemed to have been hit with the head cover still in place. He followed with an iron shot that hit soft in front of the green, and stayed there.

A chip was hit too hard, over the back of the green. He chipped back too easily and two-putted for a double-bogey six.

The storm would have broken then and there, except that Harry was still mentally in bed. The next few holes were played routinely, a couple of pars, a couple of bogeys. But with every hole played, particularly those bogeyed, the clouds gathered more ominously on the horizon.

At the eighth hole after a fair drive, Harry had an 8-iron to the green. But there were a few branches ahead that could bring trouble. It wasn't a hard shot, but at the moment Harry was not one for finessing. He hit a good shot, but too close to the boughs, and it hit, tinkled around in there, then fell straight down. That did it. The 8-iron went whistling into the same tree as though fired from a cannon. The club battered around for a few seconds, then came down—in parts. First the clubhead and lower part of the shaft, then the top of the shaft and the grip. When the Moose saw this his neck veins protruded like sausages. Without a word he stuffed the pieces into the bag. War had been declared.

The next shot was a honey, six feet from the cup. But that did not stay hostilities. A long, arching toss of the club followed the shot. He made the putt and then threw the ball—a high, hard one—into a nearby pond.

At the next hole he drilled an iron three feet from the cup and flipped the club halfway down the fairway. It was a par-three hole and he had a chance for a much-needed birdie. But the greens were fast and he had a downhill twister. I feared the worst was coming.

I finished my putting quickly, headed straight for a high knoll beside the green, and crouched down behind it. I was safe. I peeked over the rise. The other players in our foursome had also fled, and Harry stood terribly alone on that green. A few seconds later there was a croaking growl, a second of quiet, then a whooshing sound. I duly marked 3 on the card under Harry's name and left for the next tee. Harry recovered his club from the crotch of a tree.

That was how it went for a long stretch of holes. After every shot, be it good, bad, or indifferent, we heard the whirring and whipping of a club flying through the air.

Finally, at the middle of the 17th fairway, 9 holes after it had begun, Harry subsided. He had hit a big drive and followed it with a Herculean heave of the club. He now had a four-wood shot to the green. He hit a screamer, then positioned himself for what was becoming a traditional conclusion to his golf shots. The right leg was braced, the left raised up slightly like a baseball pitcher's, the arm, with club, went back . . . but it never went forward. There was a heavy, sighing grunt and the club dropped meekly to the turf behind him. His body sagged as though a great weight finally had been lifted.

"I'd like to," he said in a whisper, "but I just can't . . . throw it . . . anymore." And so it ended where it began, in a state of complete frustration.

Harry the Moose dragged himself, spent, through the rest of the round with a strange smile on his face. It was the eerie, slack-jawed smile of a man who had fought a losing battle with himself, yet somehow had survived.

THE
DELUSIONS OF
RIGHT-HAND
SUPERIORITY

(Golf Magazine—1970)

Why, it's a looking-glass book of course! And if I hold it up
to the glass the words will all go the right way again.
—ALICE, IN LEWIS CARROLL'S *THROUGH THE LOOKING GLASS*

If by mere chance in the development from fetus to birth the right cerebral hemisphere is heavier than the left and one emerges a left-hander, he is doomed to suffer many inequities. Left-handedness is not common. It is not as uncommon as most people think, but right handers are an overwhelming majority and have duly stacked the deck against the minority on the left. Punch-bowl ladles are spouted so left-handers need to be contortionists to fill their cups. Auto ashtrays are situated where dangerous feats of twisting are required. The left-hander is shunted to the far end of a dinner table, where his eating elbow will not soil someone's soup. The Italian word for "left" is *sinistra.* Alter the suffix slightly and you have the English *sinister.* Going back beyond biblical times, left-handed people have been accused of, and punished for, black magic, witchcraft, and other necromantic devilries. And only because they were left-handed. In at least two major religions,

Christianity and Islam, practice of certain rituals must be with the right hand. That's dogma.

One of our least admirable human characteristics is that, when a relatively few of our fellow men differ from the norm, particularly in something so elemental as handedness, we are capable of acting upon the difference with fear and trepidation. It's the very stuff of superstition. As absurd as it may be, even as we have passed through the Dark Ages and the Age of Reason flush into the superscientific Space Age, there are parents today who, if they see their infant child grabbing his rattle with the left hand, will firmly snatch the toy away and place it where only the right hand can get it. Medical evidence indicates that forcing a natural-born left-hander to be right-handed causes stuttering, hypertension, and general irascibility. But never mind. Being left-handed is worse. It will bring the gods down on your head. One wonders how far we really have come as reasoning animals.

Left-handers who play golf have been no less victimized by a right-hand-dominated world. Most ball and stick (or paddle) games have had a fair share of southpaws (a term coined, it is said, at a Chicago ballpark, where left-handed pitchers faced west, hence their delivery came out of the south). Many lefties, Babe Ruth and Rod Laver to name but two, have been and are very powerful greats. Why golf, one of Western civilization's older games, has had but one outstanding left-handed player, Bob Charles, is an interesting question. It is answered by a perverse, fright-filled inability to countenance the unusual with equanimity, or at least indifference. The fact of Charles's recent vintage perhaps marks a change in attitude toward the matter in golf circles. We may see more left-handed players like Charles in the future. But old concepts still persist and if a total turnaround in thinking and acceptance does come, it will have fought through a morass of ill-conceived notions.

Golf surveyed professionals around the country to learn something of how and what golf teachers think about left-handed golf, and why. We asked first whether they (the pros) consistently advise left-handed people just taking up the game to play right-handed. Sixty-one percent replied no, which is rather encouraging. On the other hand, a not unsubstantial 39 percent answered yes, they do advise playing right-handed. One of the most repeated arguments for playing right-handed golf is the presumption that golf courses are designed to suit dextrals, or right-handers. Golf architect William Mitchell agrees and justifies it by the numbers. Some 95 percent of the golfers in the U.S. are right-handers and about 80 percent of them slice. So Mitchell generally sets up a course with less trouble on the right. If he builds a fairway bunker, for example, it is usually at the left side of the road, from where the right-hander's slice veers away. The lefty's slice, obviously, has that bunker very much in the way. Mitchell feels that a 10-handicap left-hander is actually a 7, because every course he plays is about 3 strokes harder.

There is considerable disagreement on this. Jimmy Demaret, who played golf left-handed for a brief time as a beginner, then switched, discounts the right-hand-favored-course idea altogether. For Jimmy, a course's design is first and foremost dictated by the piece of land on which it is built. Architect Ed Ryder agrees that the land itself bears most heavily on how holes take shape. Demaret, it should be noted, does not advise left-handers to switch over. Bob Charles remarks that over the long run there are as many doglegs to the right as to the left and feels the left-hander is at no disadvantage. Of course, Jimmy and Bob view the matter from the vantage point of their ability at shot-making. If a hole turns three different ways, ascends an alpine cliff, and descends across the River Styx, they'll have the shots to handle it. In that respect, however, architect Joe Finger says that in building a championship course he will generally trap his fairways on the left at about 250 yards (out of the average player's range), because good players tend to hook. Actually then, good left-handed players, who also tend to hook, but the opposite way, have an advantage on the "big" courses. But, Finger goes on, a well-balanced course will favor neither port- nor lee-siders.

On balance, speaking in terms of courses that are more than heavily played "fast tracks" designed with minimal trouble for maximum speed of play, the left-hander is no worse off than his dextral brother. That's the feeling of Bill Sharp, executive vice president of the 200,000-member National Association of Left-Handed Golfers (NALG), and as you might imagine, the subject is close to his heart.

A second "alibi" given for switching left-handers is equipment availability. Southpaws are often told that good equipment for them is hard to come by. This was undoubtedly true to some extent 20 or 30 years ago, and so was a somewhat legitimate reason for making the switch. It is nowhere near the case now. The manufacturers have definitely filled the gap in this area. Bob Rickey, of MacGregor, says left-handers are a significant part of the market and, his company considers itself very much in the left-handed club business. Jim Shea, of Spalding, reports that his firm offers five different grades of left-handed clubs. The NALG has a special arrangement with the First Flight Co. to produce left-handed sticks for its members. Forgings for left-handed clubs are quite expensive, yet all the manufacturers maintain a price parity with right-handed equipment. No extra charge for left-handed clubs.

In short, clubs can be had for southpaws. Club pros do not usually stock them and for this they can't be blamed, since demand seldom warrants it. All it takes, though, is a phone call or an order by mail and in a few days left-handers can have the clubs in their hands that they need, and should use.

The third major argument for switching to the right is the most involved, and controversial. It has to do with the swing itself. The 61 percent who do not advise switching reason that it's wrong to make anyone go against his natural instincts, that a person should play the way he feels most comfortable. It's as simple as that. The implication is clear that swing fundamentals are the same no matter which side of the ball you do it from.

Those who say "switch" insist that golf is a left-sided game, that you need a firm, bracing left side at impact and a strong left-hand lead through the ball. Let's grant the validity of this, although there is an equally valid counterargument we'll get to in a moment. In its survey, *Golf* also posed a hypothetical problem: Is it not logical that a left-handed person's presumably stronger left hand (and side) will serve a right-handed swing better and, thus, shouldn't he switch to right-handed play? More than half of the 39-percenters disagreed completely with this logic, an odd contradiction of their strong-left-side theory. Fact of the matter is, there has been no concrete proof, as yet, that the left side of the human anatomy can do things the right side cannot. In other words, there's no reason why a left-hander can't have a firm *right* side.

Probably closer to the truth is what a number of pros said in answering *Golf's* questionnaire and phone survey. Golf is a two-handed, two-sided game and both must work in coordination with each other. Swinging a golf club is largely a learned process and if a right-hander has a weak left hand, or vice versa, he must only strengthen the weakness by steady play and exercise. Again, swing principles are precisely the same, and it is certainly much easier following natural instincts to achieve enjoyment and even highly advanced ability. Johnny Bulla, who played some fine golf in the '30s and '40s, as a right-hander, is actually ambidextrous. Around age 40, Bulla began playing almost exclusively left-handed, his original, more natural way, and he says today that if he had played left-handed throughout his career he would have been a better player and won more.

The 17th-century philosopher-mathematician Leibniz said that right and left are indiscernible, until the choice is made. The earth revolves to the right if you face the magnetic pole, left if you face south. Right and left, then, are relative concepts. Darwinian evolutionists will point out that handedness among the apes does not exist. They snap up peanuts, peel bananas, and bang rubber tires with the right or left hands, indiscriminately. Only man, for no truly known reason, has developed handedness, and sanctified it. However, rather than reopen the Scopes Trial, the left-hander can defend his position against the adamant righties by pointing out that Michelangelo was a left-hander, and on his Sistine Chapel ceiling Adam receives life through his left hand. Leonardo da Vinci also was sinistral (left-handed). Paul McCartney is a Beatle lefty. Charley Chaplin and Danny Kaye are lefties, too. Harpo Marx confounded the music world by playing beautifully from the "wrong" side of the harp. The Boy Scouts' handshake is left-handed, and who could dishonor them? The Amazons had to amputate their right breasts in order to shoot their arrows from the right side, which is food for contemplation. And for closers, speaking of mirrors, does the right-hander ever consider that when he examines his golf swing in a looking glass he sees himself as a southpaw?

THE THEORY OF POSITIVE DEFLECTIVE TURMOIL

(Diversion—1979)

In my checkered, make that smudgy, competitive golf career, I have played best and accomplished most when the circumstances were not what would be commonly considered the most advantageous. For example, while I was editor in chief of *Golf* magazine, a very busy job involving myriad production problems and decisions (and which left me time for maybe 10 rounds of golf a month), I took a day off to try to qualify for the U.S. Amateur championship. And did. Another time, during my last season of collegiate golf, I kept up a heavy academic schedule, played the lead in an August Strindberg play, and carried on an active romance with a young lady. At the same time, I finished fifth individually in the National Small College championship and was a member of the winning team in that event.

I mention the above not to boast, but to illustrate from personal experience a theory that I have conjured up. To wit, the more you are distracted by the pressures of one discipline, the better you are apt to perform in another. I call it the Theory of Positive Deflective Turmoil.

I hesitate recommending my theory to brain surgeons, pharmacists, and auto mechanics, not to mention dentists, plumbers, and computer analysts, but all others might give it a go. In any case, to prove my theory by a kind of inverse deduction, or reverse induction, or ridiculous perversion, I played in that U.S. Amateur at a site some 500 miles from my editor's desk. Having nothing to do but practice and play golf, I failed (miserably) to qualify for the last two rounds of the tournament. Catch my drift?

DAMNED YANKEES

Another example. In 1978 the New York Yankees went through about half a season of uncommon and well-publicized clubhouse turbulence, most of it stirred up by manager Billy Martin's rancorous verbal and physical battles with his star home-run hitter and the club's owner. As we all know, the Yankees won the 1978 World Series. Now, conventional thinking might have it that the Yanks were able to win it all because an easygoing Bob Lemon took over as manager in midseason and calmed the team's storms. However, recall that Lemon and his '78 Yanks needed an extra-season game to get into the playoffs, whereas the year before, when Billy Martin led the club throughout and fomented his usual brew of on- and off-field fracases, the team won it all going away. According to my theory, Bob Lemon so eased life among the 1978 Yankees that he damn near blew the season. The Yanks won on the ebbing dregs of earlier discontent.

Positive Deflective Turmoil can also be manifested through an illness, real or otherwise, that draws off exceedingly intensive—ergo destructive—concentration on technique, game plans, etc., as well as the psychological tension stemming directly from the competitive situation. So it's not surprising, then, that there have been a number of instances when athletes have done very well when not full of the stuff and vinegar of brimming good health.

Olin Dutra came out of the hospital, and still feeling the miseries of a serious stomach ailment, won the 1935 U.S. Open, his only major golf victory; when he was 100 percent, Dutra never won much of anything. Ben Hogan's body was crushed and he nearly died when a speeding bus hit his car head-on. Hogan was never totally fit after that, and as the years went by he had to soak and bandage his legs before a round of golf; yet he won six of his nine major championships after the accident. Mickey Mantle hit most of his home runs swinging on diseased knees. They say he would have been even greater had he been on good pins. I say that "The Mick" was a superstar because the pain of his bad legs relaxed his mind for

baseball. To those of you who think I am off the wall, then you should live
and be well; or be well and play; or remember how you play when you are
not well.

ALL IN YOUR HEAD

Of course, I am not suggesting that on the eve of your next big
tennis/golf/racquetball match you should order out for a migraine
headache or contract pleurisy. However, you might conjure up something
along those lines by way of hypochondria.

One of my boyhood baseball heroes was Luke Appling, the Chicago
White Sox shortstop, who was known as "Ole Aches and Pains" because
he was forever complaining that some part or other of his body was hurting him badly and that he was two steps from the grave. For all that, Luke
played in the majors for many years at his strenuous position, rarely missed
a game, and twice led the American League in hitting. Luke knew what
he was doing with all that kvetching of his.

Over the past few years, Tim Gallwey has become quite popular in
sports instruction with his books and classes called *Inner Tennis* and *Inner
Skiing* (*Inner Golf* is coming up). His premise, based on Zen and other
Eastern philosophies, is to get persons into their game by getting them out
of themselves—their superego, ego, or what have you. It is deflection without the turmoil; slow down both your physical and mental metabolisms
and play better as a result. I understand Gallwey's essential idea, and agree
with it, although it occurs to me that if you get too "spaced out" you won't
know if you won or lost. I suppose that makes no difference, though, so
long as you play well, which is what Grantland Rice more or less said
before Gallwey was born.

I'm told that to truly incorporate Gallwey's notions into your system
with any degree of permanence you have to hang out with him a lot—
people who have taken his instruction "live" say that he is spellbinding—
but the stuff doesn't last in his absence. Or you can read Tim's own source
material—heavy, somewhat windy books by Sri Tantehinda, Krishna
Muhktavayismir, and folks like that. This also entails significantly altering
your worldview, let alone your backhand drop shot.

What I offer is simpler by far. If winning really is important to you,
just get a little sick, or feign it. Or have a nice argument with your wife,
your boss, or a pencil sharpener.

A TERMINAL
CASE OF
OVERTEACH

(Golf Magazine—1970)

Golf is an easy game once you've
conceded you're not going to beat it, that it will always have the upper
hand. Accept this and you'll come to enjoy the game, and suffer it with the
passive indifference of a Buddhist. Refuse to accept, and you could face
the tragedy that befell one Putney Swipe.

Putney came late to golf, having misspent his youth making model
airplanes, playing baseball, and learning to dance, instead of using the time
nipping 5-irons from the hard dirt of a caddie yard. Schooling himself in
the mundane simplicities of buy and sell, Swipe read the *Wall Street Journal,*
learned about debits and credits, and only when financially secure did he
take up the game. He then expected to overcome golf with the same force
and determination that beat the stock market.

But plagued by an office paunch and cocktail-softened muscles,
Swipe's bone and sinew would not respond to the new, unnatural exigen-
cies of the golf swing. His sturdy foundation of self-confidence, construct-
ed over years of enriching business deals, began to crumble like soapstone
beneath a sculptor's chisel. At an age when he should have been a resigned

loser, he persisted in believing that he could solve the riddle of golf and bound joyously into the light, free air of scores in the 70s.

Of course, Swipe took lessons. He acquired the fundamentals of grip, stance, posture, and eight million admonitions to keep his head down. He was told that with some regular play and practice he might acquire a modicum of ability. But no, no, modern man that he was, he wanted instant par. Nothing less would do. A man in a hurry, he reached for any instruction straw in the wind that held the promise of straight tee shots, crisp irons, unwavering putts. He was inundated with a cascade of suggestion, recommendation, advocation, and exhortation. Even had he wanted to, he could never avoid so much advice. *AND HE DIDN'T WANT TO.*

He read, with the voracity of an underprivileged kid at a banquet, reams of closely printed and elaborately illustrated "instruction": everything from HOW TO HIT A LOW DRIVE OFF A HIGH TEE to A HIGH WEDGE OUT OF LOW GRASS. Nicklaus, in the morning *News-Call-Bulletin,* told him to GRIP THE CLUB TIGHTLY AND SMASH THE BALL WITH THE RIGHT HAND. In the evening *Examiner-Bugle-Times,* Palmer intoned, GET THE RIGHT SHOULDER UNDER, KEEP THE LEFT HAND SQUARE TO THE LINE OF FLIGHT, DON'T GRIP THE CLUB TOO HARD, AND DON'T UNCOCK THE WRISTS TOO SOON.

As if by some omniscient timing, every tip applied to Swipe's most current problem. On the locker room bulletin board there was tacked, STAND ERECT AND KEEP THE BODY TURNING LIKE A CORKSCREW. True, he'd been swaying too much. Inscribed on the dining room menu was, USE THE FORWARD PRESS TO RELIEVE TENSION IN YOUR HANDS, ARMS, AND CLAVICLE. Yeah, yeah. Been too tight lately. A pro on TV demonstrated, in slow motion, TWITCH THE EYELIDS JUST BEFORE AND JUST AFTER HITTING PUNCH 6-IRONS INTO THE WIND ON COURSES ALONG THE EASTERN SEABOARD. Right. Must try that.

On Swipe's bookshelves gathered volume upon volume written by U.S. Open champions, or anyone who had finished 10th in the Cajun Classic, and who felt a sublime duty to offer up panaceas for the duckhook, the banana ball, and the apple in the throat. A PGA champ smiled from a box of breakfast food and beckoned him to TAKE A DEEP BREATH BEFORE STARTING THE BACKSWING, AND HOLD IT THROUGHOUT THE STROKE. Gasp!

Swipe listened raptly to a cab driver who feverishly explained that the proper wrist action for hitting sand shots was the same as he used to flip his meter. Uh huh.

All the material of golfing erudition that came funneling into him finally became impossible to retain. He needed it all—ALL. But how to keep it? He devised a system of writing pertinent tips on his wrists so they would be with him wherever he went, be it trap, rough, fairway, or boudoir. Not enough room! He filled his bared arms with indelible, sweat-resistant reminders to KEEP THE KNEES RELAXED, KEEP THE RIGHT ELBOW POINTING DOWN, THE HEAD IS THE ANCHOR—DON'T DARE UNMOOR IT. There was not enough skin to hold the profusion. On to the clothing!

Dark-hued clothing made reading difficult. He took to wearing all white. Black-inked memoranda rapidly saturated his clothing. He was swarmed over with print. He resembled a living, breathing newspaper. Were he to fall and lie prone for any length of time he might have been wrapped around a fish.

It began to take its toll on him. Standing before a golf ball he would become paralytic, his body corpse-cold and rigid as he sought to remember: ESSAY THE BACKSWING WITH A LATERAL MOVEMENT OF THE LEFT PATELLA AND A FORCING OF THE WEIGHT TO THE RIGHT, PARTICULARLY ONTO THE INSIDE OF THE RIGHT HEEL. One day Putney tried to incorporate into one 8-iron shot Nicklaus's flying right elbow, Casper's left leg flax, Player's firm right side, Boros's grip, and Palmer's desire. After some 10 minutes of getting the concepts arranged in his mind, he tried to hit the ball. He wound up like a machine in some crackpot inventor's workshop, and swung. A ligament in his knee was torn, he ruptured blood vessels in his hands, got an upset stomach. The ball skittered straight left and almost maimed a fellow on another fairway practicing Middlecoff's pause at the top of the swing.

Physically, Putney was becoming a cripple. Psychologically, he was approaching the same impasse. He was unable to sleep. Pills were called in, and he dozed. Yes. But he dreamed, too. He dreamed he was in a pro shop. There were thousands of cardigan sweaters standing around, ghoulishly empty but in various golf swing positions. An echoing babble of golf instruction emanated from the mohair shrouds.

Another dream. He was walking alone on a tree-lined fairway. From behind a tree popped a tan face that whispered, "HIT IT WITH YOUR RIGHT HAND," then disappeared into the dark forest. Another face from behind another tree. "HIT IT WITH YOUR LEGS." And another. "HIT IT WITH YOUR HEAD." The anonymous voices hissed the advice, tittered madly, then faded way. Swipe awoke from these dreams in a sweat, hands clutched together in an interlocking grip.

More pills, and finally, a concluding nightmare. He is sitting at a huge round table. All around are famous and not-so-famous golfers. There's the short, pudgy Sarazen, the silver-haired Armour, the lean, hard Hogan. Many, many more, living and dead. There is Nelson and Snead, Locke and Casper, Palmer and Finsterwald. There is Moody and Coody, and his home pro and his playing partners. All are talking at once: "SWING SLOW . . . SWING FAST . . . SWING EASY . . . SWING HARD . . . RIGHT HAND SHOULD FACE THE SKY . . . WATCH the V'S SO THEY POINT TO THE RIGHT SHOULDER . . . LEFT SHOULDER SHOULD POINT TO THE . . . KEEP YOUR EARS STEADY AND YOUR NOSE CLEAN . . . THE HANDKERCHIEF MUST STAY UNDER THE ELBOW THROUGHO . . . DON'T PURSE YOUR LIPS ON 7-IRON SHOTS, BECAUSE . . ."

Putney turns to each speaker, but they are talking too quickly for him to seize and hold all this rich lode of information. And he wants it all VERY BADLY. What an opportunity! All these greats and near-greats together, doling out, free of charge, priceless filberts of golfing method. "Give me time," he pleads.

But the voices continue, now all at once, bleating their messages. Swipe searches for pencil and paper, but there's none to be had. Surely he'll never remember it all. A sinking sensation comes to his chest. He can no longer understand a thing being said. All of a sudden there comes a tremendous flush of paper onto the table. Quires of golfing counsel are strewn about. The bulk is so great that the voices are muffled. Putney picks off a sheet and reads: HIT DOWN ON THE BALL WHEN YOU WANT IT TO GO UP, HIT UP ON IT WHEN YOU WANT IT TO GO DOWN, AND DON'T HIT IT AT ALL WHEN YOU WANT IT TO GO STRAIGHT. Putney gathers as much as he can, stuffing his pajamas.

Meanwhile, the people around the table are picking up sheets and, pounding them angrily, denying or affirming their contents. The voices grow higher in pitch. Shrill arguments break out. Some fold the sheets into airplanes and hurl them at each other. The inside-out swing is having a dog-fight with the outside-in swing. Like a Stuke divebomber, the stiff left arm seeks to destroy the lateral pivot. There is bedlam, a wild cacophony of do's and don'ts, how to's and how not to's.

Swipe looks up. Beyond the table he sees, in a pale light, an old wizened man wearing a tam o'shanter and a 12-button jacket of plaid wool. He is calmly smoking a pipe and has under his arm a huge hunk of curved lumber—an ancient golf club, perhaps the first. The old pipe smoker is smiling gently as he watches the people around the table. He shakes his head sagely and nods to Putney to leave. But no, Swipe can't leave now. Someone might tell him the cure for his pull-hook, or flabby 5-iron. The ancient gentleman motions one more chance for Swipe to leave the madhouse of instruction. Putney wavers briefly. But then, Sarazen barks that "ALL GRIPS SHOULD BE THE CIRCUMFERENCE OF DRAINAGE PIPES, AND THE HOLE AS BIG AS AN APPLE BASKET." Swipe takes a firmer grip on the edge of the table. "More, more," he wails. The tam o'shanter and 12-button jacket dissolve into the woodwork leaving only a tendril of pipe smoke.

Sam Snead begins to drawl something about a li'l ole idea he came up with that made the big difference in his game. "AH BEGAN TO . . ." but Snead's voice is lost in the din. "Begin to what?" Swipe asks wildly. He missed that. Snead's voice comes back into range. "SO AH MOVED THE CLUB OVER JUST A MITE TOWARD THE . . ." and again it dims out. "Over a mite where?" Putney shrieks. It is too much for him. There is a cataclysmic tightening in his chest. Swipe slumps from the chair. He is lying under the table and is being kicked by hundreds of two-tone shoes. He gasps for air, tries to raise himself, but is no longer strong enough. He hears Snead again ". . . AND THAT WAY AH COULD GET IT THE WAY AH LAHKED."

Swipe is in severe pain as he wakes from his nightmare. He grabs for the telephone to call his doctor. But he takes the wrong grip on the phone, and he dies.

TIMES
&
PLACES

HYPOCRISY IS EVERYONE'S HANDICAP IN THE RYDER CUP MATCHES

(New York Times—1993)

The American professional golfers playing for the United States in the Ryder Cup match next week in Britain go on at great length about what it means to tee it up for their country. In hushed tones with a hint of tears, they talk of representing the Stars and Stripes, and suggest that their knees weaken when their national anthem is played at the opening ceremony.

But after the comments some of them made recently about making the traditional visit to the White House, you wonder if they fully understand the symbolism that so moves them.

Paul Azinger said he wasn't pleased with the idea of shaking hands with a "draft dodger." Lee Janzen, Payne Stewart, and Corey Pavin said they did not like the president's plans to tax the rich and give the money to, in their words, "people who don't give a damn."

Of course, they have every right to express their views, which points up why they are more than a little naive about a visit to the White House. The appearance as a team is a gesture that honors not the details of the nation's policies at the moment but the principles it stands for, as well as its much larger stance in the world.

NATIONALISM OVER FELLOWSHIP

But then, misunderstood goals are not new to the Ryder Cup. The match has long been heralded as a meeting of golfers to foster international good fellowship, a kind of communion to enrich the game; who actually wins is irrelevant.

Is this true? Not on your life! The competition has always been larded with a heavy dose of nationalism satisfied only by victory. Gallery reactions have always been a good indicator of this. When playing in Britain, American players who hit poor shots are often applauded. Their good shots are greeted with a great roar of silence.

American fans respond similarly here. If winning is not the point, why did Fred Couples break down in tears for failing his teammates with a poor shot in the closing moments of the 1989 match? He's never been so emotional in losing a close one before.

In a competition touted as promoting golf and camaraderie and not crass capitalism, the European Ryder Cup side has sold itself to a liquor maker and promotes the event as the Johnny Walker Cup. What's more, the Europeans will for the third time in a row stage the match at The Belfry in Sutton Colfield, a resort course, not in any way up to the architectural standard this competition demands. But the British PGA did a deal with The Belfry. For a very nominal yearly rent, the PGA makes its headquarters there. In return it has to hold the Ryder Cup there at least twice. The match, of course, gives The Belfry considerable, valuable exposure.

The PGA of America, which administers the U.S. Ryder Cup side, has steadfastly refused to go commercial with a title sponsor, but its choice of the site for the 1991 match, the Ocean Course on Kiawah Island, South Carolina, had a sniff of commercial interest. The course, barely completed a few months before the competition was played and without many peripheral amenities needed, was owned by the Landmark Land Co., a major golf resort and homesite developer that is now out of business after struggling with a savings and loan problem.

So the Ryder Cup is not all it has been trumped up to be as an international communion of the golfing spirit. But that is in keeping with its origination. According to Herb Graffis, who wrote *The PGA,* a history of the association, the idea for a competition between British and American pros was hatched in the early 1920s by the PGA of America as a way to get its members better jobs—just like a labor union would do.

George Sargent, an influential American club professional, was quoted in Graffis's book as saying, "Too often when American clubs needed professionals they would get lads from the old country, and we had been training very good American boys as pros. So, to show a strong offense as the best defense we . . . began the Ryder Cup Matches . . . [which] stopped the idea that British golfers were easy superiors of American professionals."

CUP FULL OF COMMERCIALISM

The first foray was in 1921, when a group of American pros traveled to Britain a couple of weeks in advance of the British Open. That led to the official Ryder Cup competition, begun in 1927. But a tint of commercialism existed even then. For example, the U.S. team's expenses for the '21 trip were picked up by *Golf Illustrated* magazine in an effort to increase circulation and generate goodwill among golf professionals. And consider the name of the competition itself: The cup was donated by Samuel Ryder, a British seed merchant who was a late convert to golf. Extolled as a prince of golf for his support of the old Scotsgame, and a proponent of inter-Atlantic goodwill, it seems Ryder was also doing a bit of business on the side. As Graffis points out, his firm also "had British and American [golf] courses as patrons."

Which brings up a remark Payne Stewart made a few weeks ago in discussing the fact that the Ryder Cup players are not compensated except for expenses. "As players, being on the Ryder Cup team is the biggest honor you can have. But now the media and the PGA have made it a money deal, big business, and the character of it is being lost. Maybe we players should start sharing in the pie, get a cut of the action."

Spoken like a capitalist, a real pro. But one thing is wrong with Stewart's statement: The character of the Ryder Cup isn't being lost, only revealed.

MERION: THE OPEN COURSE

(Golf Magazine—1971)

What is a "great" golf course? The term has been so overused, and thus abused, that it has lost much of its real qualitative force. Yet there is such a thing. Golf architect George Fazio thinks that if a course is to be considered "great" it must have no more than one weak or ordinary hole. A sound judgment, but it doesn't go far enough. St. Andrews has a number of ordinary holes and is still thought of as "great." There's more to it then, than a full or near-full run of fine holes. Another course builder, Pete Dye, gets more to the whole point when he says, "A great course should have the Atlantic Ocean on one side, the Pacific on the other, and Ben Hogan or Arnold Palmer winning a tournament on it." That last part is the key expander on Fazio's remark. Greatness, in the case of a golf course anyway, derives from a combination of good architecture *and* human events of significance occurring on it. If you accept those criteria then Merion's East Course, scene of this year's U.S. Open, has a claim to greatness that, to snip a phrase from Joseph Conrad, "rings like unto bullion."

I'm inclined to give a slight nod to man-made happenings in evaluating "greatness." A beautiful piece of ground by itself is essentially bloodless until some of us upright mammals *do* something on it. If not for the Charge of the Light Brigade, the Valley of Death would be just another flat spot between mountains. As it happens, though, Merion has a beautifully balanced mixture of superb golfing terrain and events of historical consequence to the game—plus a lagniappe of interesting and entertaining anecdotes.

Since the opening of the course, in 1912, wicker "baskets" have topped the pins on Merion's greens. It's the only golf course in the world today with this distinctive innovation. The course's designer, Hugh Wilson, had taken an extended trip through the British Isles to get ideas for what would become Merion. It's generally believed he saw such baskets at one of the layouts he visited and incorporated them at his course. No one has been able to say where Wilson might have first seen them used. To theorize, it was probably on some Scottish links where cloth flags would be tattered in a fortnight by the sea winds and the local parsimonians found the baskets pleasingly and properly economical. The baskets used to be handmade locally around Philadelphia, but the cost became prohibitive (many are stolen every year) and they are now made in, and imported from, of all places, Hong Kong.

Merion is sown in a fine dwarf strain of Kentucky bluegrass, a hardy, heat-resistant grass that can be cut as low as a half inch. It is called Merion Blue, and for good reason. A patch of it was first discovered behind the East Course's 17th green by Joe Valentine, Merion's first greenkeeper (course superintendent it is, now). Valentine, an outstanding agronomist and a legend in his field, brought the strain to the attention of the USGA's Green Section in 1937, and it soon became a standard fairway grass on American courses.

No golfer's career is more intimately woven into the history of Merion than Bobby Jones's. Merion is the front and back covers that enclose this great player's book of achievement. It was at Merion where Bobby, at age 14, played in his very first major championship, the 1916 U.S. Amateur. Childe Bobby stunned the golfing community with his prodigal talent, and temper. He led the first round of qualifying, and beat two older, established players before bowing out to the defending champion. He also banged a few mashies to the ground, which got him more than a few questionable glances and something of a "bad press." Eight years later, at Merion, a far more mature Jones won his first major title, the U.S.

Amateur, and of course, it was at Merion where, in 1930, he defeated Eugene Homans in the finals of yet another U.S. Amateur to complete his famous "impregnable quadrilateral," the Grand Slam.

Jones closed Homans out on the 11th hole, and a bronze plaque set in a drinking fountain beside the tee commemorates the occasion. But the 11th hole has even more to make it one of the richer stretches of golf turf in the game's history. It's only 378 yards long and from the tee is not very prepossessing. You can't even see it all. But when you come to the crest of a steeply descending hill about 130 yards out, its aesthetic charm and strategic beauty become readily apparent. The green is fronted by the "Bubbling Brook," an alternately wide and narrow water hazard that courses around to also guard the right side and rear of the putting surface. While the second shot is rarely more than a seven-iron for the big players, it is a shot that can bring, and has brought, a jerk to the smoothest swings of the finest players. In the third round of the '34 Open at Merion, Bobby Cruickshank, leading the field at the start of the day on the strength of two 71s, struck a weak approach to 11. The ball descended into Bubbling Brook, but the ball landed on a rock in the shallow stream and bounced onto the green. Cruickshank went from deep depression to high elation in a moment. He was so excited at his good fortune he threw his club high in the air and shouted, "Thank you, Lord." No sooner were his words out than Bobby was knocked in the noggin by his falling niblick. It was a forceful blow that felled him. His playing partner, Wiffy Cox, immediately turned fight referee and began to count Bobby out (they had a sense of humor in those days). Wiffy wasn't all wrong. Bobby was so shaken he finished 77–76 to end up two strokes off the pace.

The 11th was the platform for another tragic, if not comic, event of note. It was the same '34 Open. Gene Sarazen, leading by two going into the final round, came to the hole and decided to play safely from the tee with a two-iron (today's power players, almost to the man, will lay up on this hole this year). But Gene hooked badly into a creek at the far left, took a drop in the rough, hit the next shot into the water behind the green, and eventually made a seven. He lost to Olin Dutra by a single stroke.

The television people would do well by their audience if they showed the action at this 11th hole, rather than keeping to the customary last five. Those final "quarry holes" are good ones (the 17th, in particular, is a tremendous par-three), but 11 has a special quality all its own. Walter Hagen once called it "Black Friday."

In one respect, Merion has had the luck of good timing, which is essential to the development of "greatness." Bobby Jones might well have slammed grandly at Winged Foot, or Baltusrol. Chance was again good to Merion in 1950, the year Ben Hogan returned to championship golf after his terrible car-bus collision. It was the Golden Anniversary U.S. Open, and while Hogan's body may have been shattered, and only marginally mended, his determined spirit, his unique genius for hitting golf shots, and his acute golfing intelligence were never impaired. As to the latter, Hogan played his first practice round over Merion with his good friend Francis Sullivan, a Philadelphia lawyer and member of the club. As Sullivan relates it, at the 18th, a long, strong par-four, he told Ben that the line off the tee was the flagpole directly behind the green. Ben drove precisely where told. The next day, same hole, Sullivan reminded Hogan of the line. But this time Ben said, "No, it's five yards to the right." The day before, Hogan's drive finished on the sidehill slope in the middle of the fairway. It's a bit shorter shot in from there, but five yards to the right there is a level piece of ground, which also affords a better view of the green.

The first three days of the championship Ben drove to the flat spot. On the 72nd hole, however, he pulled his drive to the middle of the fairway. It was not a propitious moment. He needed a four to tie Lloyd Mangrum and George Fazio for the title. Hogan's two-iron shot from there has gone on record as one of the game's finest and most memorable. But in fact, Hogan told writer Charles Price afterward that it wasn't a very good shot at all. It did finish some 60 feet from the hole, on the green, but from Hogan's perspective on shot-making his demur is understandable. But those who were merely spectators saw only this small man in a white cap, under the consuming pressure of an Open, limping on legs no one ever thought would walk on anything again, let alone a golf course, striking a ball with the toughest club in the bag from an uneven lie. To put it anywhere on the green, hell, just to hit the ball at all, was enough to raise hosannas for a lifetime.

Hogan, of course, two-putted that final green and caused a three-way tie. Again Charles Price recalls that Ben's first putt went some four feet past, and that Ben hit the second putt so quickly he (Price) was amazed. When he asked Ben, normally a deliberate putter, why he stroked such an important putt so quickly, Hogan replied that his legs were aching so, he was so tired, that he just wanted to sit down somewhere. By the way, Hogan's two-iron was stolen right after that fourth round and the next day he played with only 13 clubs.

The Hogan, Mangrum, Fazio playoff featured one of the more bizarre incidents in golf history. At the 16th green Mangrum had a medium-sized putt to stay within a shot of Ben. Fazio was pretty much out of it by this time. As Lloyd stood over the putt an insect perched itself on his ball and would not move off. Finally, Mangrum lifted the ball and blew the gnat away. He then holed the putt to stay close to Ben. At the 17th Lloyd prepared to take the honor. As he was teeing up, USGA official Ike Grainger broke through the crowd and informed Mangrum that he would have to be assessed a two-stroke penalty for removing a foreign object from his ball, which was against the rules at the time. George Fazio remembers that Lloyd was stunned, then damn angry. He slammed his four-wood into his bag, and Fazio had to work hard to keep Lloyd from making a scene. Lloyd didn't, and Hogan won by four shots.

With this upcoming Open, Merion will have been a stage on which every era of American golf in this century has performed; from Jones-Hagen, to Hogan-Snead, to Palmer-Nicklaus. Jack, of course, did not play in the '50 Open, but he has already played in competition at Merion. And my how he did play. It was in the 1960 World Amateur team championship, and the 20-year-old Nicklaus had rounds of 66, 67, 68, 68. His 269 total was 18 better than that of Hogan, Mangrum, and Fazio. It was phenomenal golf, and for many people portends the end of Merion as a venue for future Opens. The feeling is that the East Course, at 6,700 yards (par is 70), may have become too short for today's players. Perhaps. Many other respected people in golf think that only if there is a lot of rain a week to 10 days before the start of play will the course be wracked up.

Nicklaus played those four rounds of his in something much less than an Open. This can be largely discounted, though, since he is one of the all-time great "championship" golfers—when he wants to be. For the "majors" he usually wants to be. But those four sub-70 rounds were also shot in the fall of the year, in damp, misty, windless weather. The course was soft physically, and therefore figuratively. The point is, Merion has long been noted for its very firm greens. You have to play approach shots from the fairways to hold hard greens, and Merion promises to be tight off the tee and long in the rough. Even if playing from well-clipped grass with tight corner-pin placements, of which there are plenty, players will take great risks in flying it right to the stob. Also, under normal conditions, Merion's greens are extremely fast and have always had many very subtle rolls and breaks. If they are firm at Open time, and only the gods can make a difference because the proud Merion people in charge of the course's condition may cut off the drinking fountains, that factor will probably balance the short yardage.

So the matter of timing, destiny if you will, is going to play a role once again in the history of Merion—in its "greatness." Up to now it has been lucky. Then again, no matter what the conditions of play this year, Merion may still prove to have served its time and have been passed over by a game that, in terms of the best golf played, has outdistanced it.

In any case, that L-shaped spate of golfing earth that has served the game so well for so many years will always be etched in the heraldic pageantry of the old Scotsgame—will always evoke images of Bob Jones on number 11, Hogan at 18, Nicklaus everywhere, and a legion of others who brought what nerves and talent they had to its turf.

WASHINGTON'S WHEELING DEALERS

(Golf Magazine—1970)

Visiting the nation's capital one day, I
was driving down Pennsylvania Avenue from the great-domed Congress.
Easing past the White House, I spun around the pristine Washington
Monument, took a few more turnings, and found myself in East Potomac
Park. Strangely enough, there was a golf course there, and a group of
golfers who gamble at the game under a system as intricate as any lobby-
ing techniques used on the Hill, as frenzied as business transacted on the
Stock Exchange.

The participants were night-shift cab drivers, ex-vaudeville hoofers,
government hacks (to be confused with hackers), and just plain hustlers.
Their action, far removed from civil rights, dams in Colorado, or parity for
Iowa farmers, revolved around what is called the Wheel, a system bringing
good players and bad together on somewhat equal terms, and allowing a
large number of men to compete against each other at once. The system,
fraught with financial hazards and strategic maneuvers, reduced my customary quarter nassaus to something as uncomplicated and simple as a
newborn babe's diet.

The Wheel is this. Say there are 12 golfers on the floor of the exchange. That is, the clubhouse. Two of them, fearless investors in the mold of Jay Gould, form a partnership called the Wheel. They match their best ball on a hole-by-hole basis against the Field. The Field is comprised of as many two-man teams as wish to compete. For simplicity, if each of the 10 men outside the Wheel collaborates with each of the 9 others, there are 81 teams in the Field. Each of those in the Field can gamble as much as he cares to on each match. The usual is two dollars. So, the man in the Field with nine partners has $18 riding against the Wheel. That super-gutsy duo, the Wheel, plays all 81 teams over a nine-hole distance, and for total money of $162. Now that's a nice little game.

A business day is not a business day unless there's a Wheel. Without one it is a black night in which men wager in boring skin games, or fiddle around the putting clock. Dull, dull. Some go home, of all places. Others meander over to the bowling alley to find a bit of action. Still, getting two men to Wheel is not easy. The fear of losing a bundle fosters caution. While the Wheel doesn't usually lose all its bets, or win them all (the more bets the less chance of "taking a bath," so they say), the pressure is obviously terrific. Should the Wheelers bogey the same hole there's due cause for a leaping-type depression. Yet, since these gents do like their daily "trick," a day rarely goes by when two men will not dare the Field.

The exchange opens around 11 A.M. every snowless day that temperatures exceed 35 degrees. The round of offers and counteroffers leading to the formation of a Wheel takes about two hours. The bargaining points involve the pairing of golfers to form the Wheel, and compromises made regarding handicap.

The handicapping system is suitably unique—hardly USGA-approvable. Actually, it is quite simple. There's no such thing as a 2-, or a 10-handicapper, which is always questionable anyway. There are top-men and bottom-men. A top-man can hit the greens of par-five holes in two, usually makes at least one birdie in every nine holes, has a full set of clubs, and "swings good at it." Bottom-men are prone to killing snakes with tee shots or hitting chip shots twice with a single swing, and own little canvas bags. Each man on the floor of the exchange knows very well his own and every other man's full market value under this system, which smacks more of the ancient Greek *agora* than the coldly modern computerized marketplace.

Handicapping, then, is not by strokes, but by other compensatory methods. For example, a short hitter is given steps. This novelty allows him to move 40 steps ahead of the tees on par-four holes, 50 steps on par-fives, and to drive from these advanced positions. If steps are in order, a typical scene has three players driving from the regular tee, then the stepper striding out onto the fairway like Mickey Mouse playing Paul Bunyan. He grunts and he groans as he stretches for every possible inch. Split breeches are commonplace, hernias a constant threat.

Another feature in this very special handicapping system is the option clause. A bottom-man will Wheel if his partner is a top-man and he, the bottom-man, can forsake his own drive, drop a ball where his partner has driven, and play his second from there. You can see why the bargaining sessions take up so much time. Everyone stands around the pro shop–cafeteria waggling irons, stroking putters, drinking coffee, discussing women, money, horse races, meanwhile keeping a keen ear open for an interesting offer—waiting for someone to "make a mistake" is the term— and fish-eyeing the others for signs of vulnerability.

The men on the floor have to be *struck* with an offer. A few may like one, but there is no common agreement. Everyone just shuffles around, hemming and hawing like congressmen weighing constituency vote demands against private interests. With things at a standstill, the arrival on the floor of a known Wheeler may spur excitement. Or a real crisis may stampede bears into bulls. It may be late autumn and a day threatening early darkness. Or, "hey, the first tee is open, we can get on the course." All the cunning calculations are thrown to the wind, everyone says "what the hell," and the Wheel spins. In the rush to the first tee, the slips are written.

The slips are the Wheel's buy-order forms. Each man in the Field marks his name on a piece of paper, then his partner's names and how much money he is betting on each match. These are handed to the Wheelers, who, for the first time, find out how much pressure is on them. If the Wheel finds they are responsible for more money than they would make in a month if, God forbid, they had a regular job (a Wheel has run into thousands), they will, if they can, lay off some of the play.

Mingling with the golfers are sidemen, investment brokers in Wheel play. These well-heeled sporting gentlemen, who would rather watch than play, but will bet in all cases, pick up a percentage of the total play on the Wheel. Sometimes a Wheel is formed when sidemen coax two men with their support. These deals are consummated in the manner of those made on the floor in Wall Street. The pact is closed with a nod, or a point of the finger. On to the golf course!

The rules of play offer another bizarre improvisation on the Grand Old Game. All players, excluding step men, tee off from the very front of the raised tee, no matter where the markers may be. It's a standardization of procedure that keeps everyone honest. Improvement of lies may be made anywhere on the course, except in bunkers, an odd quirk since the traps haven't been raked since the last coming. But so it is.

As for improving the lies on the grass, this is an outlet for each individual's ingenuity and creativity. There is no simple nudging of the ball to a bit of full turf with the turn of a clubhead. No no. Turf is kicked up with the heel of a shoe, then twisted around by hand until it looks like the turret on a Gothic castle. The ball is set atop this pinnacle, and if you can't get it into the air from this lie you need a shovel. Putting a ball on a real tee, however, is a serious breach of the rules.

A golf ball may be changed anywhere on the course. Some fellows, confident of their driving game, use a new buck-and-a-quarter pellet from the pegs. But in the fairways, where an iron is required, the shiner goes into their pocket and an old graying warhorse, bruised and nicked, is dropped to the ground. Notification of a ball change, usually from a newcomer, is met with a condescending "he'll learn" smile. You see, it's the essence of the game these fellows are interested in. Why get boggled up with all the nuances? Leave that for the purists. The game itself is the gamble.

The golf course itself is as flat as a fashion model. No major championship, hah!, no minor championship will ever be decided on this track. It's a wide-open course of no distinction, but that's not the point. The layout facilitates a communication system between all those in the action. The Wheelers play in the first foursome, carefully paired with two birdie-shooting top-men to keep the heat on them. As if their burden of 81 matches were not enough. The two men paired with the Wheelers are responsible for notifying everyone behind them of the progress of the Wheel. They transmit hole-by-hole results by a method not unlike that used on the high seas.

Signals begin with a sweeping circular movement of the arm, followed by any of three additional movements of that same arm. Should the Wheel birdie a hole, the arm comes out of its spin and plunges down to signify one under par. If a birdie seems inevitable (a one-footer, let's say), the signal man has his arm spinning while the putt is being addressed, and the full signal is out before the ball hits the bottom of the cup. If the "sure thing" is somehow missed (could the spinning arm directly behind the putter have done that?) there's every chance the signaler may break an arm. Should there be an eagle by the Wheel, the arm plunges down twice, like a man with a nervous tic, which may not be far from the truth.

If the Wheel pars a hole, the signal is a sweeping gesture like a base-ball umpire's safe sign. A bogey, understandably, is the cue for some enthu-siastic gyrations of histrionic proportions. The arm jerks straight up like a fevered Nazi at a Bund meeting. An accompanying leap adds a note of jubilation to the news. A BOGEY, a BOGEY. One over! For three holes behind, other men are jumping up and down like kids on pogo sticks. As they all approach the scene of the bogey they saunter easily, knowing a par will win. And they still bogey the hole themselves. But that's another story, isn't it?

After the nine-hole spin of the Wheel there is a conclave behind the final green. It's settling-up time, and reckoning is swift. The Wheelers stand with slips in hand and tick off their wins, losses, and ties. No scorecards are kept. The signal system is more than sufficient. Hole-by-hole results are vivid in everyone's mind. By the time a player prepares to putt on the last hole he knows to the dime how much the putt is worth. Like any good business, this one runs simply . . . to those who know what's going on.

From any angle on the course one sees impressive reminders of the nation's past, and present. The white-domed Capitol is off to the east, the Jefferson Memorial is but a long par-five north. However, the timeless beauty of these grand structures is lost on the Wheelers and the Field. These speculator-golfers live only for the moment, not the monument. The Washington Memorial? It's just the line for a tee shot. Which, by the way, it is.

THE MASTERS, AN IDEA BETRAYED?

(Golf Magazine—1971)

On television you can follow the flight of a golf ball beautifully against all the trees at the Augusta National Golf Club. Simpleton that I am, that was just about enough to make the Masters a terrific tournament for me. Pah! Most everyone acts toward the event like neighborhood priests at an audience with the Pope, and such a skimpy evaluation as mine is next to saying St. Peter's is a great cathedral because it has such an impressive apse. Strange things happen to people when it comes to the Masters. Television announcers broadcasting from Augusta lose their usual sharp-edged crackle and sound as if they're murmuring pars, birdies, and eagles while running a string of golf balls through their fingers. Most of the writers become church scribes and brush their copy with ecclesiastical reverence. Only drop the name—*Masters*—on a professional or amateur golfer and he practically collapses in a state of divine delirium.

While not a particularly religious man, I do like golf quite a lot, and whenever anyone waxes evangelistic about something to do with the game I can be sold. Which is undoubtedly why, having never actually attended a Masters, I began to feel like a monk who had yet to kneel before a crucifix. At the same time, however, there's a strong streak of pro-letarian back-porch-Chicago-bred cynicism in me, and such piety over what is, in the end, only a golf tournament, leads me to question the atti-tude and that which provokes it. So when last year I finally did "journey to Jerusalem," as it were, I was of at least a couple of minds about the halo of sanctification that appears to encircle Mr. Jones's and Mr. Roberts's annual Georgia Passion Play.

When you enter the main gate of the Augusta National Golf Club and move down its tree-shrouded lane toward the simple white clubhouse it's like a trip back into the twilight zone of early-20th-century moneyed-class America. There is an air of quiet gentility free of commercialism. That's part of the tournament's charm, and intention, it is said. I had an impression that the town itself was in this mold—a pokey village with pointed spires punctuating the skyline, and where prosperous burghers bought all their provisions at Priscilla Tompkin's hardware store. Not much of any of this holds water.

The western approach to the city is over a ribbon of four-lane con-crete. Downtown opens with the Georgia Railroad Bank building, a tall steel-and-glass birdcage out of current architecture's standard playbook. The building may be a move toward urban renewal. Across from it is a row of cheap restaurants and various hangouts for young soldiers out of near-by Fort Gordon. "Our boys" are sidewalk-hawked into two-bit photos and "joolry." For a couple of blocks there is the normal run of merchandisers and movie houses, then loan agencies, Realtors, and gaudy discount shops. Downtown finally folds into the shantytown wooden dwellings of the blacks. That peters out fairly close to the Augusta National, which may once have been sequestered from any taint of the commonalty, but is now fronted by banner-festooned and neon-lighted gas stations, an acre of blacktopped shopping center, and by all means, an Arnold Palmer cleaning establishment.

Modern times do not stop at that cozy Old World entrance to the club. Under the spreading water-oak tree that shades the golf course side of the clubhouse, there gathers a consortium of golf's buyers and sellers of one thing and another. The tournament's timing, geographical location, and developed prestige brings everyone in the game to Augusta during Masters week. Little Ernie Sabayrac, the biggest man in the golf distribut-ing business, is under the tree shaking hands with those who buy, or may buy, his pants, shirts, shoes, sweaters, and other gear. John St. Claire, the

Spalding custom-club man is there; the graying Jack Whitaker is soaking up terminology like *speed-putt* and *fanned it,* none of which will get into his broadcast because there is never time; Bob Drum, the insult king, a sportswriter turned publicity man, is standing around "Don Rickling" friends and foes alike and keeping an ear out for something to do; Gene Sarazen sits in a cloud of nostalgia outside the locker room greeting the thousands who saw "the shot"; rosy-faced Warren Orlick is smiling forth for the PGA, of which he is president; Joe Dey, Jr., radiates his particular Calvinesque sobriety, by which we may always rest assured The Game will not fall to the depths of pro wrestling; Toney Penna is telling Byron Nelson to tell Roberto Bernardini to just take the club back and hit the damn ball; George Fazio, Robert Trent Jones, and Bob von Hagge are telling everyone about the most recent courses they've built; Dan Jenkins is mop-ing around trying to figure out yet another angle for a Dave Marr story; Herbert Warren Wind, in tweeds and with umbrella, glorifies nonetheless in the Georgia sun, happy to be free of his bare *New Yorker* office and to be once again into his game; Charlie Price comes back into the world-at-large from his retreat on Hilton Head Island; a host of other sportswriters from all over the nation get shut of pale faces and essence of basketball court and luxuriate in the warm, clean air reasonably sure their reports will see print. And there is handsome Mark McCormack, the world's tallest agent, selling Arnie and the rest of his horses to shirt-makers, pant-makers, shoe-makers, watch-makers, car-makers, and enthusiasm-makers. It's all going on, the wheeling and dealing, but it's all muted by a special ambience peculiar to the Masters.

A few months after last year's Masters the town of Augusta experi-enced a full-fledged racial uprising—something to do with poor treatment of blacks in the jailhouse. But inside the gates of the Club, Negro waiters slither about with silent antebellum obedience. The black caddies huddle beside the bag room and are not allowed anywhere on the course if not lugging a set of clubs, unless they are on a cleanup crew. There are next to no black faces in the gallery, just as there has never been one among the tournament's contestants. The race issue aside, for the moment, signs des-ignating parking areas for PREFERENTIAL PATRONS, and what seems like one Pinkerton man for every 10 citizens, signal to even the ordinary white folk that they might do well to walk softly in a place where they really don't belong, no matter how much they've paid to get in. It's been said that the genteel decorum of Masters crowds is because they consist mainly of southerners, who are, as we know, bred to politeness. Could be, although the drunken brawls at the Greensboro Open stretch that presumption. You could also say they are bred to "place," which it seems to me is what really pervades the atmosphere of the Masters. It's not religious reverence for the game, as intimated earlier, although in the name of tradition that's what you're led to believe. It's exclusivity—snobbery, really—under which everyone is mesmerized, or cowed, at the Masters. Invitations to play in, or tickets to watch, the Masters are tendered like ducats to a Newport Beach cotillion. The people are given to feel Mr. Astorfeller has let them stroll on his lawn. The golfers get a sense of being country club members and for a week lose something of their real identity as working stiffs earning a buck. It's old-fashioned privilege they're selling at the Masters.

The U.S. Open, in earlier years, had a similar elite quality. Even today there are remnants of it in the gray-mustachioed gentlemen in blue blazers wandering around an Open. But they are really anachronisms, and look it in the light of Opens that have moved with the tenor of the times; that have a more brittle, glossy character representative of golf as it has developed in the country. Everyone can play in the Open. They get in solely on the merit of their current playing ability. This above all else is what makes it a genuine premier golf championship. The Masters has a great course, and the field of players is a good one. But that last is essentially selective, with many in it who do not measure up to the overblown name of the event; who are there at the whim of a few people. The Masters is a half-major championship.

The Masters would like very much to get out from under the weight of ever-growing criticism that no Negro golfer has ever played at Augusta. They might have helped themselves by inviting, under the "sprinkling of non-American players" clause in their qualifications list, the South African Sewgolem. His record, compiled under the most severe restrictions, should be as worthy as that which got Gary Player into the event for the first time. Gary's father wrote a nice letter to Cliff Roberts asking if his son could play in the tournament, and Gary was sent an invitation. The Masters would just as soon *not* have a black player, but they will take one if he should win the Open, say, or at least finish eighth, or if he should garner enough Masters points on the tour. But even if a Charley Sifford or Lee Elder just misses by the Masters point system, there is still a way in. One player (either professional or amateur) not on the invitation list is selected by ballot of Masters champions. In 1969 Sifford won the L.A. Open and some $35,000 up to Masters time. However, he just did fail to put together enough Masters points (it's 30 points for a win, 24 for second, 23 for third, and on down). By an act of will the champions could have broken the barrier and brought Charley into the field. It's difficult to be a fan of Sifford, who can be sullen and surly, but he did prove he was an accomplished professional. Wouldn't you say that one L.A. Open win (Charley has won a couple of other tour titles) is worth as much as Hsieh Yung-Yo's record of tieing for third in a World Cup and winning a Thailand Open? Hsieh was at Augusta on the strength of *that*. But most of our professionals are rooted in traditional racial bias, and they weren't about to let their clubby little tournament be infiltrated by a black man . . . if they didn't have to.

I got my first look at Cliff Roberts in the flesh at a golf writer's meeting the day before play began. While announcements were being made, lots of green-coated men began to appear at the entrance to the room. They had the clean-cut, serious, officious look and manner of federal agents—the kind who hover around presidents of the United States. Somebody big, really big, was coming. I thought. Dick himself? And even *before* a winner was crowned? A hush fell over the room. A woman at a switchboard cautiously pulled down an already long skirt and nervously primped her bun. Black waiters shuffled quietly. Then the green coats stiffened, and into the room came a slightly bent, rather slender old man wearing thick-lensed, plain-framed glasses resting on a narrow, pinched face that seemed not to have smiled since Hagen was a pup. It was Clifford Roberts. That's all. Just old Clifford Roberts, known as sir, or Mr. Roberts to the heathen, a man who makes a lot of money on Wall Street, and through an association with golf and Bob Jones has become a quasi-celebrity because he runs a golf tournament. What a letdown.

Was this kind of pretentiousness what Bob Jones had in mind when he created the tournament? As Dick Schaap points out in his book on the event, no one quite knows for certain who dreamed up the name *Masters*. "I must admit," Jones has said, "that the name was rather born of immodesty." It's original title was the Augusta National Invitational. Golf writer Al Laney has remarked that Jones was never much interested in the organization of the tournament, which he left to Cliff Roberts, who was a cofounder of it. So the original intention of the event—a get-together of some of the best players on a good course for a week of good golf, nothing more—may have gotten away from Jones.

Still, with Jones's abiding interest, his golf course, he has left something very real and lasting. Everything that has been said and written about the course itself is right on the mark. The architecture of that part which actually comes into play is the product of an acute golfing intelligence. The general landscape—the flowers, trees, and undulating terrain—the whole thing, is such that you *feel* like playing golf there. You even feel like *watching* golf there. One gentleman I know told me of a brother of his who came to see a first Masters, and after two days was somewhat bored. It was becoming just another series of arms and legs flailing at, then walking after, golf balls. He was on the verge of leaving early. But then he changed his mind. He decided he had to see more of how those 18 passages would respond to the playing of them. The golf course kept him on, and in effect the golfers somehow became secondary to it. An intriguing turnaround. The course is something of a great green symphony. The more you see it the more secrets you discover. It reaches its height of power when orchestrated by the best players. But even when sawed upon by fifth-rate fiddlers the intrinsic worth of its music will shine through.

So I too, after all my carping about abstractions, have ended up rhapsodizing about the place. Well, the golf course is the only genuine thing that exists at Augusta National. All the rest, the posturing of a Cliff Roberts, including that ultimate production of boredom, the televised presentation in a club room (which was rather nice when Bob Jones was able to take part), is just panache, so many feathers in an oversized helmet.

HEY, FLYTRAP!

GETTIN' TO KNOW YUH!

(Golf Illustrated—1992)

A lot of guys around the K&L is beginning to think that maybe the media is starting to go too far in the way of divulging the interior character of the athletes as in the case of this kid Daly. I mean the deal is does it make any difference whether they are boozers or whatever. The idea is to see the game played real good and that's that.

When he hears this Three From the Edge gets his thinking cap on and talks about how if we know more about the athlete as something beside a ballbeater and competitor then we can more appreciate his performance. Enriches the show Edge says using one of his big words. Then of all people Shag Bag pipes up and says he cant see how if some pro covers the pin with a cut four iron out of an old divot into a wind that that shot is going to be any better enjoyed if he knows the guy hated his father.

Which sounds about right to me until Augie the Snipe chirps up with another example in which a guy blows a three footer and you wonder why because hes always been a great pressure putter but then you find out hes been on the outs with his missus. Now you cant blame the guy so much and call him a loser and choke artist. Right says Shank City who as you may recall has always tried to blame his laterals on the fact he was the middle child of three and no body payed any attention to him. Yeah well sometimes a shank is just a shank as Ziggy the Fraud once said.

Then to refute Shag Bag Fat Shot says it can work for good shots like if you know a guys kids are in trouble with the law or his fathers sick with something bad and he can still nail a downhill 4 iron and hole eight footers when he needsem then he must have some kind of fortitood. Now the game is richened. Yeah I says but if your going to punch up the good things about guys you gotta deal in the bad stuff for the sake of equity as they say in the usga rules of golf book.

Anyway it looked like Edge was up or at least had us dormie. But he wasnt about to just take his winnings and buy the beers. Hes gotta press. He gets on another pedelstall about how athletes are in the public eye playing on the tube and are all role models for the youth of the nation and so the jocks have to be modicums of behavior because if they act up they are setting a bad example.

Well I decide I dont buy that one on the grounds that just for the very reason a jock can hit it pure time after time under the gun then he aint like everybody else and so shouldnt be thought of as such. I mean to get as good as those guys get you gotta spend a lot of time beating balls and thinking about the game your playing and that doesnt leave much time for figuring out how youre supposed to behave as most people do and for another thing when you get that good you begin to think you aint like most people anyhow. You catching my drift. I suppose what you have to do is stop treating these kids like they were special just because they can hit it so good. Yeah. But then you watch one of them make four birds in a row after going for a double bagel the last one coming when he turns a spoon out of some fluff around a corner and gets it back to a pin behind a bunker and stops the ball 10 feet from the stob and your mouth drops and your eyes go up into your forehead and when you get up close to the guy you want to ask him who to vote for in the next election and if he could take a minute to explain nuclear physics. Thats just the way it goes huh.

Hey seeya round. Jocko.

DIFFERENT FOLKS, DIFFERENT STROKES

(Golf Illustrated—1988)

I see where Jack Nicklaus and some of the other ones who are getting long in the teeth are trying to get the square grooves banned because they think the kids who are using them are getting an advantage and can stop the ball on a dime out of the long grass but which they are really saying is that these new kids on the block arent as good a player as their record would leave everyone to believe and are making big checks only because of their equipment.

Yeah sure. And the old folks are also saying the young guys out there now arent the shot makers that was in the game in the old days which makes me wonder if they are actually watching those kids play and if they are if maybe they have some kind of gauze over their eyes because just on teevee alone you can see that theyre all wet. Im thinking for instance about Checkoslovakia at the Masters this year which he almost won. At the last hole he needs par at the worst and he hits him the most beautiful high cut tee shot with a driver that fits right around the corner and ends up what 120 yards from the green.

And that kid Azinger in the PGA at that par five everybody got to in two. When he needs a big high cut with a 3 iron if he's going to do any good and does just that very thing dropping the thing like it was a lump of bitumulus coal four feet from the hole. T Bolt or S Snead or big Jack hisself couldnt have done it any better.

So what are they talken about?

Age is what. You gotta figure the old guys want to kill square grooves because they cant stand seeing the kids doing what they cant do no more. You oughta ask em about that even if they wont give you a straight answer. And ask Jack by the by about his using a metal wood these days which is a bigger help than square grooves.

Hey how about guys like Vardon having to play with those guttie perches which were hard as stone and didnt jump off the club and spin and stuff like the ball that the guys in Ohio invented which is kind of like what we play with now. And whattaya think Bobby Jones and Walter Hagen and those guys coulda said about Nelson and Hogan and Snead getting to play with steel shafts instead of hickory which torked all over the joint. And whattaya think Hogan and Snead and Nelson could say to Nicklaus and Watson about the kinda grass they had to play offa and putt on which is like comparing a brillo pad to a hunka silk. Yeah a guys gotta pretty good chance of hittin 2 irons as high as the tallest building when hes hittin it offa the kind of grass Nicklaus grew up on. And what about the better steel for the shafts and better balls that go farther and are more consistent.

Which brings up the bit about Nicklaus being named the Golfer of the Century the gimmick one of your rivals put together. I heard through the grapevine that when it was announced everybody in the room stood up except Hogan and Snead and that they just barely clapped. Cant blame 'em.

Player of the century. Maybe when everybody plays with the same equipment off the same kind of ground for a hunnert years running then you maybe can name somebody that. Best player of his time Nicklaus. That Ill give him. How could you not.

Hey, see ya around Jocko.

KIZMET

(Golf Illustrated—1992)

So were sitting over at the K&L having breakfast before heading out to the Bumps and Augie the Snipe is digging away at a half of fresh grapefruit of which they are very good right now with a lot of juice and he gets a squirt dead in the eye and he revolts back in his chair and howls out more than you ordinarily due when you get one of those because hes got his contracts on which are especially unfavorable to such insult. Three From the Edge is in one of his philosophical moods and after Snipe gets over his convulsions chimes up with how the squirt could just as soon of caught him on his forehead or cheek or the front of his shirt and which is the same thing with putts that get right in front of the hole then turn away from it as if its got morning mouth. So like what made it turn away from the hole. Kizmet says Chili Dip in a low voice as his mouth is full of bagel and peanut butter and Edge says right its fate and then he interprelates about how its the same thing in golf as it is when it was decided hunnerts and hunnerts of years ago that last night at 11 pm two ships could collide in the middle of the ocean.

Well at first flush we all start groaning that were in for one of his seeges about golf and god and like that. Which we were but also as usual we couldnt help getting into it ourselfs and thinking about all the what ifs that have sunk us through no fault of our own into depths of repair. Like spike marks which you cant fix and which is still the worst rule in golf as why can you fix a pit mark some guys ball makes and he didnt fix but not a clod he brings up with his feet and how if you hadda little more cut on your iron youda maybe been to the right of the clod that knocked your ball off line and instead woulda hadda free run to the pot.

That gets Blue Dart thinking about at least a few dozen of his snaphooks that caught the left side of a tree and went farther into the woods and how if hed hit it a little less out on the toe the ball woodna darted as much and woulda caught the right side of the tree and ended up on the fairway with a short iron home. Yeah and it could also have missed the tree alltogether and finished in a bush or hit an acorn when it landed and bounced straight up and stopped against the trunk.

Yeah says Fade It and what if his banana which he always calls a fade gets the good bounce out but finishes in the middle of a divot. Does that mean two different gods or whatever are in the action he asks.

Which is a good question. Anyway it starts getten pretty giddy with each guy coming up with a what if of his own. Pin High was the farthest fetcher when he goes on about what if he didnt have a taste for fresh pineapple the day he tried to qualify for the county. So everybody says what do you mean and he says he was peeling the thing with a sharp knife which is tough enough as it is but its worse yet because his kid is playing a tape of some guy they call the boss whos making a racket on a guitar and screaming at the same time so its like the world is one big bowling alley and Pin High hates it so much hes going up the wall and isnt paying enough attention to the knife which slashes his left hand and now he cant take his regular grip what with the bandage and hes pushing everything on a course with all the room you want if you miss on the left and he goes bogey bogey double at the go and its all over.

So he says what if his lady didnt have a headache and he didnt have to do the shopping which is when he spots the pineapples. Or what if the truckers who deliver the pineapples had went out on strike and they never got to the market. Or what if the weather stank in Gualamala and ruined the pineapple crop so it didnt make any diff if the truckers were on strike or not. Or what if hed been tougher on his kid so he studied instead of listening all the time to those screamers with their elective guitars. Heeda won the county he says and woulda got the exemption into the state and mighta won that too and woulda been inspired to qualify for the senior tour and woulda made it and then beat Trevino in a playoff and won 75 gees. So that pineapple cut cost him fame and fortune.

Thats Kizmet for you says Chili Dip.

I guess so. Hey see yaroun. Jocko.

GUYS &
DOLLS AND
SHAG BAGS

(Golf Illustrated—1988)

Augie the Snipe king of the duck-hookers got married. Honest to God. The guy weve been saying for years would never get hitched except if he found a chick that looked like a 2 iron. We were right. But its okay. Shes up to date. Got great perimeter weighting.

Still and all who woulduv ever thought anything would replace golf in Snipes devotional armoire. Heres a guy who turns down free ducats to the Super Bowl for 18 holes at a muni. How about the time Snipe is out there in early March ground all mush or raining icicles because he cant wait to try out a tip he picked up in the *Sun Times* that would make him Snipe no more.

Then he stuffs newspapers in his shoes to dry them out before he puts the saddle soap on. After he picks all the bits of grass and mud out of the spikes with a tee. Hours he takes for that which hardly leaves him time for the pursuit of the opposite gender.

I mean like it was fateaccompleed that during the season Snipe is out of the house by 5:30 to hit some balls or play nine before going to work even when he was at the time doing the voolyvoo acushnet with one of the waitresses at the K&L. Which is no wonder why those little dailyances never lasted too long. As I understand it from my various studies ladies are especially soft and ameanable first thing in the morning. Lot Snipe cared. And what about the time one of the waitresses was so enameled of him that she offered to clean his shag balls if he would stick around at least one ayem a week. Do them one by one out of a pail of warm water filled with supersuds and wipe them off with a terrycloth towel making sure every dimple is clear just the way Snipe does. And Snipe kicks her out for even suggesting such a sacroligious idea as someone else just touching his shags.

Which brings up the conclusion of why Snipe has to be in love like Burt Lancaster with Shirley Booth in that one about the sheep. At first the thinking around the K&L was that Snipes 2 iron had a father who owned a golf course so Snipes green fees troubles were over forever. We could see him making this tradeoff. Or she had the secret to the duckhook which he wasnt about to let get away. Or let anybody else in on.

But it turns out Snipes 2 iron doesnt know a golf club from a nightstick until she meets Snipe and she even asks him to give her lessons. Now get this. Snipe is seen at the stop and sock in Lincoln Park putting her hands on the handle and all the rest of it.

But the clincher is this one. At the K&L the other night Snipe is going on about his 2 iron and lets it be known that one afternoon they are taking a drive up to Lake Geneva for a little Thanksgiving holiday deal and she spots a golf course which is closed for the season. It is an unusually warm and sunny day so the 2 iron stops the car beside one of the fairways and suggests to Snipe that they might hit a few balls. Now the question arises what do they use for golf balls. The 2 iron spots Snipes shag bag and says well use them. AND SNIPE SAYS YEAH SURE.

You hear! Augie the Snipe lets a lady hacker use his shags. Actually hit them. Anyone comes around asking for a definition of true love you can tell him this one.

See ya around

Jocko

DONALD
ROSS
DESIGNED
THE *WORLD!*

(Golf Illustrated—1990)

Excuse me for living but the thinking around the K&L these days is that all the chatterbox and hoopla about this and that arkitect building this and that golf course is getting to be a little too much like a con job for jacking up the greens fees.

I mean like the Bumps as you know was built by a committee of city engineers who didnt know a golf course from a bananacal garden but they got the bunkers in and got some roll in the greens so its a pretty decent layout. It aint Pebble or the Monster but you still have to read the greens and gage the speed and hit the teeball in between stuff and get over bunkers in which there is the same sort of sand you can catch too fat or thin as there is in the bunkers built by some celerated arkitect. I mean the game is still mainly about hitting the ball.

Augie the Snipe says he sees a market in becoming the first golf course discounter selling cheaper greens fees for famous designer courses that he says were built by guys such as AW Tillinghanst and Henry Colt. And especially Donald Ross. All guys who are dead and long gone. If some wiseguy comes in and says it didnt look like a Colt you just say it has been changed a lot over the years but its still got plenty of the original. Look at that mound over there which is called a sedan by those of us in the know. Only AW his own self could build one like that. Snipes got it all figured.

What brings this up is we made a couple of trips around the country lately to play some golf and everywhere we stopped it was a Donald Ross course. We came across so many Donald Ross courses that if he built them all the man had to live til 125 working 24 hours every day of it. After a while we got to thinking Donald Ross designed the whole world and in seven days as Three From the Edge put it and which got a laugh. We figured out that however meeger a way Donald Ross got involved they threw his name on it.

Like we heard where Ross was driving down this country road once and glommed a nice piece of ground over to his left and he mumbled to himself that he thought it would make a good course and the guy he was with overheard that. So now years later the guys grandson buys the land and lays out the holes himself because he is on the shorts and he remembers what his grandpa told him what Donald Ross said about the ground so he calls it a Donald Ross because afterall Ross did recommend it sort of and calling it a Joe Schmo aint gonna get it written up so that the tab can be up there.

But the best was out in Arizona. Heres this little bullring out in the desert called Ocean Meadow we figured wed try and we ask the guy taking the fees if hes selling a good layout and he says sure its a Donald Ross. In Arizona! We start snickering and saying yeah tell us about it and Snipe goes on about how Ross was from the east and did just about all his work around North Carolina and Massachewsits and as far as anyone knows was never in Arizona.

The guy at the register is not even fazed one bit. With his face straighter than any drive youll ever hit he lays on a song and dance that old Don Ross was in his office one day at Pinehurst looking at a map of Arizona thinking some day he might like to take a vacation out there and he put his coffee cup on the map then forgot it and it left a ring around this area that became Ocean Meadow. He ends up by saying that his Ocean Meadow is a product of divine grace.

Right. Its a better chance she built it than Donald Ross.

Hey see ya around

Jocko

PURE AS THE DRIVEN BALL

(Golf Illustrated—1992)

So im sitting in the K and L noodling over a piece of poppy seed pound cake waiting for the guys to show up as we were going to play over at the Bumps and no one shows for way past the time which is when I realize i goofed and had the wrong date. Must be getting old. So since I already arranged everything at the job and with the missus I figured Id go out anyway and pick up a game but when I get there nobodys around. Now this is when i get this revolution such as when guys all of a sudden see god or whoever. I guess this isnt that big but anyway I decide to go out by myself which i have never thought was my cup of tee since you aint got anyone to make a bet with or help you look for a ball or to put the needle to when hes going too good and it turns out i like it.

Yeah. Like for one thing it was so quiet without Augie the Snipe barking about his duckhooks and Three From the Edge moaning about his lousy chips and Wormburner about how he cant get it up. It was like I was hearing things for the first time. Like the birds which they sound okay when you get around to it. And when the wedge poofs in the sand when the dig is just right and how the putter sort of cushes up against the ball at least when you use balata. I guess when you got all the bets going in your mind and the guys are yappin about this that and the other thing you get away from the essetics or whatever you call it.

The other thing was how when youre out there alone you can drop another one to get a shot right or try something different which you wouldnt dare to when your in with your crowd because of all the action. Like hitten knockdown spinners with the sandwedge which you get by closing the face up and which its surprising how much juice you get on it. Or a soft 3 iron which you get by kind of slowing your arms down and which youre afraid to death of trying anytime but especially when the presses have got the points tripled or fourpled. Actually you get most of the shots done by slowing down the arms but when you tell guys that they think your crazy because they figure slowing down means you wont hit it far.

But what got me the most about being out there alone was all the thinking i ended up doing about stuff that has nothing to do with the swing and hitten shots. I mean you cant think of only the golf every minute or youd go nutso which everybody knows but when youre out there by your lonesome you cant always control what youre going to think about otherwise and so what came in was stuff about me and the missus and how we get along. Went way back on that one. And how my kids have come up and some of the goofs ive made with all of them as weve been going around the horn and how i think i straightened them out and maybe didnt when i thought i did and how things could have been a lot worse or maybe better if i wasnt so much into the game but how i could-na helped that for anything since the game is what the hell the game. Right. The missus has never understood that except i thought she did once at the start but maybe i never figured out a way to explain it to her prob-ably because i had all those bets and swinging with slow arms and other such stuff always rattling around in my bean.

So now I start thinking about ways to make it clear to her what its like to hit it pure just once. Like its even better than sex sometimes which i said to her once a long time ago just sort of joken around although not all the way and she gave it a hoot which i still dont understand what it meant.

What im saying is these are the kinds of things im thinking about on the golf course. This is stuff i never thought about anywhere else even and if i did you figure itd be in the motel on the road when you cant get to sleep or in the lounger in the den and i hear her rumbling and growsing upstairs. On the golf course Im thinking such things! Right while im enjoying those pinched wedges and soft 3 irons. You went to college maybe you can figure it out.

Hey seeyaroun.

Jocko

THINGS CHANGE THAT SHOULD BE THE SAME

(Golf Illustrated—1990)

So the guys around the K&L were cranking about the game the other day since there was nothing else they can do about it what with it being colder than your putter has always been and we came up with some stuff we were thinking oughta be done this year.

For instance how about not giving anymore exemptions to Nicklauses son and Caspers to play a tour tournament which they get only because of their old mans clout. Theyre taking a payday away from guys who have paid their dues and then some going through the qualifying school and hustling and scrapeing around to get the dough to be out there and so on.

And how about putting the kibosh on the guy on television whose always carping that the all exempt tour makes life too easy for the American players so that they are only mediocre. Mediocre. Maybe his monitors fuzzy. Those cats out there can play and for the very reason that they dont have to qualify on Monday and maybe miss because they happen to have a lousy day. Which is also why there are so many more good players and why nobody dominates the show anymore. They get to play a lot under the gun. Hey what if Hogan had to qualify on Mondays in the days when he was hooking it all over the joint. Wed never of heard of him. And they should look out who theyre hiring to be club pros as we were at a few resorts lately and saw a couple of the young assistants hitting balls and holding the club like they were working the chains on an oil rig and when they swung at it looked like a derek taking a fall. (Hey writer did you notice I didnt mix my semaphores?)

Anyways these young guys are out of a school that teaches pros how to sell shirts and pants and keep count of how many they sold on a computer but doesnt tell them how to hold a club or swing it and I can tell you this that I am not inclined to ask anybody who hacks at it whats the best ball these days. I would also not be inclined to buy anything from him just out of peak. A golf pros got to be a player first otherwise he aint gong to get my respect let alone my dough.

Hell its hard to tell youre in a pro shop at most of them you go to now. You cant find the sticks because theres so many clothes hanging on racks you think youre in a Howards store. Which reminds me of a couple of years ago going to one of those old time resorts thats been around for a 100 years and which I had been there the last time maybe 25 years before when it was like it was in the beginning and I have this putter I dont like that I figure Ill trade with the pro for one he has in his barrel. Well for one thing they dont have a barrel of odds and ends anymore. So then I ask this young blond kid behind the counter about making a trade. My putter for something I like and if I have to put up a few extra bucks Im willing to deal. Hes got a club in his hand and I can see hes out of the new school for merchandising golf pros and when I tell him what Im after he smiles contrasendingly and tells me they cant do that kind of thing because all their merchandise has a computerized inventory number and that would just completely gum up the works. I kind of humph and ask him if he ever smelled the smell of shellac on a newly refinished wood. I didnt even wait for an answer.

Hey seeya round
Jocko

THAT'S GOLF

COMING TO
TERMS
WITH GOLF

(Travel & Leisure—1978)

Why is golf called golf?
It comes from the Dutch word *kolf,* meaning "club."

Then the Dutch invented the game?

Some people claim so, but not in the presence of Scotsmen. Actually, it depends on how you define *invent.* Paintings and written documents, dated before Scots began sporting their game, indicate the Dutch did indeed play a game in which a small ball was pushed around with sticks curved at the bottom end and resembling an ice or field hockey stick. The Dutch played *kolf* in courtyards, on fields and streets, and especially on ice, but not necessarily toward holes in the ground. So they may be more closely responsible for ice or field hockey. Still, the first clubs made for golf in Scotland were much like Dutch hockey sticks, and Scottish golfers apparently saw enough likeness between the game they devised and what the Dutch had been playing to use the Dutch word for their version.

Is it true that 18 holes make a round of golf because that's how many shots of Scotch it takes to finish a fifth?

A romantic canard. The rule that 18 holes make a round was codified arbitrarily. Prior to 1764 no standard number of holes made a round of golf. The earliest Scottish courses had anywhere from 5 holes (at Leith), to 25 (at Montrose). St. Andrews originally had 22, and it was here where 18 became fixed. For some time, the St. Andrews golfers played 11 holes in a straight line going out to the end of the narrow piece of land on which their course lay. To get home they played 10 of those holes again, in reverse order, plus a solitary hole near where they started. Now, in 1764 the powers-that-be at St. Andrews decided they did not like their first four holes—either they were not long enough or not wide enough, or something—and converted them into two holes. This eliminated four holes, leaving 18. At the same time, the Society of St. Andrews Golfers became the most influential golf club in Scotland, the arbiter of rules and regulations throughout the land; thus 18 holes became the official number for a round.

Is a links so called because the holes run together?

Not at all, sensible as that seems. A golf links is that which is built or laid out over basically sandy soil risen above the ocean water, which was in fact once part of the ocean floor. Thus, it is "linked" to the sea. Pebble Beach, for example, is not a "true" golf links; it is a seaside course. The only "true" golf links in the world are in the British Isles, mostly along the coastline of Scotland and Ireland, although some courses on Long Island, New York, and in Australia have a few holes built on true links land.

Is *caddie* short for *Cadillac*?

No, it is from the French *cadet,* pronounced cahday and Anglicized to caddie. *Cadet* at first described a younger person, then a young military officer—either way, something of an underling. It is believed Mary, Queen of Scots first dubbed golf-bag toters as cadets/cahdays/caddies. By all accounts Mary, the first woman golfer, was more enamored of the game than she was of her husband, Lord Darnley. Legend has it that she learned of Darnley's death while at golf (this in 1567) and at the news played on— and quite well, too.

Why do golfers holler "Fore!" instead of "Look Out!"?

Fore is an Old English word. It means, basically, "in front," as in foremost, foreground, etc., and evolved as a warning to golfers playing ahead.

Why is a tee a tee? The shape of it?

No, it derives from the Greek for the letter "T," *tau,* and was once used as we now use X, to mark the spot, or the place where things begin. The wooden peg on which a ball is propped—the tee used on a tee—was marketed in the 1920s by Dr. William Lowell, a golfing New Jersey dentist who worried that his hands would get too chapped and insensitive for dentistry from having to build small mounds of dirt or sand on which to place the ball—that was how the ball was "teed up" before.

The mulligan, or second chance to drive on the first tee; who is it named after?

Mr. David Mulligan, a Canadian. In the late 1920s he was one of a regular foursome of golfers who played together at the St. Lambert Country Club in Montreal. The course was some distance from town and, having the only auto among the group, Mulligan drove everyone out. The trip was over rough roads and an especially bumpy bridge at the course entrance that had a "pavement" of cross-ties. Because Mulligan's hands suffered the shock of the bumpy ride while holding the steering wheel of the auto, he was graciously given a second try with his drive off the first tee. Hence, the "mulligan."

Was the bogey also named after someone?

Sort of. The word *bogey* stems from *bog,* probably. Celtic for that treacherously soft, darkly sinister ground. A bogey, or bogeyman, was a ghost, goblin, or some such scary specter from the bog. In 1891, a very popular song in Great Britain was "The Bogey Man." Keep that in mind for a minute as we backtrack a bit.

The year 1759 saw the first golf competition at stroke play—the winner the one who took the lowest total number of strokes for so many holes played. Until then the only competitive format was head-to-head match play—the winner the one who won the most individual holes. However, golf holes were not rated to be played in a standard number of strokes, or par, until 1890. In that year, Hugh Rotherham, of Coventry Golf Club, in England, devised a competition using a handicap against a fixed score for each hole. The fixed score, or par, became necessary for Rotherham's "game," and caught on to become the general mark of golfing excellence. Par also became the "opponent" as much as other players, and something to be feared—a bogey. At the same time, the real live other fellow with the stick in his hands who regularly played around par was also feared and, picking up on the popular song of 1890s, became "the bogey man."

Then a bogey actually was a good score: par?

Right. But, when the lively "modern" golf ball was invented in 1898 by an American named Haskell, it quickly replaced the solid-rubber "guttie" ball that could not be hit nearly as far. The bogey established in previous years for each hole became too easy; the Haskell ball shortened the length of the holes. Thus, a bogey was not so fine an accomplishment and came to mean "one over par." At least in most of the world. The British, retaining tradition, often still call a par a bogey.

Why is a birdie so called?

A birdie, a score of one *under* the par of a hole, is from a slangy expression in vogue around the turn of the 20th century for anything or anyone attractive, unusual or extraordinary, e.g., "That bird is the cat's meow." A.W. Tillinghast, a fine American golf architect and historian, claims the term *birdie* got started in golf one day in the early 1900s. During a round he was playing with friends, one of the group hit a terrific second shot that reached the green of a par-five hole in two and resulted in a four on the hole. After that second shot, another of the group exclaimed, "That's a bird."

Two under par on a hole would soon after be called an eagle, the most extraordinary bird of all. An ace, for a hole in one, which is also an eagle on par-three holes, comes from card games. The ace is number one.

Why are poor golfers called duffers, or dubs?

Duff is a variation of the Scottish *dowf*, "lacking in force; dismal and gloomy." *Dowf*, by the way, reminds that there is a Scottish word, *gowf*, for striking with the hand. With this in mind, the term *golf* may come from the Scottish, after all, if you think of the club as a surrogate hand.

Dub is a Middle English word derived from both the German and Frisian *dobbe*, "pool of water," and "pit or hole." If you hit a golf ball into a pool of water or a pit you've dubbed it, you duffer you.

What does *dormie* mean?

Dormie is probably from the French *dormi*, "asleep." In match-play competition, if you are three holes up with only three holes to play, you have your opponent at dormie. You can't lose in the regulation number of holes, and the last three are a yawn. However, you will be rudely awakened by losing those last three holes; you may get dead in overtime.

The nassau bet—does it come from the Bahamas?

No, it's from Long Island, New York. Findlay S. Douglas, the 1898 U.S. Amateur champion, tells us that players in team matches among golf clubs in the New York metropolitan area around the turn of the century did not enjoy seeing newspaper accounts of their being badly beaten. So one day, when team matches were held at Nassau Country Club, Glen Cove, Long Island, the home team devised a scoring system in which one point went to the winner of each 9 holes, plus one for the entire 18. Thus, it became impossible for losers to be defeated by more than three points. Face was saved, in the public prints, anyway.

Are you supposed to talk to a golf ball when you address it?

Not really, although many golfers do, either in frustration or in vocalizing high hopes or intentions. In setting up to hit a golf shot, you address the ball. One meaning of the term, obsolete except in golf and taken from the French *adresser,* is "to direct oneself in a given direction."

The chunk of turf taken out with a golf shot is called a divot. Why?

Except that the word is credited to the Scots, no one knows its roots. Golf's mystery word.

Why is a hazard called a hazard?

The word may stem from the Spanish *azar,* "an unforeseen disaster." The definition applies to golf because on the first golf courses, the links of Scotland, you could not see from a distance the deep holes filled with sand, which—if you get into them—can be so disastrous to your score. The first sand traps were formed by sheep burrowing straight down into the flat terrain to get protection from strong, chill winds off the nearby sea. Scottish links land was originally used for grazing sheep, and continued to be for centuries even after golfers began using it to nibble at small balls. These sand pits, or hazards, also came to be known as bunkers—Scottish for "a large bin."

Why are there grooves on the striking faces of golf clubs?

Supposedly to impart backspin on the ball, especially one hit with irons, and to otherwise control the flight. However, scientists have shown rather conclusively that clubs with traditional width grooves that are widely separated, have no more effect in these regards than those with smooth faces, which was how clubfaces were until the late 1800s. At that time, Scottish club makers etched grooves into clubfaces for the first time, probably for cosmetic reasons, or to define their product from that of other club makers. There were chevron-shaped grooves, circular, and so on. For many years now, the grooves in clubs have been regulated. They can only be horizontal lines (from toe to heel), separated by a specific distance, and of specific width. Grooves that are too close together roughen the surface of the clubface in such a way as to import excessive spin on the ball.

Why is a handicap called that?

It is widely accepted that the term is from *hand-in-cap.* There are two theories of its origination. In the racing tradition, numbered slips were dropped into a cap, then drawn out by hand to determine the post position of each entry in a race. The other theory is from diarist Samuel Pepys, who wrote of a swapping game he learned in 1660. Each player put a small possession and some money into a cap. In the exchanging, an umpire decided how much money each player should receive to keep shares equal. The ump's hand was regularly dipping into the pot, or cap. The game was called Hand In Cap.

THE
MOTHER OF
INVENTION

(Golf Magazine—1978)

Off the top of your head, how many variations on a golf tee can you imagine? It's but a bit of a thing with a point on one end, a shallow cup on the other. What's to vary? No big deal.

Okay, but keeping in mind that to be patented an invention must have at least one unique feature, did you know that from 1927 through 1929 *alone,* the U.S. Patent Office issued *64* patents on golf tees? In fact, there are hundreds of variations on that bit of a thing on which golf balls are propped.

Man's inventive genius in all things mechanical must never be under-estimated, as volume upon thick volume of registered patents attest, but golf seems especially susceptible to the "better mousetrap syndrome." In that same 1927 to 1929 period, a grand total of *437* patents was allowed on golf items ranging from the basics—clubs, balls, tees, and so on—to ball re-formers and warmers, shaft preservers, range finders, and enough practice devices to keep a body busy until the Old Course at St. Andrews becomes a shopping mall. Overall, since golf was introduced in the United States in 1888, literally thousands of patents have been taken on golf stuff.

Such a wealth of creativity must be credited to the frustrating character of golf combined with the engineering aspects implicit in the nature of the game, both of which drive players to seek a better way through industry. Frank Thomas, a trained engineer who had much to do with the invention of the graphite golf shaft and who is now technical director for the United States Golf Association, amplifies this notion. Thomas is in charge of testing and evaluating golf equipment to determine if it conforms with the Rules of Golf and conjectures that for all the how-to instruction available to golfers, each must in the end make or invent his own swing, and that spirit carries over to equipment.

Since this is not an encyclopedia, we can only list a fraction of all the golf inventions extant. A sampling, though, will reveal the turns of mind taken by some golfers in the never-ending quest for The Secret, or whatever else urges their golfing souls. Some turns have redirected the game's essential playability—the steel shaft, the three-piece rubber golf ball, the sand wedge—others are simply bizarre, albeit fascinating, twists.

Tees first. The golf tee pretty much as we know it was first invented in 1899, by Dr. George Grant, a golfing African-American dentist from Boston. He thought so little of it, though, he never tried to market his device and eventually let his patent expire. However, in 1920 another dentist, Dr. William Lowell, of New Jersey, devised a similar tee (the cup was a bit bigger), got a patent and tried to make a fortune from it. (The theory is, dentists came up with the tee because their hands were getting badly chapped from building the small mounds of sand or dirt on which the ball had always been propped.) Dr. Lowell's wooden peg was painted red, and called the Reddy Tee.

Lowell got Walter Hagen to use it, thus popularizing the device, and when F. W. Woolworth ordered a billion Reddy Tees the idea was off (or in) the ground forever. At the same time, it stirred the precocity of many another inventor. Unfortunately, Dr. Lowell did not get an airtight patent on his tee and spent the rest of his life and all his money in the courts fighting what he deemed infringement on his invention.

Since 1920 the Reddy Tee has spawned numerous progeny: a tee with a smooth "front" edge on its cup to cut down resistance to ball departure; a tee with a carpenter level assures a straight peg when in place; another is made to stand on a bias angled toward the target, perhaps to give a more forward sense of flight or more practically so that a too-low stroke will simply drive the tee into the ground unbroken and easily retrieved. Another fascinating effort is a three-way tee: Three pegs, each at a different height, are mounted on something that looks like a moon-landing vehicle.

Frank Thomas reckons that about 80 percent of all golf inventions sent to the USGA for advice and (hopefully) consent are putters. This is because a putter is not subject to the stresses of clubs used for hard hitting and does not require the more refined engineering and manufacturing techniques of the irons and woods. Thus, it can be put together in a basement workshop by anyone handy with tools. In this regard, the quintessential "workshop" putter is one Arnold Palmer received from a fan anxious to help Arnie get in the hole. The "blade" is an actual hammerhead, claw and all, attached to a shaft.

Putter invention also engenders the most idiosyncratic methods. There is a putter with two mirrors on the head, one by which the golfer can keep an eye on the line, the other angled so he can see the target. Using the mirrors, the golfer does not have to keep looking up to see where he is going, or memorize the line and target for that interminable few seconds before stroking.

In a more mechanical vein someone produced a putter that, I swear, has a motor, a push button, and a flywheel on the toe of the blade. When ready to putt, the golfer pushes the button to activate the flywheel, which spins and provides a gyroscopic effect designed to keep the blade square during the stroke.

The search for a "perfect pendulum stroke" by putter inventors is as consuming as that among the explorers who sought the headwaters of the Nile. For instance, one patent describes a putting system whereby a metal, C-shaped "tripod" is placed over the golf ball. A putter hanging from the center of the C is merely pulled back and released; another perfect pendulum stroke, and no shaky knees or hands to fret about. When Frank Thomas suggested to the inventor of this one, "Why don't we just make a hole as big as a bushel basket," the inventor, either ignoring or unmindful of his system's ultimate reason-for-being, replied, "No, no, that would make the game too easy."

Making the game too easy is a guiding principle behind the USGA's rejection of most inventions, rejections, by the way, that cannot stop manufacture, distribution, and use, but only makes the use illegal in competitions played under the Rules of Golf. The essential USGA thrust is to maintain the traditional form of golf equipment and manner of swinging the club.

Frank Thomas does judge on the basis of specific Rules of Golf, though: Number 2, Appendices II and III, which he calls his "national anthem," deals with the design of clubs and balls; Number 9, on Advice and Assistance and Numbers 37–39, on Artificial Devices. One basic rule says no moving parts are allowed on clubs, which also eliminates those one-shaft, one-head-with-adjustable-loft clubs, an idea that goes back to the 19th century.

The carpenter level is a pet device among inventors, who evidently fear being tipsy (golfwise) on the course. One has put the level under the peak of a cap. The golfer raises his eyes only to see how he's standing. Sorry, it's an artificial aid.

So is the gauge or meter attached to carts or belts that click off distance measurement.

Golf ball warmers taken onto the course are nonconforming as artificial aids to play. One of the more elaborate of these was patented recently. An oven is mounted over the exhaust manifold on gas-powered golf cars; For electric cars resistance coils are wrapped around the housing underneath an insulated cover. The balls are kept in pipes under the seat. In a way, then, the golfer "hatches" balls that will travel a few yards farther by being warmer.

Many putters used in the manner of a shuffleboard stick have come along. One, Patent #3,220,730, has a cylindrical head with a small wheel on each side. Imagine, your putter is liable to flat tires! A key advantage to these instruments, one inventor points out, is that after bending low behind the ball to sight the line of putt you do not alter your angle of vision by then standing up beside the ball to hit it. A nice idea, but no soap. For one thing, you can't stand behind the ball, or straddle the line of putt. And even if you moved to one side (while staying low) and sort of peeked around the corner, the "stroke" constitutes a push or shove and is not by the rules "fairly struck."

Inventors have not left imagination out of grips. Clubs have been designed to be held with an actual shoehorn, or an eyebolt at the top in which a finger is projected. There is also a putter with two grips that looks like a divining rod or cripple's crutch. No deal. Only one grip to a customer and that must be "substantially straight and plain in form, may have flat sides, but shall not have a channel or furrow or be molded for any part of the hands."

So far this article has dwelt on the negative, with what does not conform to the Rules of Golf. This is not to be pessimistic, and anyway will surely not dissuade inventors, who are by definition thorough optimists. They have reason. No less an innovation than the steel golf shaft, first patented in 1910, was finally ruled legal in United States golf in

1925. Other inventions have been immediately accepted, such as Dr. Lowell's tee, the rubberized grip, and the heel-and-toe weighting of clubs we hear so much about today, but which was patented in the United States in 1915.

It may seem, also, that in the description of many inventions the tone has been somewhat mocking. More accurately, it is a kind of amazement at the ends to which golfers will go to plumb the deep mysteries of the game. Today's equipment manufacturers are certainly not as haughty as they once were in the face of new ideas, although they have been burned in the past.

But attitudes change, and both a Wilson and a MacGregor executive recently remarked that, whereas in the old days the Ping iron, which looks like a plumber's nightmare, would have been "laughed out of the office," nowadays they are taking a second look at new inventions. The great success of the Ping clubs and the Zebra putter is nothing to laugh at.

Still, it is difficult in this observer's corner to resist a giggle at some golf inventions. Patent #3,195,891, for instance, is for a hunk of metal that is strapped into the space between the sole and heel of the golf shoes—the right shoe for right-handers—and by elevating the outside edge of this foot is meant to prohibit swaying on the backswing. The metal wedge is worn through the entire round. Best you use a golf car, or you'll look and feel like the Hunchback of Notre Dame by the time you walk up the 18th fairway. (The metal wedge, by the way, does not conform to the Rules of Golf.)

Finally, going from the bottom to the top of the golfing anatomy, in 1966 a patent was issued on a pair of glasses to be worn by golfers to control head movement in the swing. The glasses are opaque except for two small apertures, one in each lens. At address, with the head properly positioned, the ball can be seen through the "peep-holes." Now, in making the backswing, if the head moves out of position *the ball disappears from view!* What to do, then? Why, you simply stop your swing and start all over again.

Consider the possibilities. A golfer who just cannot keep his head still could take from five minutes to a year to hit one shot. In any case, stopping a backswing, especially the faster ones, which most of us have, risks a wrenched back, slipped disk, or broken arms. Furthermore, it is the rare individual who can stop a backswing of any speed once it gets going. And if he does stop it, the golfer is in a situation akin to the lights going out at the very moment a surgeon is inserting a new heart. The thing could end up in the patient's mouth, which is by no means a metaphor.

The inventor, though, does offer a slightly larger aperture in one lens so the golfer has enough peripheral vision to spot those who might get into the danger zone *before he begins to swing.* Thank you, sir.

I CADDIED
FOR THE MOB

(Golf Magazine—1970)

Chicago, my hometown. The mere mention of that fact to people I've met around the world has invariably elicited a reaction such as, "ah, Tchikago. Rat-tat-tat. Scarface." Or, "Chick-ago. Boom, boom. Capone." I'm then asked, half jokingly, to show my gun, called a gat. City-proud, I used to respond by pointing out in high-flown passionate language, the "good stuff" about that broad sprawl of the Middle West; how it's always been a leader in architecture; how it has a brilliant symphony orchestra; an art institute with one of the world's great collections; the last remaining naturalist in baseball, a club owner who refuses to light his ballpark for night games; how Chicago had a golf tournament worth $100,000 to the winner, which hasn't been topped yet. My listeners only smile condescendingly, look for a bulge in my jacket, turn their hand into a pistol and go, "boom, boom. Capone." So goes the influence of old movies, among other things.

Inevitably though, it must be said that gangsterism and the Syndicate, or Mafia, is inextricably woven into the fabric of Chicago's life. Try opening a tavern, or going into the laundry business, or putting a jukebox in your basement den. Such as that gets you a visit from the "boys," as Syndicate men are usually referred to, not necessarily with endearment. They offer their *services,* and you accept. Quickly. Unhesitatingly. It's something all Chicagoans accept, some with another kind of pride than my own, a strange phenomenon I won't get into here.

The "boys" have no less added their swatch of darkish goods to the Second City's golfing raiment. There was a man named "Golf Bag" Hunt, although he really doesn't count since a niblick ever saw the inside of his unique holster. As a caddie at Tam O'Shanter CC (where that 100-grand first prize was given, incidentally, and whose turf is now buried under a labyrinth of factories), I came very close to certain of the town's leading gambling and brothel masters.

Tam O'Shanter didn't have the kind of exclusivity usually associated with private clubs, because it was owned outright by one man, George S. May. That long-deceased entrepreneur extraordinaire let anyone into his club who could raise the money. So Tam was composed largely of nouveaux-riches, people who had just made a score in trucking, auto sales, coffeepots, and didn't have their money long enough to satisfy the membership requirements of the stuffier country clubs. Also, Tam O'Shanter was in a suburb directly adjacent to Chicago, a town called Niles, and was somehow able to have slot machines in its massive clubhouse. Slot machines are very good raisers of revenue, and when such very good raisers of revenue are around, so are the "boys."

On the surface Tam might have been any of the more genteel places, North Shore CC, Olympia Fields, Bryn Mawr. It did have a veneer of traditional country clubness. The grass was well tended, very green and soft. It was actually in the country, and was quiet. The members were obviously doing well, as their cashmere socks and sweaters indicated. But the chimera of total respectability was punctured by such events as the arrival of Tony Accardo for his daily game of golf. Around the curving driveway leading to the locker room entrance came the longest, widest, blackest Cadillac ever conceived and created by man. When the doors began to open, cautiously one at a time, out came four enormous human beings. No brown and white loafers, pink pants, and white linen sportcoats for these sportsmen. They wore padded black overcoats, wide-brimmed gray fedora hats, and spiky-toed spit-polish black shoes. In early spring, midsummer, or late fall, this was their outfit. With unremittingly menacing expressions on their shadowed faces they lined up tall and firm at the door out of which Accardo, the don of dons, would come. It was indeed a scene out of *White Heat, Key Largo,* or *Little Caesar* except that Accardo in no way resembled Cagney, Bogart, Edward G. Robinson, or even Rod Steiger. As he emerged from his upholstered cavern the first thing we saw of Accardo was his nose, which gave him his name. He wore frameless glasses on a pinched and ashen face, and had a warped little body that measured no more than 4½ feet in length. You would have to say that Accardo, also known as Big Tuna, either had a very deep voice, or was quite a fast and sure shot. Take your pick. Accardo moved to the locker room, and eventually onto the golf course virtually enveloped in the flesh and flannel cage formed by his guards. He always played alone, save for his overdressed "gallery of four," and always shot 78. No one ever questioned his score.

In charge of slot machine collections was a curly-haired man known as Morrie. Only Morrie. For some reason he took a liking to me and I caddied for him often. He was a good "loop"—six bucks and a lot of golf balls, which served to balance out my aesthetic distaste for his golf. Morrie, playing for his shank, lined up west to hit the ball north. When the Kefauver Commission came to town to "clean up the mob" (poor Estes, he had a better chance running for president), the only man he could not locate for an appearance downtown was someone known only as Morrie. Who was this mysterious man? Estes asked. I read his question in the newspaper the same day Morrie drove me home from the course, stopping first at his own house to pick up his wife. I might have trotted right down to tell the senator who Morrie was, where he lived, etc., but something told me that course of action would have been less than circumspect.

One tried to avoid getting the bag of Lou Rosanova, chief muscle ripper of recalcitrant loanees, who had the physical eminence and style that suited his position in the organization. Rosanova was a master of the "improved lie." You were unavoidably involved in his ball-nudging contretemps, and thereby constantly in dread of being asked point-blank by the other players whether the ball was moved illegally. It was not a question you cared to answer.

Not all the boys were such obvious heavyweights, though. One gnomish little character walked around in fishnet shirts, was quiet as a marshmallow, counted all his strokes, and seemed quite pleasant. It was later determined that he was the man in charge of murders.

They're like that, the "boys," talk softly, seem like real gentlemen. Perhaps even be one sometimes . . . if you don't get into their pocket. Which brings me to the main episode in this Two-Penny Opera. One early-summer morning I was assigned the bag of a moon-faced, heavyset, rather shortish man called John Thomas. His foursome included two bookies, called Czar and Trophy, and a bondsman named Eli. They all played for more than a few dollars, but Eli and John Thomas had more going for them—like a thousand dollars low man wins, no handicaps. Actually John Thomas could have used a stroke or two. He could move the ball pretty well, was kind of strong, but had a way of occasionally sticking his pick in the ground and moving the ball only a foot or two; especially after the clever Eli had half-topped a shot a couple of feet from the cup. Maybe John Thomas was too proud to take shots from the pudgy Eli, who looked like the guy everyone figures they can beat at anything.

In any case, they played all even, and the first time around Eli, with his uncanny chipping and putting ability, took the "thou" from John Thomas. Thomas casually skimmed the bills off a stack of money so thick, so heavy, it defies description. Enough to choke a horse? Enough to gag a gargantua? In his pocket it looked like a giant goiter that had slipped to his hip. When Eli was paid, Thomas picked off a single ten-dollar bill and gave it over to me. That was a fine bit of pay, but I knew, and it had been hinted, that if John Thomas were to beat Eli out of a thousand my portion would be substantially, gratifyingly increased. That wasn't how it was put, but so be it. I understood, and from that point on I did all I could within the rules of golf to bring my horse home a winner.

No caddie ever lined up putts for his player with the precision I did. I chose every club John Thomas used, put it in his hand properly, folded each of his thick and bejeweled fingers into the correct position on the leather, set the clubhead perfectly square to the target, got his feet aligned, did everything but actually swing the club. Yet time after every time John Thomas sat hunched before his locker after the round, heaved up that quire of green and off-white, and peeled steadily in favor of the hated Eli. I was then tendered my skinny one-page note. I was onto a good thing as it stood. I was making ten dollars a day four times a week, and had plenty of time to play myself. But with one John Thomas victory I would have been rich. Rich! Some of the other caddies looked at me enviously, but there was also something else in their eyes. They would ask me whose bag I was carrying. I told them John Thomas, and they said, "Oh yeah. John Thomas. Sure enough."

It was not to be, and as John Thomas continued to lose thousand after thousand his personality slowly, inexorably began to take on another hue, notably red. Words like *jadrool* and *madonne* began to filter through a deep growl.

Then one day John Thomas came very close. Everything he and I did went right. He had Eli down with but a few holes left to play. A thrill ran through me. My instruction was working and the money to come would put me in real golf shoes, not old street brogues with tacks screwed into the soles, new clubs, a bag, who knows what else. Then Eli holed a putt from the other side of heaven, followed that with a noodler from the trees that skidded past a bunker, hopped over a rake, bonged against the pin, and stopped an inch away from the main cavity. John Thomas was back to even again with one more to play. Every ounce of blood must have flooded to his brain. He was livid, magenta, cerise. He was catatonic. On the last tee he couldn't get the driver back. It just wouldn't go. He stood over the ball for a full five minutes. Then he burst. The club came off the ground, but it was not intended to return to the ball. He tucked it under an armpit, aimed it at Eli, squinted down the shaft with glazed eyes, and with a maddened voice began to "shoot down" his despised adversary. "Rat-tat-tat. Ra-tat-tt-tt. Rat-tat-tat-t-t-t," he went. Eli's eyes opened as wide as a fish. Thomas kept peppering away. "Rat-tat-tat. Rat-tat-tat-t-t-t-t." Eli walked slowly off the tee, broke into a trot, and finally took off at full speed, running with the ungainly bouncing plop of an ostrich through a bunker, over a green and into the trees, never to be seen again. Trophy and Czar removed the "machine gun" from John Thomas and led him, blubbering, back to the locker room.

It was ended. John Thomas lost upward of $20,000 and myself say a thousand, maybe more.

Periodically the other caddies asked me how my pal, John Thomas, was. I shrugged, still not understanding their innuendo. Only the following winter did it come clear. Idly flipping through the pages of a magazine, *Coronet* or the *Police Gazette,* my eye caught the picture of a familiar face. I looked carefully, and lo, it was my man, John Thomas. Then I read the caption, but it didn't say John Thomas. The man in the picture was my man, and was also the older brother of Scarface himself. I had been caddying not for John Thomas, but for John Capone . . . in Chicago, Chicago, that toddlin' town.

O, FOR THOSE DAYS OF SPRINGTIME COLLEGE GOLF!

(Golf Magazine—1976)

I used to deeply envy, even hate, those lucky southerners who could tee up a golf ball any time of the year, their hands always elastic and good-feeling on a dry and giving club handle, their bodies loose and free in light clothes. But I have come to realize that as a native of Chicago who has experienced spring golf in the North, I have known more fully the passion for the game, of golf's Calvinist essence, and of the pleasure-pain principle.

Any golfer who has calculated the effect of a simple pitch shot that will bounce 50 feet straight up off a frozen green, has choked down on a driver to compensate a stance ankle-deep in mush, has felt the hot sting on the buttocks of a "handwarmer" left too long in a back pocket, must be a more rounded person who has been closer to Life. And if you say Life, Schmife, the North has not produced any great players, be reminded that Arnold Palmer came from Pennsylvania and Jack Nicklaus from Ohio, places where deep frost is not unknown. What's more, Nicklaus played his college golf in his home state. In fact, I almost played a match against Jack and am eternally grateful I did not . . . and not merely because I would have lost. More on that, later.

Sure enough, there are dedicated northern-tier golfers who will spot a few balls with red paint, prop them on handmade, Scotch-taped squares of paper, and go at it in midwinter, and not only on rare January days when it happens to warm up to 30; I mean in subfreezing, call-of-the-wild weather. Many legends have been frozen in time out of this. It is said that on a February afternoon with the mercury at 10 above 1 Alex Kameczura started a swing he did not complete until April; the man froze stiff at the top of his arc . . . tic. They say a Frank Wisler, on a similar day, managed to get the clubhead through but when the ball got 50 feet out it stopped cold and remained suspended in air until mid-March. A fellow named Blaha, legend has it, about to stroke a 12-foot putt, got hit in the eye with a puck struck in a hockey game played on the upper level of the green (a Robert Trent Jones course, no doubt). Blaha three-putted, threw his club at the skater, and was given a 10-minute major penalty. Slight exaggerations, of course, as legends tend to be.

There are also the less hearty—or loony—who will essay their first round of the year as soon as the snow has edged back to reveal 10 feet of fairway and the temperature reaches 40, sometimes hedging on a windless day of 38. But all the above don't count here. They don't really *have* to play. However, young lads who yearn for the pride of a school athletic letter or are getting their tuition paid for playing golf, must play. College golf in the North, always played in the spring, is, of course, competitive, and we all know what competition does to the heart and soul and to what ends it will take us to be in the action.

My college golf was played for Western Illinois University, a small school on the flat prairie of the nation's breadbasket where there is nothing to restrain a wind that blows with the steady force of a mighty river. It is traditional in the American North to not only say that the winds come out of Canada, but that it is Canada's fault they are so hard and cold; that Canadians are getting in their licks at their richer southern neighbor by somehow making sure we get *their* wind's full fury. So persistent is the tradition that one dark and howling night in December a teammate of mine named Rysko wrote a letter to Buckminster Fuller, inventor of the geodesic dome, suggesting he build one of his masterpieces over the whole of Canada so we could get an earlier start on the golf season. Rysko told us Fuller replied that he couldn't help as he was busy planning a dome to cover Midtown Manhattan. Rysko would not show us Fuller's letter, though. Strange things happen to golfers locked in a west-central Illinois icebox.

In any case, we were never able to get in any golf before early March, at the earliest. The winter months were spent painting our dormitory ceilings and walls with overswung two-irons, squeezing rubber balls back to their natural state, and stretching out on our cots dreaming perfect swing planes and winning with a rush of birdies the "Mattress Open."

Finally, though, the snow did melt, the air lost enough of its chill, and the Golfers Equinox was upon us. There was no time to lose. The coach would be holding the team qualifying rounds any minute and there would be the Easter vacation trip south to sharpen up for our own conference meets. The month of March was half gone and school was out in early June; a short "season."

Out we went wearing rubber-pegged galoshes, sweatpants under chinos under corduroy trousers, a flannel shirt under a heavy woolen sweater under a nylon jacket, and an Ace ice-skating cap turned down over the ears. Go *think* of a good club extension with all that gear on, let alone *make* one. One of the guys used to fight the chill factor by wrapping newspapers around his chest then piling on all the other stuff. Every time he swung it sounded like someone wrapping a piece of fish. A punning political science major and a liberal, he used to say with a particular relish that the *Chicago Tribune* was the World's Greatest Windbreaker.

Being "players," we did not step onto the first tee without having hit some practice balls. Everyone found their own spot from which to hit a few by dropping a ball to the ground from shoulder-high. If it didn't disappear in primordial ooze, that was the place. Now to hit it. Pro golfers will say that some days their hands feel "fat"; no feel, an insecure grip. If that's so for those who play 390 days a year, the feel in our hands the first day out was as though they were shot through with novocaine. The initial stroke was invariably like an earthmover making a cut in a hillock. The clubhead never touched the ball, which, if it moved at all, was shoved by a mass of mud coming up from behind. We didn't hit it fat, we "obesed" it.

Not all the mud went forward, either. Much of it flew up, at, and on us. It wasn't long before we were vertical stacks of encrusted gumbo. The shag balls were an even sorrier-looking lot. Cooped up all winter, they had a yellow pallor in the early-spring light that accented the nicks and bruises of yesteryear. They didn't last long, anyway. If it was soft where we stood to hit them, the ground where they landed was softer still and they were sucked down and away until July, when by some kind of earthy gurgitation they would reappear.

Team qualifying rounds began the next day and immediately after we were thrown into battle. Western Illinois had an exceptional golf program for a school its size, and good teams—one year we won the national small college championship—but the coach was wise and started us off with some easy matches. The confidence builders were against such teams as Eureka College, in Eureka, Illinois, Pumpkin Capital of the World; Nauvoo Polytechnical; and Table Grove Methodist. How confident our victories against such schools made us is moot. A player from Eureka took 10 minutes for each shot—93 of them. Irritated at first, we learned later he was playing as therapy for a nervous disorder; some doctor he had. When the Table Grove team knelt behind a putt they looked to heaven more than to the line.

By Easter vacation time we were ready, so to speak, and were off to play matches against everyone from the University of Houston, Texas A&M, and Florida State, to Ouachita (Arkansas) State. We looked forward to these trips, although I'm not always sure why. Five golfers and a coach, all with irregular digestions, each with a suitcase, a trunk-sized golf bag, and shag bags, which added up to 12 bodies, shoehorned into an ancient station wagon for a 10-day, 1,800-mile round trip.

Byron Nelson has said that in his early days on the pro tour driving a rattle-box Ford across the nation, it took him two days to steady hands that held a vibrating steering wheel before he could hit a putt with something less than a palsied stroke. Too bad. Most days on our spring trips we didn't have more than 15 minutes to get the crick out of a neck not made for sleeping upright in cars and stamp the pin-needles out of long-dormant feet before we had to defend our golfing honor against a Phil Rodgers, Tommy Aaron, or Bobby Nichols. Our honor despoiled, we squeezed back into the wagon to retrieve our neckaches and pin-needles.

I don't know what Nelson did about falling asleep at the wheel, but our coach tended to take his naps while driving and we became expert at recognizing when he was preparing for one. One of us was assigned, like a sentry, to keep an eye on the coach. When his head started bobbing up and down like a marionette's, or the wagon accelerated to 80, slowed to 40, and revved up to 80 again in the space of a few seconds we knew it was time to tuck him in back among the golf bags.

We did stay in motels at night, but the golf budget was slim for all our success as conference champions, which bought no shoulder pads for the football team, and Coach Mussatto was necessarily careful; two, sometimes three of us to a room in a place like Mac's Rest Haven, in Zolfa Springs, Florida. It was difficult to get the sleep that makes champions with the vibrant hum of trailer trucks echoing off concrete floors and the smell of kerosene burners keeping whatever was growing in the groves just outside from going to hell in a basket.

Neither were the meals too glamorous. Contrary to what you may have heard, grits do not tighten up loose backswings and hamburgers by any other name are still hamburgers. George Sauer, the athletic director at Southern Methodist University, must surely have known how susceptible we were to good food when we straggled into Waco one year. No doubt he was being friendly-hospitable, but he may have had other motives when on the morning of our match with his boys he fed us breakfast in SMU's athletic dormitory cafeteria.

It was not a meal, it was to our famished eyes and bellies a James Beardian gorge; magnums of fresh-squeezed orange juice and rich white milk, slabs of warm bread thick as dictionaries, tureens of crisp dry cereal smothered by cream a churn away from being scooped, eggs no normal chicken could possibly lay, their yolks as big as footrests, sausage patties the size of bulldozer tires, and the *coup de menu,* a platter of fried chicken. Oh how we ate, and oh how on the first tee we hit one drive after another straight right into a field of alfalfa. It took us nine holes before we could bend properly over a putt. A nice man, George Sauer; cagey, too.

We played often in the rain, wrapping handkerchiefs around club handles and skipping shots off standing water. One of those days was the time I almost played Nicklaus. It was a quadrangular match including us, Indiana, Purdue, and Ohio State, at Purdue. We drove to Lafayette through a dark, rainswept night and the child of morning was wet-fingered Neptune. That is, it was still raining when it came time to play. No postponement, of course, nor waiting for the rain to stop. It was a 36-hole, one-day affair, and there was no lightning.

The Purdue course is a very good one—narrow and long, its length increased now by about 12 miles from the steady, unabating downpour. It never stopped. It was the Ark scene with, in my case, double bogeys. Nicklaus, naturally, played number one for OSU. I didn't play him because my teammate, Emil Esposito, beat me out for top spot by giving the best oral presentation of the par he made in the one-hole team qualifying that year. Played in a snowstorm, no one could see anything. The coach had to go by word of mouth. I too made a par, but Esposito had a better mouth. I played number two. As I say, just as well.

I watched the Nicklaus group play from the first tee. It was the last I saw of them. It was the last I saw of anything. It was my glasses, mainly. No hat was wide-brimmed enough to protect them from the wet. I had no umbrella, no budget for that, and furthermore, my golf bag, which was on a pull cart, had no hood (lost in South Carolina). So many towels were wrapped around my clubs it looked as if I was pulling a turbaned midget around the course.

I played by the following procedure: Dock the cart beside my ball, wipe my glasses to see where I had to go, finger through the soaked towels for a club, put its grip under my jacket to keep dry while I rewiped my glasses, address the ball, step back for another lens wipe, then rush to hit before I was again looking through the kind of window they put in lavatories. No chance! One reason Nicklaus is so great a player is he has infinite patience. Some of it may be God-given, but I submit he honed it to a fine point playing in such conditions as those at Purdue that day. It also helps that he doesn't wear glasses.

It was the longest day I ever spent on a golf course. I don't recall who I played, and did not care. I didn't even keep score after the first hole, when the card became as soft and limp as a sick cat. My shoes curled so badly at the toes that my shins ached. On the back nine of the second 18, by which time I resembled a flaccid fig, final, total disaster struck. From the constant wiping, my glasses frame broke . . . dissolved. I just caught the fallen lens before it floated away. Then a wheel came off my cart, adding to the other wheels that had come off long before. I carried my bag and walked with my head up to keep the lens in the frame. I finally gave that up and played with one eye. Tommy Armour I am not. I started shanking the ball. The final, unspeakable tragedy.

Nicklaus, by the way, was not all-conquering that day at Purdue. The host school's number one, John Konsek, a tenacious competitor who knew cold as only someone born in Buffalo would, had been preparing for the Nicklaus match all winter; not with an indoor net or a Christmas holiday in Florida, either. A medical student, he must have pumped himself with some kind of human antifreeze, because he went out in the middle of winter, scraped away some of the ice cap, and banged balls into polar-ized Indiana. When the time came he got his man, defeating Jack, one up.

Any golfer who has ever beaten Jack Nicklaus will have something to remember for a lifetime, but Konsek's victory has to be a little bit sweeter. His effort involved more than some straight drives and good putting. It came, too, from a kind of character only Yankee country produces, which may have something to do with the success of Nicklaus himself. You Californians, Floridians, Texans, you don't know *all* of what this game of golf is about.

GOOD OLD DAYS AROUND THE CADDIE SHACK

(Golf Digest—1965)

My introduction to golf began on a warm motionless, lonely, school's-out summer day when I was 13. A pal said I could make some money carrying someone's golf clubs. Fine, I thought. I'll make enough to buy a pair of baseball spikes and a fielder's mitt.

On that summer day I found my way out of the brick and stone of Chicago to suburban Tam O'Shanter CC and entered a world of unbelievably clean green grass on which men walked wearing red pants and white shoes, and little white caps with the tops cut out of them. It was a polite, gentle world where, if you were in someone's way, they shouted "fore," instead of "look out, buddy." Soon after, Ben Hogan replaced Stan Hack in my idol room, and the money I made went for golf clubs, shoes, tees, balls, green fees, and entry to amateur tournaments.

On that first day I was directed to a tall, stern, white-haired man called the caddie-master.

"What do you want, son?"

"I want to caddie."

"Ever caddie before?"

"No."

"No, sir."

"Nosir."

"You're a little small, but I'll give you a try. Go wait up at the caddie shack until you're called."

He pointed to a white house on a hill overlooking a creek. Up there fellows were swinging golf clubs and chipping golf balls toward a hole someone had dug with a heel of his shoe. A branch was sticking in the hole. They were betting on who could get closest to the hole in one shot, and talking in terms of fade, and hook, and Texas wind ball, like Demaret, whoever he was.

Soon, myself and a few other sunstruck neophytes were herded down to the second green, where the caddie-master was waiting. It was the first golf green I had ever seen, and I couldn't believe it was made of grass. Fresh from the city streets, the only grass I knew was those strips of chained-off straggle that separate the apartment buildings from the asphalt street; those little havens for the neighborhood's dogs. This soft, smooth surface I was kneeling beside was a rug. I was afraid to touch it for fear I'd make it dirty. But there was the caddie-master, walking all over it, with spiked shoes yet.

With the caddie-master was a deeply tanned fellow of 15 or 16, wearing a neat white cap and a very confident half smile on his face. He was a regular caddie, and as the caddie-master instructed us on golf course behavior, this fellow demonstrated. How calm, poised, and easy he was as he walked all over that fine carpet. He must have remembered to wipe his feet.

"The caddie whose player gets the ball on the green first must take the pin . . . Never walk in a player's line . . . The man farthest from the hole putts first . . . Hold the pin and flag together so the flag doesn't flutter . . ."

Some touchy guys, these golfers.

"Stand on the same side of the hole as your shadow . . . Clean the club off before putting it back in the bag . . . Keep the balls clean . . . See that white box with the stick in the middle?"

We looked toward the first tee.

"It's got a brush and water in it. You wash golf balls in it. It's a ball washer."

Ahhh, that's what it is.

"Never make a sound when your player is hitting . . . Always keep up with your player . . . Never fall behind . . . All right, lad, pick up that bag and carry it to the clubhouse."

He was looking right at me. I jumped up, hugged the bag of clubs to my chest with both arms, and began to waddle away like a duck. I didn't get very far.

"You expect to walk four miles holding a golf bag like that?"

The lean, bored, regular caddie took the bag from me with one of those grins the experienced have for their inferiors.

"Take the underside of the long strap in the bottom of your right hand . . . Swing the bag up and lay the strap onto your right shoulder . . . Move the bag horizontally along your backside . . . Hold the clubheads so they don't bang against each other . . . Don't forget it."

I didn't.

So now there was a new order in my life. I didn't even know how much money I would be paid when I did caddie, but every morning, early, I was out of the house and off to the course. Under my arm was a brown paper bag filled with two or three thick sandwiches, an apple, a peach, and some raisins. My mother never fully understood what I was doing on a "gulf" course, but she understood hunger.

A singular special delight on an early-summer morning is the quiet of the city, and the cool morning air that tickles your skin. A kid on a new adventure, alert to new sensations, enjoys it, and remembers it well. I was off to the golf course. The bus would get me to the end of the line, and I would hitchhike the rest of the way, aided by a new golf cap, wide, baggy, nonadjustable, and oversized. What fear could a grown-up driver of an automobile have for the likes of an 80-pound bag of small bones wearing a hat that flopped over his ears like a generous portion of whipped cream?

Each caddie had a number, the size of which was in direct proportion to his experience. My first number was 395. Out of 400. The number was on a badge, bought for 50 cents, and was worn on the shirt. It marked your standing in the society of caddies clearly, and without hesitation. I was suddenly a "flytrap," a caddie who can't find the ball, steps on it when he does, and usually walks through a sand trap instead of around it. How else could I be classified as No. 395?

But I made progress. I memorized words like *flange, hit it stiff, looper,* which is a caddie, *birdie,* and *hit it on the toe.* Good words, and bad ones. And as soon as I heard them I tried to use them. I wanted to belong. Occasionally, I left myself open for a hail of criticism.

I found that my player was two up with two holes to go. Flushed and cocky, I told my fellow loopers, three wise, experienced 17-year-olds, that "my man is stymied in his match."

Did they give it to me good. I was laughed at and derided, sneered at and smirked upon. "He's dormie, flytrap. Stymie is when he has a tree in front of his ball, or a dumb caddie like you."

I learned.

It wasn't very long before the inevitable happened: I became a golfer. A neighbor gave me some old wooden-shafted clubs that had moldered in his basement, and one of those stiff, narrow, round canvas bags.

I couldn't put the clubs down. In the house I was making shreds of the family rugs while "working on my swing," and spotting the ceilings with thin black streaks. Now, along with the brown bag of sandwiches and fruit every morning was included a golf club and a pocket full of Po-Dos, Air-Flights, and Cincinnati Tool Steels. Waiting time at the caddie shack was now spent hitting shots toward that makeshift hole.

I hit balls down the long rough of the second hole, and entered the contest, and lost, to the other caddies. At the end of the day's caddying I was back up to the shack for more practice. I hit shots down the rough, as usual, but instead of hitting them back toward the shack, as before, I kept going forward to within range of the first green, which was empty now, and out of view of the clubhouse. I played shots to that big green. I imitated every golfer I had ever seen play. I strained to get the clubhead through the thick grass, my thin wrists bending more than the shaft of the club. When I did manage to fly a ball to the green, and it took up a bit of divot, I proudly took out a tee and fixed my ball mark. What a man! I could put so much stuff on the ball. Most often I hit little shanks and dribblers into the traps.

There were very few jocks, loopers, bag-rats, and flytraps who didn't play the game. Often, after caddying all day, we would walk down the road to a public course (a housing development, now) and play nine holes, sometimes eighteen, before the light went out. Many times we putted out on the last green while matchsticks illuminated the hole.

We always made sure we caddied over the weekend, the busiest days, because that qualified us to be in on the most important day of our week, Monday—caddie day.

What an opportunity! We didn't mind that we had to be off the course by noon, or that the markers were positioned way ahead of the regular teeing ground, or that the pins were set way in front to save the biggest part of the greens. We had a chance to play off impeccable turf amid the rich splendor of the country club. Enough!

We had a chance to see how far we could hit it on the long fourth hole; what club we needed for the tough eighth; whether we could get home in two on the long par-5 ninth. We scattered over the course like locusts, hitting shots from every imaginable angle—and some unimaginable. We shouted two fairways over to each other:

"What d'ja hit on 11?" "How do you stand with par?"

With par! What nerve. Most of us would have been happy to be even-fives.

Some of us dressed to the teeth for the occasion. Despite the soaking dew, we wore our best slacks, and if we had to roll up our cuffs, so what, we could show off our new argyle socks, bought in the pro shop for the price of a round of caddying. We were playing at the country club, after all.

And if the shoulders of our finest white golfing shirt became black-striped by the end of the day because we had to carry our own bag, it was ignored. Ma could wash it out. We were emulating our economic betters. We were bankers for a day, playing a game of let's pretend.

When we were through we would gather around at the halfway house for hamburgers, Cokes, and lies.

"Match ya cards." "What d'ja hit on the 12th?"

"Five-iron."

"FIVE-IRON, YOU LYING BAG-RAT, I HAD TO HIT A 3-WOOD, AND I HIT IT 50 YARDS PAST YOU."

The next day, or even that afternoon, we shucked off the fancy clothes, put aside the golf clubs, and returned to work.

"Who's bag you got?"

"Big John O."

"How come you always get the good bags?"

"I happen to be a very good jocko."

"I got two ladies."

"See you next week."

Who were some of these caddies? Some were my peers, contemporaries who caddied and earned money and scholarships to go to college and become engineers, metallurgists, salesmen, professional golfers. Others were older men, professional caddies, who traveled north and south, as the weather dictated, making their living toting golf bags.

The professional caddies were a colorful crew. There were men like Swede, an amiable, sleepy-eyed hulk who got the best bags at the course. A huge, rotund man, his abdomen swelled out from just below his Adam's apple, reaching a point in space that denied him sight of his feet, then curved gracefully back in to join the top of his thighs. He always held his head high, Swede did, perhaps to keep himself in balance. He caddied every day of the season, made a ton of money, and used it all to drink a tun of beer every night. Swede never had a harsh word for anyone. So long as he got his bags during the day, and bagged at night, he was happy.

Then there was a tall gawk of a man named Ho, who wore a tee shirt that must have been under a thousand golf bags without benefit of laundry or repair. Ho was called Ho—we knew no other name for him—because he made a little gasping sound between words during the course of his conversation.

"I got this, ho, member, ho, who can't break, ho, eighty, ho, and he, ho, gets hot, ho, and shoots a, ho, seventy, ho, five, ho, and wins all the, ho, dough, ho. So, ho, he gives me, ho, a tenner, ho. Great, huh? ho."

Just a nervous little habit, the ho's coming out in pushes of air so fast you didn't even hear them after a while.

Another of that crowd was Indian Al, an ageless little man with two teeth to his name, and a sloping, convex posture that permanently marked his chosen profession. Indian Al had caddied so long and hard that even when free of those two leather golf bags, he walked as though he still had them on. Always anxious to "get out," Al jumped around, laughed, giggled and mumbled to himself. During the hot days of August, when caddies were in short supply, Indian Al made two rounds with double bags, his loose, baggy pants flapping in the breeze as he walked down a fairway, and if someone wanted to play a quick nine after dinner, Al would grab that bag, too. No one ever knew where he came from, or where he went after a day's work.

A caddie at Tam O'Shanter during the '50s was double lucky. He was in on the ground floor during the years of the All-American and World's Championship of Golf tournaments. As thousands of people stormed the gates, paying hard cash to get in, we caddies walked in free, our ticket the white tee shirt with TAM O'SHANTER written across the front. We had "open sesame" to the wildest, most exciting two weeks of the golfing year.

The World was the first of the really big-money tournaments in professional golf. Actually, there were four tournaments at once, each at 72 holes of stroke play. There was a men's and a women's pro event, and a men's and a women's amateur tournament. It was an extravaganza in the real sense of that overworked word. It was carnival time. Everybody was there trying to knock over the prizes. There was Joe Switzer, the licorice king, who handed out his product to one and all, and played a pretty fine game of amateur golf at the same time. There was a mystery golfer who played with a hood on, and pros with strange names such as Ugo Grappassoni and Flory Van Donck. And of course there was Babe Zaharias and Patty Berg, and Vic Ghezzi, and Johnny Bulla, and Sam Snead, and Byron Nelson, and Bobby Locke, and it went on and on.

There was George May, the promoter, who walked around the course betting the pros a hundred dollars they couldn't hit an open green with a wedge from ten yards out, and paying off on the spot when they made the easy shot. And of course, there were the people. A huge, moiling mass who roared mightily at the play, and left behind an ocean of hotdog wrappers, broken umbrellas, scorecards, and smashed grass.

While the galleries raced for position to watch the shots, we caddies walked to the front, right next to the very ball that was being played, and talked with, worked for, and advised these stars of the show—these pros. The caddies with the most rounds, or loops, got first choice of bag, and so on down the line. Those who worked hard all year and took no time off to play a little golf of their own got the top bags. They snapped up Snead and Demaret, who were always in the big money, or Joe Louis, the Bomber, who was an amateur but paid off as though he had won the top pro purse.

One kid made up his mind early in the spring of one year that he was going to caddie for Ben Hogan. He wanted nothing better out of his life than to pack the sack of the Hawk. He began his climb to high office during the cold, wet days of late March, piling up loops early. He worked hard right up to pick time, and was first in line. He knew all along that Hogan didn't always come to Tam, even if the prize money was the biggest in golf, because Hogan and George May didn't always get along. But this kid was determined, and willing to take a chance.

Hogan still hadn't committed himself at pick time. If the kid chose Ben, and the little man didn't come, the kid would probably end up with some pro who might not make the cut. All the other top bags would have been gone. He picked Hogan anyway.

And Hogan came, and Hogan won, and the kid was vindicated.

After the tournament the kid began to look like his man, so great was his love. He wore white caps, and plain tan slacks, and brown leather shoes. No fancy Demaret styles for him. He smoked a cigarette, and kept it rigid in his mouth as he squinted down fairways, or ball washers, or wherever he squinted. He walked like Ben, and he talked like Ben, and he even tried to play golf like Ben—which was a mistake. Only Hogan can swing like Hogan and the kid, who was not a bad player before Hogan, had a tough time getting it in under 90 after Ben left.

Most of us caddies were a simple, mercenary crew with a mild streak of idealism. We wanted a player who would place well in the money so we could share his winnings, but we also wanted a man who was respected as a shot-maker. It would have been easy to take a Frank Stranahan, a rich guy who always paid well, but he was an amateur, and we would rather take our chances with a bona fide professional.

We spent a lot of time on the practice fairway when the tournaments were at Tam. We ducked and dodged while in the stream of fire, never really able to follow our player's ball. But we always came up with some golf ball—they were dropping around us like hailstones. A pro may have been on the Wilson Co. staff, but by the end of the two weeks at Tam he might have had more Spalding Dots in his shag bag than anything else.

The rest of the time, when not working, we didn't chase the action out on the course, but planted ourselves behind the pros who were practicing. With sharp, critical eyes we watched and analyzed the pause at the top of Middlecoff's backswing, Mangrum's overall slow tempo, and how he really cracked at it in the hitting area, Fazio's beautiful one-piece swing, a miniature Snead, and, of course, Hogan's fade.

There were five years of tournaments for me. I caddied for Ed Furgol, an extremely talented golfer with a high temper, and I spent two weeks pulling golf clubs out of the turf after Ed fired them in like darts from the top of his high follow-through. Those were years when Lloyd Mangrum won everything—twice—because he worked for George May, representing Tam, and when he won the first prize, May doubled it. Those were the years when Bobby Locke needed a par on the 18th green to win it all but, because he couldn't hit a cut shot from the right side of the fairway, made a six and lost. On that same hole, another time, Lew Worsham rolled in a wedge shot from 110 yards out for an eagle that beat Chandler Harper out of $25,000. Poor old Chandler, the look on his face after that.

But those were years, too, when I spent near-idyllic summers out of the city, making a bit of money and learning a game I would never forget—or forgive. Quiet days in July when I would get to caddie for Mr. Horlick, the malted milk man, who played nine holes and decided it was a nicer day for flying than golfing, and gave me ten bucks for nine holes of work. Ten bucks!

They were good days, those caddie days. There were interesting people, and interesting events, and an entirely new society I never knew existed. I found out about fresh air, and trees, and grass . . . and sand. I was
tanned by the first of May and only got browner as the year went on.

And I became a walker, which is the best way to see the world, be it
a golf course or a foreign city you're visiting. When you walk you have
time; time to look around you and see things, time to think about what
you're seeing. You're not concerned with mechanical things—controls. All
you need control is yourself. In your golf game, the time it takes to walk
up to your ball is just enough to settle you down, and for you to figure out
how you want to play the shot. And with a caddie to carry your clubs
you're absolutely free to pursue the game and enjoy yourself.

A caddie is an extra pair of eyes to follow your ball, the rooter for
your big shot that will win the match, the fellow who knows every blade
of grass on the course, and shares his knowledge with you. He's the boy
who puts back the golf course for you after an iron shot; who rakes
smooth what sand is left in the bunker once you get out of it. He's an inte-
gral part of the game. He always will be.

THE AULD GRAY GAME ISNA' WHAT IT USED T'BE

(Golf Magazine—1970)

Whither has gone the game of golf, that trial of subtle economics given us by hard-boned men with wind-watered eyes, which has borne out on the gaels of progress from the stubborn craigs of Scotland? It has traveled far since its remove from the grim and misty half light of Carnoustie, the pitted earth of St. Andrews. And hoot, mon, it has taken some twists and turns in the passage. No longer is it solely the game of God-fearing, Lord-have-no-mercy-on-your-damn(ed)-soul Calvinists. Why, it's fallen even into the hands of those who glorify and sanctify the bosom of women. Do you hear, old Tom? The *bosom* of *women*. In a place called the Playboy Club-Hotel, in Lake Geneva, Wisconsin. And hoot, hooot hoooot, mon, it is nothing like you'll find in the somber half of the Royal and Ancient, where even a grain-pecking chicken has no breast.

There in Wisconsin they have young hussies walking brazenly about in their skivvies. Less. The poor things can hardly take a breath or bend forward, the skivvies being so tight around them. And so trussed up are they, a great double diving board bursting from their upper half, letter-high, as they say in baseball. It's an uncommon sight, that fleshly terrace. Almost unreal. But not. And hear this O Laurie Auchterlonie, winding a weathered brassie in your little shop by the Old Course, these lassies stand a thin sheet from the naked side, introducing themselves as Bunny Cynthia, or Bunny Wendy, although you'll not find such a hare in the Highlands, and *sell golf balls.* Right there in the *pro shop!* Doesn't that stir the haggis in your baggis, sir.

So this is where the game has come, or gone. The mind goes bonkers with wild imaginings. Would one of those Bunnies be lugging the sticks from tee to green? Could you call her Cottontail without insulting Henry? Would her mighty mammarian presence inflict you with the incurable shanks? Surely you could never ask her to bend for a divot. But then again . . . ? Perhaps each hole would spin out the Playboy theme— double-legged fairways, leading out from 10-toed tees, that join and widen at the hips then trim down to pert waists from where you hit approach shots over double mounds rising before long-eared greens. Aye now, there you would have your Valley of Sin, mon. Aye.

Not quite. Ask a Bunny if she has a Spalding Dot and she'll canvass her person in a fright for some outrageous scar. Say "caddie," and she asks what year, "bogey" and she talks movies, "nassau," and she's packing a bag. But that's all right. A little flesh, flash, around the place doesn't hurt. The man who built one of the two courses, Robert Bruce Harris, had golf in mind. More or less. He may have been taken in by the general ambience of the place, however, and tried emulating in his design female convolu- tions. On a delicatessen menu each hole might be called the Jane Russell, the Raquel Welch, or, Mr. Harris being up in years, the Mae West. One way or the other there's not a Twiggy on the lot, which figures, come to think of it. Mr. Harris was out to build a very tough golf course, but for *who,* or *what,* is another question. His first hole moves down a country lane with water on both sides, and more cutting across. After that most of it is like shooting a grass rapids. A par-five has a second shot through a six-foot gap between two high hills. A par-four asks for a drive to a fair- way banked for a toboggan race. At least two others have huge lakes to the right almost their entire length. Ninety-five percent of the world's golfers slice.

The second Playboy course is a little flatter in spots and is fashioned after Scottish links. It more or less makes it, but is so new the unmanicured look may only be because the grass hasn't come 'round yet. This course has bunkers 200 yards long, par-fours with three-yard wide landing areas, and a couple of holes that convolute like . . . Anita Ekberg? No *dolce vita,* those little beauts. And not necessarily Scottish either. This one was built by Pete Dye, with a fly-over consultation by his sometime partner, Jack Nicklaus.

It's pretty hardy golf, to say the least, with some high-powered people doing the building, so you figure it's a place for pure-blood aficionados of the cut six-iron and the pinched wedge. Besides that, to play there you must be a Playboy Club Key-Holder, or a guest of one. The key costs only $5 a year, but from there on it's not Dyker Beach or Griffith Park public golf. Green fees are $6 and $9, the lesser if you're staying at the hotel. Rooms start at $30 a day and run up to $150 for the Hefner Suite, which presumably has hot and cold running you-know-whats. Carts are $10 a round. No, Bunny Diane does not pack golf leather. Nor does anyone else, so you better know how to move the ball around.

Now to play. Let's find someone to ask about how much dogleg to cut off. Hit a spoon to the far corner? Or bomb number one over the bunker? There's someone coming up 18. Big bag, white shoes. All the gear. "Hey pal, how do you like the back nine?" "What's a back nine?" he asks. Well, lots of new blood coming into the game. Keeps it alive. Must ask someone, though, what club to use on the three-par over the water. A guy wearing either pants that are too short, or shorts that are too long, looks up from his manual on Multilinear Phase-Out Procedures for the X1zx51-9Z Computer System and asks if you can supply him with "read-outs." Read-outs! I want to know if you hit a hard four-iron, or punch a little three in there. Some guys under an umbrella. Ask them. But they're all reading pamphlets on the Cybernetics of Aggressive Wholesaling of Women's Shoes. Ah yes. Club has to pay the way with some convention business. Somewhere around are the "players." Change for dinner.

The hotel is smartly done in stone and wood—a takeoff on Frank Lloyd Wright's unobtrusive low-line horizontals. The rooms have carpets, beds, chairs, mirrors, showers, and copies of the magazine by which it all comes. Where's Hogan's *Power Golf?* Herbert Warren Wind's *Story of American Golf? The Life and Times of Willie Park?* Only Center Spreads. At least you don't get Conrad Hilton's autobiography.

The Playmate Bar is lined with college-educated, middle-to-high-income, 25- to 35-year-old sports car and bedroom roustabouts. They all have one-inch blond crewcuts and wash-and-wear jackets, and lean over drinks (7&7) staring at illuminated pictures of Playmates of the Month as they appeared in previous issues of . . . "Say, pal. What do this think of this Square-to-Square stuff? It's really kind of old hat, and no man can take a club away . . ." "Thirty-eight," says a crewcut. "You had 38? Where'd you get the bogeys?" "February. She's a 38." Bunny Felicia, all thighs and terrace, walks by saying "I'm your Bunny Felicia, I'm your Bunny Felicia." Crewcut looks her over and says, "Thirty-seven." "She shot a 37?" you ask. "Get outta here," says crewcut.

Dinner is in the VIP Room, a Joe Dey room. Lots of class. Quiet, tasteful. First one at the table is Bunny Beth. Big, strong girl. Might as well try. "Say, Bunny Beth, perhaps you can tell me something about the pinched wedge." She backs off quickly, mumbling about a no-touch policy at the club. Never see her again. A college kid from Madison plays *sommelier*, opening the wine and rolling the cork over for you to smell. You wink and tell him you don't know what to smell *for*. He smiles shyly and whispers that *he* doesn't either. How about the club to use on the par-three? No. He's studying agronomy. Wants to farm. Father farms. Father's father farmed. All his uncles farm.

After-dinner drink. The Bunny Hutch, a light and sound room. Short spurts of red, orange, blue, puce, magenta, mixed in with Janis Joplin records played at high shriek. Those lights won't do tomorrow's putting much good. Bunny Ellie comes around introducing herself as Bunny Ellie and asks if you want to dance. No, love. Got to get up early for a run at that big track old Mr. Harris set up. "Oh, are you a runner?" she asks. "No. A golfer." "A golfer. A golfer. Ohhhh, yes." Bunny Ellie walks away, turns up the Janis Joplin. "Babe Zaharias was a golfer. So is Mickey Wright. Drove it up with the men, they did."

You go into the notions shop, buy two cigars, and ask Bunny Cora for the issue of *Golf* magazine with the Alex Morrison article on the True Swinging Action. "I'm your Bunny Cora, I'm your Bunny Cora. I'm your . . ." "I know, I know. But what about the True Swinging Action?" "Oh," she says, "that's up in the Penthouse Room." Aha. At last.

Bunnies Belle, Inga, and Doreen direct you each step of the way. Bunny Arlene leads you into a large room filled with tables and Multilinear Phase-Out people. Bunny Marilyn sits you down, Bunny Marie takes your drink order, Bunny Ann serves it. Thigh and terrace are everywhere. You also know you're not going to get Alex Morrison's secret to consistent golf. The house lights dim, the curtain rises, and it's show time. The show is a burlesque. The Lido comes to Wisconsin. A burlesque show at the Playboy Club. That's like bringing a chicken salad sandwich to a banquet. Finally it's over, and everyone heads back to the Playmate Bar for another look at January, February, etc., etc. You take a pass, and head to your room. You'll dream about great golf shots. Alex Morrison once said you could do that, too, and make it work. Along a quiet corridor you pass a man standing in a shadow. He's mumbling to himself, "What's a back nine? What's a back nine?"

By the way, Sandy MacDermott-Kenzie Donald, Hugh Hefner does not play golf, "being much more the indoor sport." Heh, heh.

THE DECLINE AND FALL OF THE SHAG BAG

(Golf Magazine—1972)

I don't have statistics to back it up, but I have a notion that we are seeing the decline and fall of the shag bag. You may well say, so what? T'hell, you can name a couple of thousand other problems in the world more important than the demise of a shag bag. And you're right. But blast it, there are some old things, old ways of doing things that have a subtle way of distinguishing one man from another. We sure can use some, and the shag bag was one of them.

When I was a kid a man's shag bag marked his status in the game. Not the bag itself—that could be a beat-up hunk of canvas with a broken zipper, although anyone who came out with a few balls wrapped in a handkerchief was considered a rumdum—it was the contents of the bag, starting with volume and going to quality. If you had a collection of upward of 35 balls you were a golfer—a serious student of the game. If most of those balls were shiners—used for but one round of play and still with good paint—you were a player.

As a caddie at Chicago's Tam O'Shanter CC, where for two weeks every summer all the men and women pros and amateurs came for George

May's festival of tournaments, I saw Al Besselink arrive on the practice tee with a bowling ball bag (I swear it was that) absolutely filled to capacity with the brightest white mountain of shags I had ever seen. That gave him more standing than he probably deserved since Al was always something of a hustler of one thing or another who never reached his full playing potential. However, I once saw Sam Snead on that same practice tee break out a box of 12 brand-new Wilson Staffs and dump them into the great pile of shag balls already in front of him. I was awestruck. Snead was a great player. I knew that just as everyone else did. But when he used those never-before-hit balls in a practice session he became a signed and sealed man of pure class.

All of us watched over our hoard of shags with Marneresque greed. As youths, of course, we never had shag boys and, while retrieving our own balls, would carefully keep count, to be sure we found them all. That often led to 15 or 20 minutes of kicking around in deep grass, ditches, trees, and grown-over bunkers in search of one precious ball. One thing about that, and to the good, it made you work that much harder at hitting your shots where you aimed them.

In a junior or caddie tournament, a lot of us would be hitting practice shots to a confined, shag-boyless field. There were some terrific arguments over whose Titleist One, Dot Four, or Maxfli Five was in whose bag. No one, of course, marked their shag balls—we wouldn't dream of painting a stripe on them, which I'll get to in a minute. Finding your own beloved pellets among all the apparent look-alikes was akin to roasting potatoes in the alleys of Chicago. We built a fire, and everyone placed their spud in the tangle of branches, broken-up chairs, and *Tribunes*. In five minutes or less every blackened tuber, to the casual eye, was like every other. Those who owned them, however, could differentiate theirs by its position and shape. No two potatoes really look alike, just as every single shag ball has its very own scuffs, cuts, and color variations.

I don't know how many hours I used to spend bent over a bucket of water filled with my shags, a towel in one hand, pulling each ball from its soak and wiping it as carefully clean as a parent revamping its soiled infant. If there was no bucket around the house, the kitchen sink was filled with balata, which brought a howl from Mom. She would suggest using the john bowl, but then, mothers never understand these things.

As covetous of our shags as we were, those who had style or sought it would, while practicing for all to see, go through the bunch periodically and toss aside with consummate disdain those balls that had gone too gray or were too obviously cut. When in a mood of exceptional well-being, we might even discard those few balls of a brand other than the majority—a man reached a higher plateau of prestige if he had a bag full of one kind of ball only. When we ran short of balls with which to play, though, we would secretly, very secretly, pull out the most recent denizens of the bag and take them to the first tee.

What's occurred? The shag bag has been replaced by the horrid, classless, styleless striped "range" ball. As kids we went to commercial driving ranges (called "stop and socks" in Chicago) and hit the stripers, but only at night when there was no alternative. The balls, we knew, were rotten to the core—duds, clinkers, rocks that zigged and zagged and never went the 250 they should have. That's the image I can't lose when nowadays, at the finest clubs in the land, from Winged Foot to Riviera, you walk onto the "range" carrying a mundane iron bucket of some 25 to 30 stripers that had clattered out of a bloodless machine in response to the deposit of two quarters, half of them bouncing out of the bucket and running all over a slab of concrete. For one thing, it's not a very good buy. But more than that, the ignominy of it is disheartening.

Yet, being from the old school, I keep up a shag bag. New balls come fairly easily these days and out of habit I play with them once and toss them into the bag. But I never get to use them. Many times I've asked a pro somewhere if I could use my own shags and get a rather cold "No" on the grounds that either there is no one around to chase them or there is simply no place to even shag them myself, his "range" being cluttered with his own ghastly stripers. I don't mind the pros making a few extra bucks off "range" balls, and I realize it is easier for more golfers to practice this way, but an area might be reserved for us old-guard players . . . at least until we're gone. For tradition's sake.

It's even come to pass that at a few of the PGA's tour stops the pros themselves are obliged to hit stripers from a bucket. A disgrace. I thought there might be a chance to unveil my beautiful bag of shags last year when I happened to qualify for that most venerable of all championships, the U.S. Amateur. I was ecstatic over the possibility of pouring my saturation of shags onto the hallowed turf. But before I even got to the tournament a letter of instructions from the USGA noted that the contestants would not be allowed to use personal practice balls. Oh, they said that the "range" balls were of high quality, and they were, but it was a great disappointment. When I walked out to warm up among 150 of the game's best amateur golfers, I had to purchase a bucket of those disgustingly striped balls and hit them into no-man's-land. No chance to imperiously wave a caddie to one side or the other, or back, or to earn quiet murmurs of appreciation from onlookers when the caddie caught a ball on one bounce without having to move. It was like sitting down for dinner at the Waldorf and being served a hot dog from the vendor on the street corner outside.

What do I do with that magnificent accumulation of shags moldering in my basement? I don't have to wash them, that's for sure. I count them every now and then, just for the hell of it (got 102 in there). I can tell you right now that if you write saying, "Send them to me, I'll play with them," you'll come up empty.

No. I'll hang on to them. Perhaps someday there will be a Grand Convention of Shag Bag Owners. All will gather on the pastoral grounds of the new USGA Golf House out in Jersey and on tables before each of us will be a place to pile our collections, stacking them in the enormous rounded pyramids we used to build, for all to assess, gloat over . . . and remember.